REBEL LAND

BY THE SAME AUTHOR

In the Rose Garden of the Martyrs
The Struggle for Iran

REBEL LAND

Among Turkey's Forgotten Peoples

CHRISTOPHER DE BELLAIGUE

BLOOMSBURY

LONDON · BERLIN · NEW YORK

First published in Great Britain 2009

Copyright © 2009 by Christopher de Bellaigue

Maps by John Gilkes

All photographs reproduced in this book are from *Armenia: Travels and Studies*
by H.F.B. Lynch (London, 1901) except where credited otherwise

The moral right of the author has been asserted

Bloomsbury Publishing, London, New York and Berlin

A CIP catalogue record for this book is available from the British Library

ISBN 978 0 7475 8628 9

10 9 8 7 6 5 4 3 2 1

Typeset by Hewer Text UK Ltd, Edinburgh
Printed in Great Britain by Clays Limited, St Ives plc

The paper this book is printed on is certified by the © 1996 Forest
Stewardship Council A.C. (FSC). It is ancient-forest friendly. The
printer holds FSC chain of custody SGS-COC-2061

Mixed Sources
Product group from well-managed
forests and other controlled sources
www.fsc.org Cert no. SGS-COC-004081
© 1996 Forest Stewardship Council

به جهان خرّم از آنم که جهان خرّم از اوست

Contents

Dramatis Personae

Abdulhamit II, Ottoman sultan from 1876 to 1909, author of several pogroms against the Armenians

Abdullah, Sheikh, Kurdish nationalist commander during the 1925 rebellion.

Akbal, Nilufer, Kurdish pop star

Aktas, Ercan, entrepreneur, parliamentary candidate, son of Kadir Aktas

Aktas, Kadir, entrepreneur, sometime acting mayor of Varto, legendary Varto informer

Ataturk, Mustafa Kemal, founder of the Turkish Republic

Balikkaya, Lutfu, Kurdish nationalist living in Germany

Bayar, Celal, Democrat Party president from 1950 to 1960, ousted in the 1960 coup

Besikci, Ismail, pro-Kurdish Turkish sociologist

Bingol, Ceylan, Mehmet Serif Firat's daughter

Cakar, Salahettin and Sukran, Armenian couple living in Germany

Celik, Demir, Varto's Alevi mayor

Cicek, Yakub, Kurdish nationalist now living in Germany

Darbinian, Meguerditch, Armenian boy from the village of Baskan

Demirel, Suleyman, veteran national politician of the centre-right

Dikmen, Ali Haydar, leading Varto Alevi, head of the Feron clan

Dikmen, Ekin, Republican Peoples Party deputy, son of Ali Haydar Dikmen

Dink, Hrant, Armenian newspaper editor in Istanbul

Ecevit, Bulent, long-serving politician of the Left

Erdogan, Kamer, farmer from the village of Emeran, member of the Feron clan of Mehmet Serif Firat

Erdogan, Gulseren, carpet weaver from Emeran, Kamar Erdogan's sister

Ergun, plainclothes cop

Evren, General Kenan, leader of the junta that seized power in 1980, president from 1982 until 1989

Firat, Mehmet Serif, Alevi from the village of Kasman, leading member of the Feron clan, author of the *History of Varto and the Eastern Provinces*

Gezmis, Deniz, Turkish revolutionary, executed in 1972

Gursel, Cemal, leader of the military junta that took power in the coup d'etat in

1960, author of a famous introduction to Mehmet Serif Firat's *History of Varto and the Eastern Provinces*

Halit Bey of the Cibrans, Ottoman soldier turned Kurdish nationalist leader

Han, Abdulbari, Sunni former mayor of Varto, local representative of the Islamist Justice and Development Party

Han, Ismail, head of the Varto branch of the Sultan Pir Abdal Association, nephew of Nazim Han

Han, Nazim, a.k.a. Uncle Nazim, Varto's first Alevi mayor, a leading member of the Avdalan tribe (no relation to Abdulbari Han)

Haydar (codename), PKK commander, brother-in-law of Demir Celik

Inonu, Ismet, statesman and successor to Ataturk as president of the Turkish Republic.

Karayilan, Murat, acting leader of the PKK

Kasim, Major, of Kulan, cousin of the Kurdish nationalist leader Halit of the Cibrans

Menderes, Adnan, Democrat Party prime minister from 1950 to 1960, executed after the 1960 coup

Noel, Major E.M., British intelligence officer active in Kurdistan after the First World War

Ocalan, Abdullah, a.k.a. Apo, leader of the outlawed Kurdistan Workers Party (PKK)

Osman, Nuri Pasha, Turkish military commander who re-took Varto for the government in 1925

Pamuk, Orhan, Turkish novelist, winner of the 2006 Nobel Prize for Literature

Sait, Sheikh, leader of the 1925 Kurdish nationalist rebellion

Serif, Sheikh, Kurdish nationalist commander who took Harput for the rebels in the 1925 revolt

Tas, Nizamettin, Alangoz Sunni who rose to become a senior PKK commander

Xenephon, Athenian who led a defeated Greek army through eastern Asia Minor in 401 BC and described his experiences in the celebrated *Anabasis,* or 'March Up Country'

Yuce, Mehmet Can, former senior member of the PKK now living in Germany

Zeynel, Ottoman-era Alevi chief and bandit

Zia, Yusuf, Kurdish nationalist leader and comrade of Halit of the Cibrans

Author's note:

The terms Bey, Aga and Efendi are Ottoman-era honorifics common among Turks and Kurds.

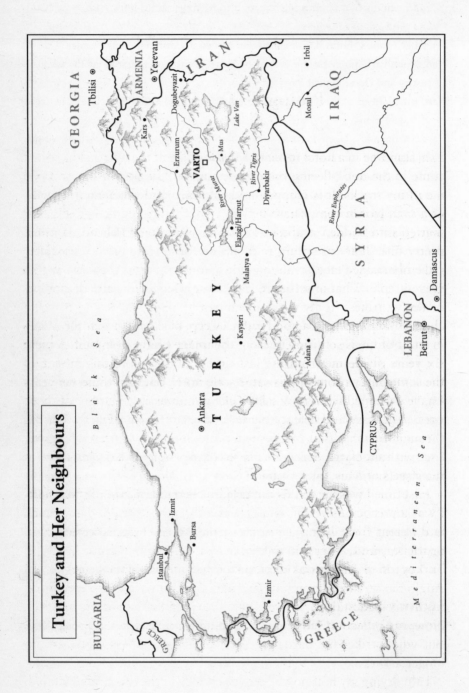

Turkey and Her Neighbours

Prologue: The Mirror

I am standing in a hotel room in Mus, looking at the mirror. I have just come in the door, fleeing the downpour, and the mirror has stopped me in my tracks. It is chipped and smudged and the view it affords, of a man frozen somewhere between youth and middle age, his hair matted into sodden arabesques over a gleaming forehead, is not a pretty one. Tears of spring rain run disconsolately off my nose; my red embarrassed face, steaming industriously, anoints the scene with a grey aureole. What unsettles me is not the effect of an utter drenching, or the weariness in my eyes, which can be remedied with a towel, a change of clothes and a good night's sleep, but the fact that the image in front of me is so different from the image I have of myself. A mere six years divide me from the last time I stood before this mirror, in the same dingy room in this same stale hotel, but into those six years I have crammed what now seems like an impossible number of those rites, of passage and defeat, that mark the advent of maturity. Peering through the nimbus at my flushed, puffed up, rain-spattered features, I see with shock the degeneration that the people outside, out there in the streets of Mus, must also see.

Last time I was here in Room 205, the room they give to foreigners, I was a precocious young man. I was a foreign correspondent, which is different from being a journalist, implying curiosity rather than prurience, and a certain mildly debauched romanticism. I was in Turkey on a glamorous assignment for the *Economist*, arbiter of Anglo-Saxon liberal opinion; I shrugged off all weight of expectation from my pedestal of self-reliance and painless expatriate poverty. Now, my reflection tells me, I am a husband, a father, a mortgagee. But what strikes me hardest – here, of all places – is that I am no longer a Turk.

I am drying my hair now. There is a knock at the door, small enough to make my heart leap. Who could it be? 'Your tea,' says the room boy, a surly, emaciated fellow. He has been watching me since I arrived this morning, asking questions someone else has told him to ask. 'I will show you how your TV works,' he mumbles, entering unbidden. Our eyes fall on the objects strewn across the desk: a camera, my notebooks and some pens; a mobile; the outline of a laptop. He leaves the TV on, tuned gratuitously to CNN, then goes into the bathroom, where he informs me that red is cold and blue is hot. Then he stands at the door, with placid, bovine insistence. 'Nothing else, Sir?' I turn off the TV, rummage through my bag and give him some lira with ill grace. A black mark from his shoes remains on the bathroom floor, but the tea he has brought is good and hot.

A love affair brought me to Turkey in 1995, from India, where I had started my career as a staff reporter on a local magazine; the love affair ended but Turkey captivated me. In Turkey, Muslim, modern and almost democratic, it would be possible to test the axiom of ineluctable conflict between Muslim countries and the West. Turkey staggered from one crisis to another: the generals, defenders of the secular order, toppled an Islamist government; the lira hit the ground with a smack; the south-east was rocked by separatist fighting; Turkey thought it was European. These were big issues, as big as any around, and there weren't enough correspondents to do justice to the story. I was proud to be the youngest member of the foreign press corps, proud to talk to the foreign minister on equal terms. From my base in the dull, well-scrubbed capital, Ankara, I sought excuses to visit Istanbul: louche, suggestive, and dazzling when the evening sun struck the Bosporus, gilding the helmet domes of Sinan's mosques while the gulls panted against the wind and whorls of detritus whipped down Istiklal Street. Here was a city of old men leaning on cigarettes and slamming down backgammon pieces, and of nubile young women, affectionate and cheaply dressed – relief from the white-knuckled achievers back in London. On the overnight train from Ankara, overdoing it with the arrack in a smoke-clogged dining car, I congratulated myself on inhabiting a rough, unruly, endlessly fascinating world, a battered oriental shield of Achilles to which I, more than most, had been granted privileged access.

I had a priceless key, other than the native friendliness and hospitality of the Turks. I had learned the Turkish language first from love, and then economy, preferring not to employ an interpreter like other correspondents, and finally, from frank and guileless affection for my adoptive country. After a year my Turkish was better than good; after three, it was assumed I was Turkish until some idiomatic infelicity, corroborated by my fair hair and blue eyes, led to the question, 'Are you only half-Turkish, or are you a Turk who grew up abroad?' Neither was true. I was good at languages, and good at mimicking accents, and single-minded in my pursuit of both. I was proud of being unlike the other correspondents, chaperoned everywhere by drivers and interpreters. It was through my enthusiasm for this rumbustuous, sociable tongue that I achieved assimilation. Back then the image staring at me was bright and sharp, the image of a man who loved where he lived and what he did.

I lived in a small section of Turkey, the western part of the rectangular landmass that our grandparents called Asia Minor and we call Anatolia. So did my Turkish friends. They, participants in the nation's march towards modern civilisation, were not content to live solely in this western section. They holidayed on its westernmost extremity, the Aegean coast, or took flights to points west: Rome, Paris, New York. We reporters were exceptional in that we made trips in the opposite direction, to the interior and the south-east, where the Kurdistan Workers Party, or PKK, shot up conscripts and agitated for independence; but it was understood that these were work trips. Few of my Turkish friends would consider going as far as central Turkey. Why languish in steerage on the great liner heading west, when the sun-kissed bridge was open to all? Take a comfortable overnight bus from Ankara and awake the following morning on the coast, sucking clotted cream for breakfast, picking over the Hellenic remains, floating towards Greece. Where, among your fellow sunbathers, was the PKK or the black-clad Islamist women – 'two-legged cockroaches' in the secularists' wicked vernacular? In another country, was the not entirely glib answer, a country so far removed from the hors d'oeuvres and the nights under jasmine as to be perfectly, sublimely irrelevant.

The Turkey I inhabited was unmistakably the Turkey of Kemal Ataturk. He founded the republic in 1923, from the wreckage of the Ottoman empire, and died fifteen years later. He remained, sixty years after his death, the country's most influential politician. He was everywhere: in massive photographs digitally reproduced on the wall of a department store; in the corner of a TV screen, his silhouette rippling over a Turkish flag; in the endless hypothetical consultations ('What would Ataturk have done?') and the lachrymose, uncritical veneration that my friends offered him. I regarded the Ataturk cult with indulgence, partly to avoid offending my friends, and partly because his values, of rationalism and agnosticism, seemed to be mine. Ataturk and his legacy, my friends told me, was all that stood between Turkey and the sort of Islamic Revolution that had turned neighbouring Iran into one of the most benighted countries on earth. The Turkish identity he had promoted had prevented malcontents such as the Kurds from splitting off and setting up states of their own. God forbid that Turkey should become another Iran, or another Yugoslavia!

Back in Ankara, at a loose end, I would perform solitary pilgrimages to the great man's mausoleum, lingering in a gallery of his personal effects, enjoying the crispness of his dress shirts and handkerchiefs, his surprisingly dainty shoes, his studs and pins and the signed photographs that testified to his standing among the kings and dictators of the world. He had been a bucolic authoritarian, but for an English public schoolboy bucolic authoritarianism was cool.

Eventually I moved to Istanbul. I spent years wandering the European quarter with my head thrown back, looking for my sea view top floor, and eventually I found it. It was a *chambre de bonne*, up five exceptionally steep flights of a nineteenth-century block of flats, right there on the second bend heading down Faik Pasha Street, perhaps Istanbul's most picturesque. Two impoverished families wanted out. Twenty-eight thousand US dollars later, it was mine. I spent more on repairs and redecoration. The work was shabby but that didn't matter. The view was my Lamborghini. From my terrace you saw Aya Sophia, the Blue Mosque, the Aqueduct of Valens, some Byzantine churches, a lot more mosques, and some slums. Standing on tiptoe you saw a shard of Golden Horn – my sea view. Visitors came upstairs, bent double from the climb, and exclaimed, 'Wow!'

The smell of grilling meat rose from nearby balconies on the hot salty summer evenings, raucous TV soaps competed with the gulls' shrieks, and the neighbours' children lobbed stones on to my roof. The crone across the street chainsmoked and prayed and bought groceries by lowering a basket to the itinerant salesman below. Gypsy weddings were held on an adjacent lot. The bride, decked in gold, exulted to a trilling chorus. I observed as a girl a few doors down became a woman in the space of a single summer; by the autumn she was no longer playing hopscotch in the street, but swinging her hips like a pro. Up the hill the transvestites cruised Istiklal, the bars and restaurants roared, and the rubbish stank. Yes, Faik Pasha was the bit of rough I had dreamed of, but it came too late. Like the girl down the road, I was changing. By the autumn, I too would be gone.

It had not occurred to me in any profound way to enquire who, and in what circumstances, had occupied the houses in Faik Pasha Street before the rural Turks who started entering the city in large numbers in the 1960s – a flood of internal migrants that has yet to stop. Greeks, Armenians, Jews and other minorities; I knew that much, but little more. Ottoman Istanbul had been a cosmopolitan place, perhaps uniquely so. But that came to an end in the first quarter of the twentieth century, when the Armenians were deported and massacred and most of the Greeks were exchanged for Muslims in Greece – and, later on, when the Jews slipped off to Israel and the remaining Greeks fled a pogrom. Clearly there was a dissonance between the pluralism of the Ottoman era and the uncompromising Turkishness that Ataturk planted at the centre of his new republic, but I didn't care to examine it. Nor did I seriously question the Turkish belief that the Ottoman empire had in its final years been the victim of imperialism, still less query the tolerance that Turks reflexively ascribed to their forebears. I was receptive to the argument that the Armenian massacres of the First World War, perpetrated by the Ottoman Turks, were now being deliberately exaggerated by a vindictive Armenian lobby and its friends in Europe and America – xenophobes and racists. I rejoiced at Ataturk's stirring successes against the Allies, who invaded Turkey following that war, and his achievement in building a viable nation state from the empire's ruins. Above all, I supported with all my heart the contention, axiomatic among the political class and manifest in my friends, that today's Turks were Europeans, and that their rightful place was inside the European Union. I was, you might say, a Kemalist.

That final summer, working in Faik Pasha Street, I wrote an article for the *New York Review of Books* about the history of Turkey from the late nineteenth century to the death of Ataturk. Drawing on several recent books, in English and Turkish, I discussed the Ottomans' hesitant, defensive reform efforts and Ataturk's more vigorous programme of national transformation – his invocation of republicanism and rationalism, as opposed to monarchism and Islam, in defining the new Turkey. I set up a fanciful meeting between Ataturk and Abdulhamit II, the longest serving of the later Ottoman sultans, to demonstrate the gaping differences between the two. And I quoted approvingly the orientalist Bernard Lewis's contention that the Ataturk revolution, by giving voice to the Turkish national consciousness, represented the 'liberation of the last of the subject peoples of the Ottoman empire'.

Publication was delayed; my article appeared several months later. Almost immediately after that, I was forwarded a response to the article, which Robert Silvers, my editor, had received from James Russell, a professor of Armenian Studies at Harvard, and which Silvers planned to publish. It was not a friendly letter.

'Christopher de Bellaigue,' Russell began, 'has done his part to keep Turkey's past hidden, with these two references to the Armenians: "Under [Abdulhamit II's] rule thousands of Anatolian Armenians died while rioting against Ottoman Muslims during the 1890s." Actually 200,000 Armenians (none rioters) were systematically massacred in 1895–1896. The second: "A Turkish identity had emerged out of the ethnic conflict, particularly the conflict between Turks and Armenians, some half a million of whom died during the deportations and massacres of 1915." Three times that many were murdered, in a premeditated genocide. De Bellaigue's curious usage, "Anatolian Armenians", makes it seem as though they were from elsewhere. The Turks were. Armenians are the natives.'

Russell repeated the Armenian argument that the Ottoman massacres of Armenians were premeditated, and not, as the Turks claimed, isolated instances of negligence and omission. Then he turned his fire on the *New York Review*. 'If a reviewer wrote that only a third of the actual number of Jewish victims of the Holocaust had died, or that their deaths came about because they had rioted, or elected to make war against the German government, would you print it? No. But if the Nazis had not been defeated, and had successfully promoted their falsified version of the Holocaust, one might write of the crime against the Jews this way, with a clear conscience. The big lie is easily swallowed ... Armenians and their allies now turn our energies from combating Holocaust denial to pursuing justice. Turkey howls as though its world – an edifice erected on a lie – were coming to an end. Maybe it is.'

I had no such clear conscience. I was appalled, not only by the tone of Russell's letter, but also by the possibility that I had made serious mistakes. Going through my notes, I found to my dismay that I had got my information about Abdulhamit II and about the Armenian massacres of 1915 only from Turkish or pro-Turkish authors. These authors had bent over backwards not to ascribe murderous intent to the Turks, which extended to minimising the number of Armenian dead. I phoned Silvers. It appeared to many readers, he said angrily, as though I was an apologist for the Turks. Now I was furious.

From Russell's hostility, and reports I received of other letters that had been sent to the *Review*, it was clear that I had blundered into a big controversy. How, after five years of living in Turkey, could I have been blind to the consequences of so casual a treatment of this subject? I had been aware, of course, of the Armenians' increasingly successful efforts to lobby parliaments around the world to recognise the events of 1915 as genocide, and of the tensions between Turkey and its neighbour to the east, the Republic of Armenia, but at the time of writing few in Turkey were aware of the prominence that the genocide issue would soon acquire. During my time as a correspondent, I had not written, nor had I been asked to write, a single article about the 1915 massacres or their contemporary relevance. No foreign diplomat I had spoken to had cited them as a big factor in Turkey's external relations. I had been charmed by the Turks, and perhaps intimidated by their blocking silence. Russell had a point. I had helped to keep Turkey's past hidden.

I was unsure how, if at all, I should react. By the time my article was published my life had changed course. Visiting the Islamic Republic of Iran for the first time, on assignment, I had been bowled over, contrary to my every expectation. My Turkish friends had teased me – 'Be careful you don't come back a fundo!' But three weeks in the sophisticated and assertive city of Tehran had jolted my assumptions not only about Iran, but also about Turkey's western orientation, making it seem shallow and derivative. Iran's enormous culture, and the attempts of many Iranians to give it contemporary meaning, had filled the city with a creative tension I had not witnessed in Turkey. The two-legged cockroaches I had been warned about, or some of them, turned out to be absorbing people. Most important of all, with one Iranian woman, distant and beautiful, an artist and a patriot, I had fallen immediately in love. Returning to Istanbul after that first trip to Tehran, I was a goner. Within a year I had rented out the flat in Faik Pasha Street, married Bita, and become the *Economist*'s Tehran correspondent.

To begin with I missed Turkey very much. I would tune to the Turkish channels from longing; Bita and I took holidays in Istanbul. Gradually, however, the longing diminished and I began to recognise in Iran, if not in the Islamic Republic, alternatives to the harsh and imitative proscriptions of Kemalism. Returning to Turkey, Ataturk's ubiquity struck me with a new and unwelcome force, and I felt ever-sharper irritation at my Turkish friends' disparagement of Iran from their position of ignorance. Most important, I began to lose my trusty key, the Turkish language. No longer did it come easily. Gone were the days when I was mistaken for a Turk. I loved Persian now; more and more Persian words barged into my Turkish. My list of Turkish friends got shorter, until only a handful remained. My ties to Turkey, once strong enough for me to envisage staying there for ever, seemed to be shrivelling.

They were not shrivelling, but changing. I pondered once again James Russell's letter and the feelings it had awoken in me, of pique and curiosity. I began to read more about the Armenians, much more than I had read while living in Turkey, and about the other minorities that were pebbles in the Kemalist shoe: the Kurds; the Alevis, a sect of heterodox Muslims reviled by many among the Sunni majority; the Greeks. Some minorities were now negligible in number; others, like the Greeks, survived mainly through their physical legacy. But all undermined the claims, to ethnic and religious uniformity, and to Turkey's historical right to Asia Minor, on which the republic had been built. I reconsidered Lewis's statement that the Turks were the last of the Ottoman subject peoples to be liberated, and found it risible. The Ottoman empire had been run and dominated by Turkish-speaking

Muslims, the same group that went on to found the republic. Then I recalled Russell's breathtaking description of Turkey's 'world' as an 'edifice erected on a lie'. This is about as offensive a statement as one can make about a country; it is tantamount to saying, 'You have no moral reason to exist.' What hatred!

While living in Turkey, I had thought about anti-Turkish feeling only narrowly, linking it to the Kurds, whose demands were being articulated too violently for them to be ignored. Now there were other minorities, or the ghosts of other minorities, demanding their place within Turkey's 'world'. Turkey's troubled bid for EU membership, and the EU's fondness for minority rights, had encouraged more groups to present claims and grievances: the Alevis, demanding a distinct legal status; the few remaining Armenians, wanting an end to discrimination and official acknowledgement of their community's suffering; the Kurds themselves, apparently convinced that EU membership, not independence, was the answer to their woes. There was a corresponding rise in Turkish nationalism, a lynch mob in the making. But the new voices were taken seriously, by the EU and a small but vocal group of Turkish liberals, active in academe, the media and various NGOs. These liberals argued that for Turkey to emerge as a full and mature democracy, and to escape from the shadow of the generals, it would have to 'come to terms' with its past. This attractive but vague formulation meant that Turkey needed to throw away its foundation myths and confront the story of how Asia Minor had gone from being perhaps the most chaotically cosmopolitan place on earth to a declaredly homogeneous nation state, with what agonies and at what cost. The myths needed to be deconstructed, the victims consoled, and the miscreants called rhetorically to account.

Slowly, over the course of several years, I took the decision to tell this story, but not in a conventional way. I would not pore over books in libraries and faculties. I would not solicit help from the Kurdish and Armenian lobbies, nor sit at the knee of the Alevis' political representatives in Ankara or Istanbul. I would go to the back of the vessel and mix it in steerage with the forgotten peoples. From them I would get the story, gritty and unfiltered, of their loves, their losses and their sins.

In the spring of 2005 I had dinner with an old friend, a Kurdish Alevi, on the terrace of one of Ankara's oldest restaurants. Working in leisurely fashion through *mezes* of superlative quality, I told him of my ambition and asked him what place in eastern Turkey he thought I should make my subject.

'If you choose a place where there's fighting, you won't be able to work. They will make it impossible for you. So you should go somewhere outside the war zone near the Iraqi border. Let's see …' We returned to the little plates in front of us, innocent plants and fish, a foil to the potent, slightly treacherous taste of the arrack. My friend exclaimed, 'There will be none of this down there, you know! You'll have to get used to eating bread and cheese!'

Then, as the *mezes* were being cleared and the calf's liver arrived, my friend started to tell me about Varto. It was a small place in the south-east, he said, but not so far south as to be caught up in regular fighting, important beyond its size. It lay a little to the north of the great Armenian monastery of Surp Karapet; yes, it had been caught up in the fury of 1915. Later on, Varto had produced the Kurdish rebel Halit of the Cibrans, architect of the great rebellion of 1925. Varto had also produced Halit's cousin Kasim, who had turned his coat and betrayed the rebels to Ataturk. 'We Kurds,' my friend smiled, 'have many famous freedom fighters, and almost as many traitors.'

My friend had got to know Varto through his wife, also an Alevi, who had relations there. The Alevis of Varto generally spoke Zaza, he said, and the Sunnis Kurmanji; both were Kurdish languages. 'But you'll be fine. Almost everyone speaks Turkish.' Then he began to tell me about the Alevi-Sunni conflict that had long been a feature of Varto life, and about the state's exploitation of the conflict to shore up its own position.

'You know,' he said, 'the Alevis of Varto suffer from a peculiar existential angst. They are divided over whether they are Turks or Kurds.'

'How is that?'

'The Kurdish nationalists say that they are Kurds. The government says they are Turks, and rewards Alevis who toe the line. Mehmet Serif Firat is a good example. Have you heard of him?' I shook my head. 'He was a loyalist Alevi who fought on the Turkish side against the Kurdish nationalists and then wrote a book arguing that there is no such thing as a Kurd – that the Kurds don't even exist! You can imagine how many enemies that made him, in the middle of Kurdistan!

When he was eventually murdered, it was personal, not political. His uncle killed him. But that didn't stop the state from claiming he'd been killed for political reasons, and declaring him a martyr.'

By the time I had finished my fish I had decided that I would write about Varto, this curious place with a name like a cleaning detergent. 'What about the PKK?' I asked. 'Did people from Varto join?' My friend nodded vigorously. 'Varto is reputed to have one of the highest rates of PKK enlistment of any district in Turkey. You know Nizamettin Tas?' I shook my head. 'He's a Varto man. He was one of the PKK's top men, until he defected and was declared a traitor.' My friend smiled. 'Another traitor.'

Leaving the restaurant that evening, walking to my hotel through Ankara, losing my bearings a couple of times because of the new building work, I was delighted at having found my subject, my rebel land. But this pleasure was tempered by a sad realisation. Many Turks, I knew, in this city and elsewhere, would see my writing about Varto as a declaration of hostilities, the definitive end of a declining friendship. The Turkey of Ankara and Faik Pasha Street and Ataturk and the Aegean, the Turkey that had given me so much and made me what I was – I would now go behind its back and betray it.

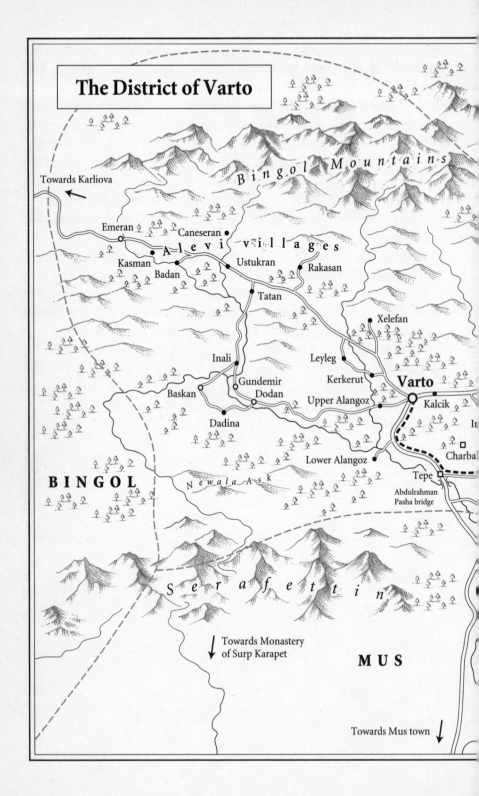

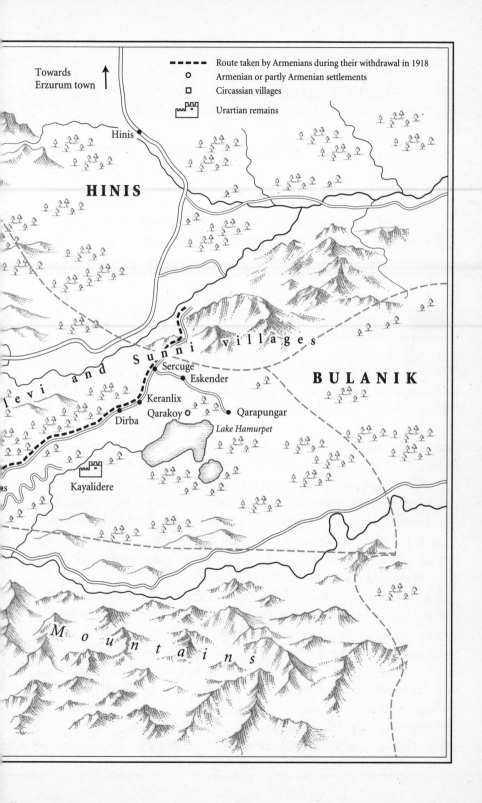

Towards
Erzurum town

- - - - - Route taken by Armenians during their withdrawal in 1918
○ Armenian or partly Armenian settlements
□ Circassian villages
Urartian remains

Hinis

HINIS

levi and Sunni villages

BULANIK

Sercuge
Eskender
Keranlix
Qarakoy ○
Dirba
Qarapungar

Lake Hamurpet

Kayalidere

Mountains

An Infinity of Shapes

Astghik, the goddess of love, beauty and the stars, was in the habit of bathing at night in the waters of the River Aradzani, which the Turks call the Murat. The local boys came to know of this and one night they lit vast bonfires on the surrounding mountaintops, in order to watch her. But Astghik was as resourceful as she was beautiful, and she immediately clothed herself in mist, which is called meshoush in Armenian, and this is how the province of Mus, within which the district of Varto lies, got its name.

IT RAINED HARD ON the first day, and again on the second. The old castle area with its ruined walls and bits of masonry and other leftovers from before the massacres was drawn over by clouds. In the main street, clerks from the governor's office leaped furtively from doorway to doorway, holding a newspaper or a briefcase over their heads, their suits damp at the shoulder and down the backs of their legs. Women in furled headscarves and olive-coloured coats stared out from the window of a supermarket. Few people held umbrellas, which was odd, for Mus is not dry and arid, not a place where people should be surprised when it rains. It tilts down a hill, like a ship taking a long time to sink, and the rainwater runs in torrents down the gutters and on to the black plain below.

Mus is a town in the middle of the easternmost third of Anatolia, the capital of a province of the same name. Its name is properly pronounced 'Mush', with a long Yorkshire vowel, a soft irresolute word that brings to mind spongy earth and brown rivers whose banks are forever bursting. The weather here, the rain and the low clouds and the mud, are accomplices in concealment. They wash away past violence and cover up present shame. Even so, very occasionally, you will hear of a secret revealing itself. I once heard of such a secret from a local who, as a schoolboy in the 1980s, had seen several fellow students playing football with a human skull they had found in a mass grave exposed by torrential rain. It was an Armenian skull, the boys had explained, the skull of an infidel, so it was all right to play football with it.

If you pass through here on your way to somewhere else, and are not much interested in history, you might come away with the impression that Mus is a town populated by Muslim Turks and that it has been this way for a very long time. In a local restaurant, tucking into lamb kebab and savoury pastries, you rarely hear a language other than Turkish. If you get into conversation with local people, they will probably tell you they are 'pure *Muslu*', which means purely of Mus, a meaningless label whose purpose is to obfuscate. It is unlikely that they will mention that they are, like the great majority of today's *Muslu*s, Kurds, for that might offend the Republic of Turkey, upon which many of them, as town-dwellers and civil servants, depend. They will not allude to the latest in a series of Kurdish rebellions against the Turkish state, the insurrection launched in 1984 by the PKK, which continues today. And they will not mention the thousands of Armenians who, less than a century ago, lived in Mus. What happened to the churches? The houses and the orchards? It doesn't occur to you to ask these questions. You get on your minibus with relief, and go on to a nicer place.

I am going on to another destination, too, with relief. These pure *Muslu*s are not very nice to foreigners. But last night, in the restaurant of another hotel, the only one in this righteous Muslim town that serves alcohol, getting merry with Lynch, there was a commotion and a big party of strangers with bulky camera bags and a profligate attitude to the Turkish lira, absorbed in their own companionship and the joy of being on the road, entered and sat down making a sibilant, hard-swallowing fuss. Armenians! Armenian-Americans, to be precise, thirty of them, and they had come all the way from LA, via Istanbul, to tour eastern Turkey under the rain. One of them came over to my table and glanced at my book. 'Lynch,' he said approvingly. 'What does he say about Mus?'

It's thanks to the Armenians and their offset reprints that H.F.B. Lynch's *Armenia: Travels and Studies* remains, even today, so cheaply and widely available. Lynch's account of two journeys he made in the 1890s, from the Black Sea coast of Anatolia, the heart of the Ottoman empire, eastwards into Russian Armenia and then, looping downwards, back again into Ottoman Anatolia, is a trove of topographic and human descriptions, maps and photographs. With the erudition and moral clarity of an opinionated, articulate Liberal Imperialist writing at the close of the Victorian era, Lynch gauges the morale of the provincial administrators, informers and freebooters who, far from their respective capitals, run two of the most decrepit empires on earth. He captures the Armenians' excruciating limbo, cocks his ear to a silence heavy with meaning. The Armenians' ancestral homeland, already divided between the Tsar and the Sultan, will soon be constituted anew, and it is in Mus that Lynch comes closest to foreseeing the imminent holocaust.

In this wretched, filthy town, where the police commissary prevents Lynch and his companions from talking freely to people, 'terror, the most abject terror' is in the air. It is 'in the atmosphere about us – a consuming passion, like that of jealousy – a haunting, exhausting spectre, which sits like a blight upon life. Such a settled state of terror is one of the most awful of human phenomena. The air holds ghosts, all joy is dead; the sun is black, the mouth parched, the mind rent and in tatters.'

The next morning, I went again to the Armenians' hotel and we got into their tour bus. We came out of Mus to the north, on to the plain, a garden for tobacco and sweet cabbages the size of tractor tyres, flecked with small villages and flocks of sheep and goats superintended by boys with cigarettes in their mouths and stocky dogs at their feet. The Armenians were in good spirits and some of them sang what I took to be patriotic songs. A few miles outside Mus, we stopped at a squat old bridge and the Armenians got off the bus to photograph it. Here, an elderly member of the party informed us, a renowned Armenian guerrilla called Kevork had fallen to the Turks in 1907. But you couldn't cross the bridge now. It had been blown in half during the PKK rebellion. There was another patriotic song and we got back on the bus.

A little further on, at a village, there was a checkpoint. The passports of everyone on board were collected for checking against the list of names that the tour guide had given the authorities. We were entering a restricted area which the Armenians had been given exceptional permission to visit. No one noticed that there was an extra person on board. Then we started to climb, escorted by an armoured Land Rover and its complement, high above the plain.

This was my first ascent towards the high tableland that divides the plain of Mus from the much smaller valley, a little to the north, to which I would devote much of the next three years of my life. The mountainside was covered in rocks and spiky grass over which the flocks picked their way. We passed lean-to shacks with thick walls made of boulders and rubble-stone. These shacks had earth roofs which sprouted green tufts and were held up by poplar trunks. At first I took them to be stables or roofed pens. Then I saw smoke rising from them, mingling with the mist and steam from the sod, and I realised that they were houses, or at least partly houses. Later I would learn that these houses often have false interior walls and a secret room for hiding livestock during the visits of a tax inspector. Then the bus could go no further because of the mud and we had to get out.

The Armenians disgorged happily in their specialist walking boots and sucked and popped through the mud. A buffalo stood at the entrance to the village, which was made up of the same lean-to houses, built on terraces looking on to the plain. The villagers came out to look, the women from their homes and the children from the simple, robust school that was the only visible government building. The women stood at the side of the road in their loose headscarves and cardigans and pendulous patterned trousers, a baby on a haunch and a leathery hand up against the vague, horizontal sunlight. The children watched slyly, some of them in dirty, sky-blue school uniforms, or tugged at their mothers. There were hardly any men. Rich, entitled, the Armenians made gracious contact. They said, *Merhaba*, the customary Turkish salutation. The Kurds replied, *Merhaba*, and the children cried out, again and again, *Merhaba*!

We walked into the village and the Armenians pointed out stones, inscribed with Armenian Cyrillic, that had been incorporated into the walls of houses. In some cases the stones had been turned upside down, requiring our guide to bend over almost double in order to read what had been written. A little further on we came to the bulging base of a brick wall whose apex had been ruined, and which was now a woodpile. We walked around to the other, concave side, which was higher up, and I realised that this had once been an apse. The Armenians gathered on the higher ground facing where the altar must have been, and the elderly man who had told us about Kevork's bridge led some prayers and hymns. Around the Armenians stood the Kurdish villagers, looking on curiously, but not so curiously as to suggest that this was their first party of Armenian tourists. And then, around them, forming the final circle, stood the eight Turkish soldiers with their rifles, wondering about the activities in the woodpile.

Until 1915, this place was the Armenian monastery of Surp Karapet, or St John the Baptist, and it was founded near the beginning of the fourth century by St Gregory the Illuminator, the Cappadocian who brought Christianity to Armenia. According to one tradition, Surp Karapet was the first, the 'mother church' of Armenia. It received important relics, such as some bones belonging to the Baptist, and its library contained texts that had been translated and transcribed by the celebrated Mesrop Mashtots, a local ascetic who devised the Armenian Cyrillic alphabet and rendered into Armenian a huge body of Christian literature.

The Surp Karapet that Lynch saw was not part of a village, but stood fortress-like and alone, its gaunt profile relieved by the cupolas of a belfry and two chapels. Everywhere, under his feet, Lynch found slabs, the resting places of princes and warriors, 'of whom we read in the pages of Armenian historians'. But then, at the end of the nineteenth century, Surp Karapet lay emasculated, enchained. Kurdish tribesmen had pillaged its riches. New buildings, designed to hold a printing press, lay empty through government orders. Of the monastery's meagre complement of twelve monks, six were absent, 'one being confined in a Turkish prison'.

Now there is a woodpile. The great monastery of Surp Karapet, the sum of fifteen centuries of labour, accretions, modification and repair, has been reduced to its separate parts. Black stone, smoothed by the centuries, incorporated at the base of a hut; a relic stolen and sold, perhaps to an Armenian thousands of miles away; a book torn up; a surplice given to a woman and used, in bits, for worn out knees and elbows. And the princes and warriors – what happened to them in 1915, after the monastery was emptied and the monks sent off to death and exile, and the dirt-poor Kurds moved in to formalise the annihilation? Are they still here, under our feet, as the Armenians sing and the soldiers look on?

Some rich westerners are performing a ceremony before a fragment of ruin, surrounded by a much larger number of poor people, Muslims

– and, further away, by soldiers holding guns. There are three distinct circles in this scene, and yet there is something in the look, or the way of standing stoically, proprietorially on the ground, that is common to all.

This is mine, says the Turkish soldier, politically mine. I am in control.

This is mine, says the Kurdish villager whose husband took up arms against the Turkish state and now rots in prison, and who occupies this land in the most basic sense, because she lives on it.

This is mine, says the worshipper in the middle, and my taking the trouble to come this way with my American passport, to stand here and say my prayers in my own language – this should make it clear that I am not giving up moral title.

And then there is me, the outsider and Nosy Parker, looking pious among the Armenians so the Turkish sergeant won't wonder who this fellow is.

We can all possess property. You find that in a deed, you get it notary-stamped: it's yours. Then the market goes up or down, or you need some money, and you sell your property to someone else. But ownership, the way I imagine the word here, at Surp Karapet, across the whole of eastern Turkey, is less a legal than an emotional term. It isn't simply the privilege to exploit. It is also the responsibility to build, to plant, to mend, to stand guard. Owning triggers primitive emotions. When three men say they own the same piece of land, such as the one I am standing on now, you get three circles, and circles have a tendency to tighten.

There it was on the map: Varto, thirty-five miles north of Mus. Varto was a district of Mus province. The small town in the middle of it, the district centre, was also called Varto.

Catching a minibus from Mus to Varto used to be a hazardous business. In general, *Mus*us remain hostile to *Vartolu*s and the reason is that people in Mus, a city dominated by orthodox Sunni Muslims, know Varto as a district of Alevis, the *Kizilbas*, or Redheads, named for the red cloth that, the historians attest, their ancestors wound

around their heads. It's not that Varto is populated by Alevis, for
Sunnis are equally if not more numerous there, but in Mus, where there
are no Alevis, Varto is synonymous with them. As every good Sunni
knows, Alevis are renegades and heretics. They are not Muslims at all.
Insulting them, beating them up, even killing them; these activities, it
has been said, are pleasing to God.

That, at any rate, was the situation until two or three decades ago.
*Muslu*s still despise *Vartolu*s but now, since the Kurdish insurgency
that started in the 1980s, the sectarian enmity has eased. When I
announced at the minibus station that I wanted to go to Varto, the
people there did not look shocked or try to dissuade me. The minibus
arrived, all but empty, the driver gunned the engine and the plain-
clothes policeman who had been following me since my return from
Surp Karapet slunk away, relieved, no doubt, that his duties were at
an end.

We left Mus towards the north-west, as if we were going to Surp
Karapet, but soon swung off to the right, crossing one headwater
of the Euphrates, the Karasu, in order to follow another, the Murat,
along its broad, solitary course. There was little cultivation on either
side. My eye started to recognise the recurrent features of this part of
the world: the clumps of dwarfish oak that dapple the escarpments;
willows straining the light through their fine, fibrous leaves;
plantations of poplar, ubiquitous, silvery. And the flocks, dotting the
soft green landscape, and the conscripts at their checkpoints.

After a while we crossed the Murat and started to climb, over the
Serafettin Mountains, the barrier between Mus and Varto, the hills
that receive a first dusting of snow in October. Now the mountains
were covered in a fine grass and the air was warm. The minibus hauled
itself up, lumbered down and around the bends.

I was on a road from somewhere to somewhere else. Others had
followed it, but few had paid much attention. There were the Victorians
Brant, Ainsworth and Lynch. The Ottoman Evliya, on his way to
Persia in the late seventeenth century, passed close, as did his French
contemporary Tavernier, breaking his journey further north. Gallant
Burnaby was well to the east, and Lehmann-Haupt and Hoffmeister,
trotting pleasantly in the nineteenth century, didn't see the Ottoman
gunk for the gentle lines of antiquity. There was one very ancient
coincidence, cause enough for celebrity, for I was now on the route

that had been followed, in 401 BC, by 10,000 Greek rowdies and their Athenian leader Xenophon. This, perhaps the greatest retreat in history, became the subject of Xenophon's celebrated travelogue, the *Anabasis* or 'March Up Country'.

The 10,000 were defeated mercenaries. They had elected Xenophon, friend of Socrates, amateur philosopher and hagiographer, to guide them home from Mesopotamia, where the Great King of Persia had given them a thrashing. Their route took them north, through the plain of Mus, as far as the nearest refuge, the Greek city of Trapezus on the Black Sea. Imagine the terror of the inhabitants, Armenians and other unremembered peoples, as the 10,000 slogged through, choosing your village, your anthill hovel, to satisfy their primitive needs. Imagine, too, the unpredictability of travel here, through lands that belonged to the Great King but were not controlled by him, and the weather turning in.

We emerged over the brow of the Serafettin Mountains. There was a grey cliff in the distance, the Bingol Mountains, and before this a valley gently hollowed and glassy where the meltwaters had spread. Closer to me, at the end of the road we were on, was a jumble of poplars and low buildings with slanting roofs, Varto town. To the west, beyond a startling blue box (the Ustukran state boarding school, I would discover), beyond the main road running past large, flattish villages, there was a second rank of villages, higher than those along the road, nosing into the spurs of the mountains where the summer pastures were.

Looking eastwards, I realised that there were three main roads running like the spokes of a wheel from Varto town – to the south (from where I had come), to the north-west and to the north-east. I saw as well how the political borders of this district followed a natural frontier formed by the mountains. I was in a small republic, population 41,000, with an elevation and climate slightly different from those of the adjacent districts; this would bear on the inhabitants' temper. You could see how winter would have the effect of turning a place like this in on itself, of preserving events under the snow.

I thought then of my friend in Ankara, and of the dinner we had had the previous month. My friend had told me a lot about Varto, but he had forgotten to tell me of its stupendous beauty. In Iran I had got used to thinking of the landscape as prone before the elements – precious water acting on a dry, jagged plain, the sun turning dismal peaks blinding white, purple and mauve. Here in the valley of Varto, I had an impression of water as landscape, masterful and unruly, swilling drunkenly and breaking banks of its own making. Above all there was this whale, poised and immense, sending out its challenge over the valley floor. The flank of the Bingol plateau inspires one not to recumbency, as the Aegean groves, nor to poetry, as the oases of Iran, but to action. I felt joy that fate had brought me here, to Varto.

The next thing I knew I was standing with my bags around me, rather exposed, near an intersection in what was evidently the centre of the town. All hopes that I had harboured of entering Varto unobtrusively vanished. An old white Renault stood there, a Renault that I would come to know well. Two men leaned complacently against the bonnet, and considered me. 'Welcome to Varto!' one of them said.

Looking back on that moment when I first stood in the upper bazaar and was greeted by Ergun, the cop with whom I would uneasily rub along, and his sidekick, the tall bald one, I feel three things. Affection, because of the time I would spend in the company of the people of Varto, looking at maps and books, recording, writing and transcribing, making this place my own. Triumph, because I outlasted the state officials who did their best, while remaining polite, to obstruct or divert me. (Ergun; the tall bald one; the district governor; the gendarmerie captain; all were posted to other places well before I finished my research.) Finally, guilt, for these *Vartolus* never invited me to come and peer into their lives or under stones they had carefully placed.

The officials, to whom I paid courtesy calls brandishing an earlier book and a letter of introduction, asked: Why Varto? I write about small things, I replied. Furthermore – warming to my theme – Varto is diverse. It has Sunnis and Alevis and it still has Armenians, the children and grandchildren of those who converted to Islam at the time of the massacres. It has a few Muslims from the Caucasus, Circassians, whom the Ottomans settled here in the nineteenth century. And it has the

Turks (though I didn't say this), the bureaucrats who get landed with this bum posting and who, with hardly an exception, long to get out.

Another interesting thing about Varto is that, despite being a little place in the middle of nowhere, its name echoes around the world. You will find people from Varto, in their tens of thousands, living in western Turkey, in the Republic of Armenia, in Germany, France, Belgium, the United States and Iraq. Of how many places as small and apparently insignificant can this be said? By writing the story of Varto, I told them, I want to write about land and identity and the way people view their past. Will you help?

Some decided to help, others to hinder. Some wanted to help, but feared they would get into trouble if they did, and others found themselves being more cooperative than they had planned. I love this prying into corners and trying to draw a design out of small instances of rage or greed or love. But there is something petty and dishonourable about it, too. You are constantly commandeering conversations, steering them on to sensitive and painful subjects. Why not let sleeping dogs lie? Why not leave this poor woman alone, why jog her memories? And then the arch of your design starts to fill, and it seems like a beautiful arch, with lessons for us all, and you press greedily on.

It is not for nothing that eastern Turkey, a.k.a. western Armenia, a.k.a. northern Kurdistan, has never been properly scrutinised. The former possession of Turkish sovereigns, a seat for Armenian kingdoms and Kurdish principalities, a place, far from the pontiffs, where the heterodox has flourished in Islam and Christianity, and a locus, during the First World War, for mass deportations and massacres of the Armenian people; modern history has not settled here. No reliable study has been carried out of the region's various inhabitants. Even the basic building blocks of identity – ethnicity, religious attachments – are loose and scattered. You might say that the science of history has been so abused and neglected here that it barely exists.

Much documentation was lost in the fighting and burning. A great deal of what does exist is guarded in high-walled repositories. One doesn't simply stroll into the parliamentary archive in Ankara and demand to see sensitive documents relating to the Kurdish rebellion of 1925. The documents are off limits even to Turkish scholars. So are many of the Turkish general staff's records of engagements with the PKK from 1984 to the present day. You are welcome to peruse documents relating to the Armenian deportations of 1915, but you will be directed to those that cast the Turks in a good light.

The Turks have written surprisingly little about the modern history of this part of their country. The reason is that the period from the late nineteenth century onwards is not considered to be history, but politics, and anyone with any sense stays away from politics. The field is left to men, many of them frauds or part-timers, who do not view history as an indispensible aid to pedagogy and human improvement, but rather as a reinforcement against particular modern perils – men with an agenda. If you want to explore the recent past, you don't do it in a library filled with their books, otherwise you will get a pretty weird idea of what happened. You get out, into the fresh air.

But even this, I soon discovered, has pitfalls of its own. Coming to Varto, I had banked on the disapproval of the Turkish state, but I had also banked on the cooperation, even enthusiasm, of the people I wished to write about. The Kurds, the Alevis and the Armenians were declaring that they were victims; well here I was, lending an ear to their victimhood. But to expect their gratitude was to disregard the reaction – of distrust, puzzlement, hilarity even – that the arrival of an Englishman in a small Turkish town in the middle of nowhere inevitably provoked.

Why had this Englishman, a Turkish-speaker living in Iran – of all places! – landed here? To write a book? To research history? A good one! He clearly had money to burn, eating in restaurants and taking taxis here and there. Where does that sort of money come from? The state of course! Which state? Britain, probably. What if the Englishman had gone native in Iran, and was now working for the fundos? Finally, most ominous of all, there remained the possibility that he was here for the Turkish government itself. An eccentric, possibly dangerous individual. Be polite to him, by all means, but tell him nothing!

Quite early in my stay, Ergun the plain-clothes cop crossed the upper bazaar to greet me with a kiss on both cheeks before forcing me to stroll with him the length of Ataturk Street, arm in arm. I hated Ergun for that.

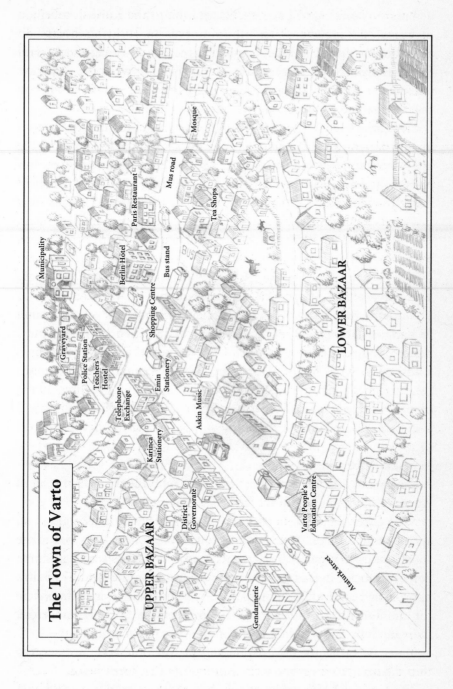

The Town of Varto

UPPER BAZAAR

LOWER BAZAAR

Municipality

Graveyard

Police Station

Teachers' Hostel

Telephone Exchange

Karinca Stationery

Berlin Hotel

Shopping Centre

Emin Stationery

Askin Music

Bus stand

Paris Restaurant

Mosque

Mus road

Tea Shops

District Governorate

Varto People's Education Centre

Gendarmerie

Ataturk Stret

Then – even worse – I was introduced to the best-known Armenian in Varto, the well-to-do distributor of a line of fridges and air conditioning units, a man whose grandfather converted to Islam rather than become another statistic in the 1915 massacres. We sat together in an office during a power cut and watched the objects on the table before us become dark stains and not once during our flaccid conversation did he utter the words he knew I was longing to hear: 'I am an Armenian. Is that what you would like to speak about?'

Eventually, when we could hardly see each other, he suggested we leave before the place became pitch dark and we ran the risk of doing ourselves an injury.

The conventional explanation for Varto's name is that it is a corruption of an Armenian first name, Vartan, from an Armenian prince, Vartan Mantagounian, who is said to have founded the first settlement here. According to this theory, under the influence of the Kurds, who often suffix their proper nouns with an 'o', Vartan evolved into Varto. But this argument has been losing ground since the Armenians were disposed of and there was no one left to champion it. Some of Varto's Alevis, Zaza-speakers, say that the word is a corruption of the Zaza 'war-e-to', which means 'your summer pasture'. In his *History of Varto and the Eastern Provinces*, Mehmet Serif Firat speculates that the name might come from the Urartians, who ruled much of eastern Anatolia in the middle of the first millennium BC.

Then there are the disputed origins of a second word, Gimgim, also spelt Gumgum, which is what Varto town used to be called – one of the town's older districts still bears this name. Some Alevis say the name comes from the drums that an Alevi holy man would beat as pilgrims approached to pay him homage. Others maintain that it summons up the clamour of a distant army. Gumgum may be Armenian in origin, meaning 'sip-sip', which would not be inappropriate, given the well-irrigated nature of the territory. Others say that Gumgum is the sound that the earth here makes at the beginning of an earthquake.

The town of Varto backs on to a low range of hills that rise gently towards the Bingol Mountains. A small river, the Xorsan Water, cuts through one of these slopes. After passing underneath Varto it issues into the valley and joins the Goskar Water; the combined waters feed the Varto Water, which in turn feeds the Murat.

The town can be divided into two distinct areas of commerce and administration, the upper bazaar and the lower bazaar, and their respective residential communities. The upper bazaar consists of one broad street, Ataturk Street, that runs from the north-east to the south-west, and this is where the Alevis gather to shop, drink tea, eat lunch and, at night, drink beer. Above Ataturk Street, heading up the slope, there are many one-storey houses and a few simple blocks of flats, most of them inhabited by Alevis. The lower bazaar, the older part of the town, is the Sunni quarter. It runs north-south along the Mus Road. The Mus Road meets Ataturk Street near the Berlin Hotel and opposite a dirty, three-storey shopping complex.

Perhaps because it became a residential area later than the lower bazaar, the upper bazaar is where the most important government buildings are. At the north-eastern end – next to the cemetery that contains, among more ordinary corpses, the remains of three unidentified PKK guerrillas who were found, frozen to death, in the spring of 1999 – is the rectangular box of the mayoralty with its Turkish flag flying and, inside the door, a photographic gallery of republic-era mayors. Walking along this street, you pass the police social club and the police station on your right. A little further on, on the northern corner of the intersection of Ataturk Street and the Mus Road, lies the Teachers' Hostel. This is where unmarried teachers who have come to Varto from other places tend to live. Ergun the plain-clothes policeman, the official face that the outsider sees when he first arrives in Varto, recommends the Teachers' Hostel as a reasonable, central place to stay.

The dormitories in the Teachers' Hostel are dusty, and the windows, at least in the month of May, resistant, having been kept closed for the whole of the preceding winter. The showers and lavatory are cold and discouraging in the extreme, the hot water intermittent, and the dormitories loud from the snoring and smelly from the feet. After a few days in the Teachers' Hostel, the new arrival becomes tired, dirty and constipated.

The Teachers' Hostel is not just a dormitory. It is a club that fills at the weekend, when teachers at primary schools in neighbouring villages come into town to send emails and have a haircut and drink tea with their friends. Then the big communal room, which contains twenty card tables, a samovar and a TV, fills with talk, the click-clack of dominoes, the muffled pounding of fists on the baize, and cigarette smoke. In a concession to non-smokers, the manager has put the TV in a no-smoking section, but the clouds of smoke do not respect the low partition around it.

Continuing along Ataturk Street, into the upper bazaar proper, you pass Emin Stationery, where the newspapers arrive from Mus every lunchtime, then Askin Music, which sells Kurdish-language and Alevi CDs, and several games arcades where nine-year-old schoolboys go to kill Vietcong. There is a fountain, and various shops selling fruit, vegetables and alcohol. Opposite the tea shops and the town's sole bar, a first-floor establishment with darkened windows and a grimy, ill-mannered clientele, is the Karinca stationery shop. Nowadays the Karinca is set back from the road. On its former site, it was torched by government agents.

The district governorate, Government House, another muddy box, is further up on the right. The mayoralty may be grander, proud and isolated at the opposite end of the street, but Government House is where the power lies and it is, consequently, where the dissatisfied come to seek redress. Unlike the mayor, the district governor is not elected, but appointed from Ankara. The mayor represents the people of Varto town alone, and his responsibilities are pretty much confined to infrastructure and culture. The governor's jurisdiction, on the other hand, is district-wide and affects everything. In front of Government House, there is a small bust of Ataturk. On public holidays, a big canvas of him, handsome, with penetrating blue eyes, flaps down the side of Government House.

The final box of consequence in Varto, a little beyond Government House and opposite the People's Education Centre, is the gendarmerie headquarters. From here an army captain, the most senior military official in the district, supervises the civil authorities much as his superiors do in Ankara – with the difference that here, being a distant and unruly zone far from the public gaze, his authority is harder to dispute. It is the captain who decides, for example, whether or not the annual migration of the flocks to summer pastures should be restricted for 'security' reasons. (The aim is to stop the shepherds providing food to PKK guerrillas.) It is he who coordinates, with his superiors in Mus, the temporary deployment of Special Team operatives to Varto to squeeze the PKK recruiters. It is he, in consultation with the men from the gendarmerie's intelligence arm, who decides on the level of surveillance appropriate to foreign writers staying at the Teachers' Hostel.

It may help to look on Varto, in common with thousands of other towns and villages across south-eastern Turkey, as a place under occupation, a place where those with authority do not generally spring from the people, where the bigwig and the common man have differing, even opposing concerns. This is what makes the office of the mayor, who does, by contrast, spring from the people, and yet must deal with civil servants and army officers who do not, so precarious. God forbid that the voters, defying the clearly expressed wishes of the state, should elect as their mayor a man who has not taken his place in the ranks of the mainstream national Turkish parties, but in a party that openly supports the PKK and its incarcerated leader Abdullah Ocalan, or Apo.

The name of this man is Demir Celik and the name of his party is the Democratic Society Party. He is a pharmacist. Someone pointed him out to me as he walked in the street, sober in his overcoat and tie, stopping to plant kisses on the cheeks of his male constituents. A stocky man, physically strong, putting himself about, eating lunch and drinking tea with the people he represents. But when I met him, I found a surprisingly restrained person, without the bombast or patter you expect to find in a professional politician, a man full of the details of running a small indebted town – and yet someone whose reading, whose culture, suggested a much broader interest in the affairs of Turkey and the world.

It's an irony of the Kurdish movement in Turkey that you occasionally come across well-educated nationalists who speak better Turkish than the officials of the republic. And so it is with Celik. His careful backing up of subordinate clause upon subordinate clause; his fondness for the discreet, distancing passive; his resolve not to let serpentine sentences dry up, but to conclude them properly, with a conjugated verb – this is the engagement of a man deeply and respectfully acquainted with the culture of the Turks, and grateful for the verbal abstraction their language affords. He speaks an efficient modern Turkish, a hands-off Turkish, not a braggart's tongue.

Demir Celik was the first person I met in Varto who seemed pleased to see me. It helped that he believed me when I said I was a writer. He hoped that I would help put Varto on the map. Sitting in the mayoralty after hours, I asked him to speak about himself and, from his replies to the directionless questions of the new arrival, I got my first idea of the memories and events that make the people of Varto – no, the people of this whole region – what they are.

For people like Demir Celik, growing up in the 1960s, an outstanding feature of childhood was the child-spies who were deputed by the village primary school teacher to hang around outside open windows with the aim of learning who, in defiance of the government's promotion of Turkish, persisted in speaking their mother tongue at home; offenders would be beaten at school the following day.

Later on, sent off to a state boarding school far from home, lonely and confused, there were the insults that the Kurdish boys received. Then there was Celik's other badge of separateness, his being an Alevi among Sunnis, and also the shame he felt, returning home spick and span from university in Ankara, and realising that no one in his family knew what toothpaste was.

Towards the end of our talk, Celik spoke about what he described as Turkey's failure to respond adequately to the Kurds' desire for peace. 'The state has fears. It fears the Kurds, the Left, Islamism. It fears each and every one of its neighbours. Everyone is an enemy. A state that has lots of enemies develops a peculiar shell as protection.'

The following day I was admitted to see the captain in an office in the gendarmerie headquarters. The captain was a hearty man, curly and blond and grainy in the way that Turks sometimes are, fit and lupine, expansive in his reaching across the table for a pack of cigarettes, in the crossing and uncrossing of his long legs. He must have felt secure here, sharing a joke with his men – the security that a military man feels, doing a job he believes in.

To start with, I found myself well-disposed to him. I was reassured by the jovial way he enquired into this and that, and the seeming indifference with which he received my answers. His shaven chin and uniform and puttees and beret corresponded, I think, to a cherished image of army officers, gallant and convivial. But this, I realised as the captain – still smiling, still calling for more Turkish coffee – showed me his perspective on the world, was the wrong image to call up. The *esprit de corps* in the Turkish army, a bristling combat-soiled army, the second biggest in Nato, rests not on social graces but on ideology. Child of an ordinary Turkish family, you enter the officer corps on merit and there is no net of class and entitlement to catch your heel as you rise. There's no requirement that you dance or speak foreign languages. The requirement is that you absorb the official ideology and history as laid down by the state, and that, furthermore, in its purest form, the form taught in the military academies. For a Turk who has done all this, a foreigner like me, poking around in the lands of Kurds and Armenians, is no friend. And so my conversation with the captain soon acquired a resentful, contemptuous undercurrent.

It was a sensitive time, but when are the times not sensitive here in the east? It was 2005. The Kurds of northern Iraq were in the process of setting up a quasi-independent state under the auspices of the American occupiers; the Kurds of Turkey, Iran and Syria felt proud and envious. The PKK had recently ended a two-year ceasefire and was resuming attacks on the security forces. Elsewhere, Turkish nationalists were offended by the increasingly overt opposition of many in Europe to Turkey's application to join the European Union, and by the suggestion of some European politicians that Turkey, if it wanted to join the European Union, must declare that the Armenian massacres of 1915 were genocide.

Part of the problem, the captain told me, was that misguided or mischievous Armenians in Istanbul, rather than thank the Republic of Turkey for its tolerance and generosity, had allowed themselves to be used by foreign enemies. Take, for instance, the Armenian newspaper editor Hrant Dink. There he was, addressing parliamentary deputies, giving interviews, preaching the need for Turkey to 'address' its past. What lay in the past, the Captain wanted to know, other than Armenian treason and betrayal? Why didn't Hrant Dink talk about that? The novelist Orhan Pamuk was another. He was all over the western papers, being lionised. His trial, for telling the Swiss weekly *Das Magazin* that '30,000 Kurds and one million Armenians died in these lands', would begin later in the year.

At such a time, when so many people wished ill for Turkey, it could hardly be an accident that I, a Turkish-speaker from a country, Britain, which had historically sought the disintegration of the Ottoman empire, was here in the east. Through his asides, his ironic smiles, the captain wanted me to know that he knew this, that he was no fool.

The captain's history started with that notorious example of western rapacity, the Treaty of Sèvres of 1920, when the Allies forced the Ottomans, whom they had defeated in the First World War, to acquiesce to the parcelling out of eastern Anatolia between the Kurds and the Armenians. This history continued in a happier vein with the Treaty of Lausanne of 1923, which Ataturk negotiated after repelling Anatolia's Greek, British and French invaders and setting up his new republic as a replacement for the defunct empire. Lausanne superseded Sèvres and restored the whole of Anatolia to Turkey.

In the captain's view Sèvres may look dead but the foreigners haven't buried it. They are longing to revive it, with their accomplices Dink and Pamuk, and I am here to push the project forward.

The captain offered me small suggestive bits of information – information to counterbalance the diet of Kurdish nationalism that, he guessed, I would be receiving from others in Varto. He opened some files and read to me the names of some of the *Vartolu*s that the PKK had murdered, for no better reason, he said, than their opposition to the PKK. There was Kerem Geldi, for instance, who ran Varto's petrol station; he was pumped full of bullets in 1993, his mouth stuffed full of money. There was Mahmut Turhan, an elected village headman, whose jaw was shot off in 1997, and Ahmet Turan, whose father was part of a state defence force and received soldiers in his tea house. The list went on.

The captain mentioned Demir Celik. The captain had never spoken to the mayor; he would not consort with a man whose party supported terrorists. He asked me what I knew about Celik and I said not much. The captain told me that Celik's sister had been a PKK member and that she had been killed in combat with the Turks. Her husband's codename was Haydar. Haydar had been the PKK's top commander in this region. Haydar had brought the PKK to Varto.

The captain asked me if I knew that Celik was from a tribe of Armenian converts. I shook my head. 'They converted and now claim to be Alevi Kurds.' In the captain's book, this made Celik's Kurdish politics, his treachery, easier to understand.

The captain had read *Those Crazy Turks*. He spoke highly of it. It's one of the bestsellers of recent years, all 750 pages of it. There are Turks who hadn't picked up a book in a decade but shocked their wives or husbands by locking themselves away in their spare time and devouring it over a couple of weeks. It tells how the Turks, led by Ataturk, expelled the invading Greeks in 1921–2 and thus took a crucial step towards Turkish independence, an achievement that was formalised at Lausanne. It's a thrilling read, packed with examples of Turkish courage and Allied cunning and greed, and you can understand why it's so popular, being an answer to all those books being written by Armenians about the massacres. 'Beloved youth!' the author of *Those Crazy Turks*, a bureaucrat and scriptwriter called Turgut Ozakman, writes near the end of his book, 'feel pride in your ancestors who brought imperialism and its lackeys to their knees, who succeeded in building a modern state from a ruin. Do not allow liars to trample the honour of your martyr and warrior ancestors.'

The book doesn't tell a new story in Turkey. School history teachers, having described the Turks' epic migration from their homeland in Central Asia, beginning in the Dark Ages, their gradual spread across the Middle East and their founding of several regional and world empires, go on to focus unswervingly on Ataturk. There is his youth as an imperial officer, his rejection of the humiliating peace imposed on the Ottomans after their defeat in the First World War, his abolition of the Sultanate and Caliphate and his setting up a modern nation state on the European model, with its capital at the Anatolian town of Ankara, in 1923. Any Turk who has been to school has a good idea of what happened at the Battle of Sakarya, when the Turks checked the Greek advance towards Ankara, and doesn't need Ozakman to spell it out in a book. *Those Crazy Turks* must therefore contain something more than a reiteration of events that everyone knows, and Ozakman's afterword spells out what it is: a defence of 'true' history, a punch in the guts for those who seek 'to destroy the republic' with their 'false history, full of lies and deceit'.

It's a striking idea, that a modern country should need shoring up in this way, that it should be vulnerable less to economic fluctuation or threatening armies than to people – Greeks, Armenians, Kurds – whose books give a competing view of events. It's striking too that when Ozakman joins the conflict he's not facing his opponents, but his fellow patriots. *Those Crazy Turks* isn't going to change minds outside the country, isn't going to alter anti-Turkish perceptions that were formed by medieval popes and perpetuated by *The Brothers Karamazov* and *Midnight Express*, because no foreign publisher would ever translate and publish a feel-good book for Turks. *Those Crazy Turks* is an interior exercise in a sealed room full of cheering people who agreed with you all along. Even the book's title, evoking the affectionate regard that the hot-blooded, patriotic, rather laddish Turk provokes in some hypothetical other, is a comforting piece of self-deception. In the frame of the dispute that means so much to Ozakman, the dispute between 'true' and 'false' history, it's as much use as dropping pamphlets into the sea.

Reading *Those Crazy Turks*, imagining the captain reading it, imagining his pleasure and that of his wife, a tall and strikingly attractive schoolteacher whom I once glimpsed in the lower bazaar, it occurred to me that this book may have sustained them a little during their posting in Varto. Since the final century of the Ottoman era, when the general staff adopted European ranks, the district of Varto has been overseen by an army captain. He appears in the reminiscences of the people, and his uniform becomes an emblem of the state and its capacity for good and ill. That was the position that my captain, the captain of *Those Crazy Turks*, occupied, and he was disliked by the people, perhaps to an unusual degree. Where, among citizens who hated him, would the captain have found his apparently limitless reserves of self-belief? In the camaraderie, I guess; in memories of staff college; in tub-thumping Turkish newspapers; in the sense of revulsion that the government servant evinces when he is in the south-east; in *Those Crazy Turks*.

What is an Alevi? Now, after two weeks in Varto, two weeks in which the Alevis have been slightly less unwelcoming than the Sunnis, I feel not much closer to an answer.

The Alevi houses have pictures on the wall, of Ali and Huseyin, respectively the first and third of Shiism's twelve imams. I know Ali, the Prophet's cousin and son-in-law, whose caliphate is synonymous with justice and peace, and I know Huseyin, Ali's younger son, whom the Damascene Omayyids murdered at Karbala in 680; these men are objects of adoration in Shia Iran. But this is where the resemblance between the Alevis and the Shias ends. Today's Alevis set store by a book, purportedly composed by the sixth imam, Cafer Sadik, which contains descriptions of the Prophet bowing to Ali and of the Prophet and Ali becoming one. To almost all Muslims, Sunni or Shia, this is blasphemous rot. Then there are the religious obligations that the Alevis disdain to perform: the ritual prayer in Arabic at specific times in the day; the pilgrimage to Mecca; the fast during Ramadan. The most important Alevi ceremony is, scandalously, a mixed affair. It is called the *cem*, is led by an Alevi holy man and involves sung and spoken prayers, the consumption of a sacrifice and a whirling dance. Asked to summarise their beliefs, some younger Alevis respond with a saying. 'Be master of your hands,' they say, 'of your tongue, and of your loins.' In other words, 'Don't steal, don't lie, don't fornicate.' Is this moral code peculiar to Alevism? I don't think so.

There is nothing perplexing about sitting in the house of a Sunni. The beliefs are there before you, no more coded than the Qoran up there on the shelf, and you gauge the piety of your hosts according to their fidelity to its strictures. Your hostess may be demure and inaccessible – her hands appear mysteriously through the doorway, holding a tray of tea things. Alternatively, in another, more secular household, she may bring in the tray, join the conversation, and remain unfazed when her scarf slips from her head. In either of these houses, there may be absences every now and then for prayers in an adjacent room; and almost certainly, in the course of a pleasant and wide-ranging conversation, invitations to confirm that Islam is the best and fullest of religions. The calendar on the wall shows the House of God in Mecca, which this slave (your host) was fortunate enough to visit – *ulhamdulallah!* – three years ago, making him something of a celebrity upon his return home. No matter how poor and wretched, no matter how isolated and ill-educated these people are, they have strength and self-esteem, and this derives from their belonging to a vast and proud community.

The house of an Alevi in Varto is harder to read. You clock the old lady wearing her scarf, but then she startles you by taking it off to show you her hennaed hair. There is no Arabic *bismallah* before lunch, no *ulhamdulallah* – where else does one find a poor home that is so empty of the name of God? You have read, in the book of a writer from Dersim, a mountainous Alevi heartland in north-central Anatolia, evidence for the indebtedness of Alevism – with its holy men and superhuman shepherds, its reverence for strange formations of stones on the tops of mountains, the esteem it teaches for the sun, the wind and the water – to older religions: Mithraism and Zoroastrianism; the cults of Hittites, Urartians and pre-Christian Armenians. You have conscientiously written down the Alevi sun prayer as dictated by a friend in Istanbul. ('Oh worthy one! You who give light and save the world from darkness! You who warm the whole world in its four corners and who give life to the eighteen thousand realms!') You clutch notes on what the same friend described as an Alevi caste system, a system that divides the holy men, descendants of the Prophet, from their followers, who are themselves graded. The holy men are known for their gifts, for their ability to fly or eat fire or turn their staff into a snake. Finally, you harbour a wicked image, picked up from some book or other, of an Alevi woman baring her breast to the moon while placing a curse on a rival.

But here, in this village overwhelmed by the cliff of Bingol, this Alevi bottle in a Sunni sea, you see none of this. You pose your questions but the answers are given warily or not at all. The older people seem to regard you as a Sunni inquisitor, come to determine the extent of their heresy. They are set on disappointing you, and stress their adherence to orthodox Islamic tenets. You are incorrect, they tell you, in your assumption that Alevis do not say the Muslim prayer. We do indeed, on certain Islamic feast days and in honour of the dead, and every community is meant to have a prayer leader, versed in Arabic and the Qoran, to lead the prayers on such occasions. Equally, it is wrong to depict us as people who do not fast. We fast for periods of eleven days (the women) or twelve days (the men), in mourning for the Imam Huseyin, and during this time we restrict ourselves to certain foodstuffs – water and meat, for instance, are out. We go without washing, sleep on the floor, and abstain from sexual acts. Is that not fasting?

It occurred to me that a good way to draw the Alevis out might be to report what the Sunnis say about them. There are the comments, for instance, of a *Vartolu* Sunni, a man who, despite having many Alevi acquaintances, remains politely mystified by them. 'If you were to ask me what Alevism is,' this man told me, 'I'd say it's a way of life that is removed from Sunni Islam. What I'm talking about is belief. If you believe that Ali is above the Prophet, this is not Islam. Even to utter this is to break the link between yourself and Islam.'

Drop these words into a crowded room of Alevis and wait for the reaction. A shrill objection comes from the old lady with the hennaed hair. 'Alevis are Muslims of the *Caferi* school,' she snorts, and goes on to affirm, in dodgy Arabic, that there is only one God and Muhammad is his Prophet. Her husband chips in, slightly irrelevantly: 'We are more democratic than the Sunnis. We are not fanatics like them. We educate our girls, give them freedom to choose.' A son shakes his head gently at the old people and says, 'Alevism is a way of life, not a religion. In any case, we're closer to Zoroastrianism than to Islam.' A second son, a member of a banned left-wing group, interjects: 'You're all missing the point! Alevism is a political movement. It's about opposition to the ruling order. We have always resisted, and we have always been persecuted.'

An important characteristic of Alevism is that there is no unified church, no central liturgy or priesthood to whom one can take the question: what are we? From the eclectic Turkish-speaking *Bektasi* Alevis of western Anatolia to the Zaza-speaking *Kizilbas* of Dersim and the new Alevi urbanites of Istanbul and the western port city of Izmir, there is a babble of competing versions. Between them, the Alevis are estimated to make up at least fifteen per cent of the country's population of more than seventy million. They are numerous, but you wouldn't know it, for they speak at odds with each other and constitute no united political force.

The main factor that has defined what it means to be an Alevi is persecution. A sense of being despised has pushed the Alevis to the fringe and induced them to bite their tongues rather than make incriminating statements of belief. It has sent them into the mountains and the forests – of Dersim, in particular – where the Sunnis cannot easily find and kill them.

The name to summon here is Selim I. To Ottoman nostalgists he is up there with the best of the sultans. Selim reigned for a mere eight years in the early sixteenth century, but he managed in that brief time to seize Syria and Egypt for the empire, and to win an oath of fealty from the guardian of the holy places in Arabia. This, in turn, paved the way for the Ottomans' assumption of the Caliphate, the leadership of Sunni Islam. But even before this, Selim had given the empire an unambiguously Sunni character. He had done this by smashing the Alevis, the *Kizilbas*.

Various in character and rite, dispersed around central and southern Anatolia, the *Kizilbas* seem to have been united, at least partially, in their support for Shah Ismail, founder of the Safavid dynasty that would transform neighbouring Iran into the world's first Shia state. During the reign of Selim's father Bayezit, Ismail's agents and proselytisers had penetrated deep into Ottoman Anatolia and, in 1511, Bayezit managed only with difficulty to put down a major *Kizilbas* rebellion.

The following year, having deposed his father, Selim prepared to roll back the *Kizilbas* and expel Ismail from those parts of eastern Anatolia that were under Iranian control. The religious authorities in Istanbul pronounced the *Kizilbas* heretics and their massacre and dispersal a religious duty. Marching east to join battle with Ismail, Selim slaughtered perhaps as many as 40,000 *Kizilbas* on the way, an act of sectarian fury that is mournfully commemorated by Alevi minstrels and poets even today. Then, in August 1514, Selim defeated Ismail at Caldiran, near the present-day border of Turkey and Iran, and the *Kizilbas* scattered.

But the *Kizilbas* credo did not die. It was reinforced in the plunging hermitages of central Anatolia by a vivid and highly poetic self-image, of martyrdom and loss. In the words of Pir Sultan Abdal – Alevi philosopher, poet and rebel – just a few decades after Caldiran:

> I gave my heart, I declared my faith to Ali,
> I shall stand firm if they cut me to pieces.
> They called me a heretic and hanged me –
> Strange, for where is my sin?

This is a question that the Alevis carried on asking well into the twentieth century, and which they ask, albeit in greater security, even today. It is to Caldiran and its turbid aftermath, a time of periodic pogroms and unrelenting harassment, that we can trace the Alevis' bent for secretiveness and seclusion. This tendency is exemplified by their nocturnal, candlelit *cem* ceremonies, often held in the manner of an illicit cult. Built into the structure of the *cem* is the role of lookout, whose job is to give notice of approaching strangers. *Cems* were not infrequently broken up by fanatical Sunnis, convinced they were doing God's will, and the participants humiliated or killed.

Here, too, lies a key to a second feature of many Alevi communities: a history of forced removal and migration, a memory of flight. In the remotest corners of Dersim, the Alevi tribes were able to live autonomously, overseen by tribal chiefs with the sanction of holy men. In more exposed areas, however, they were vulnerable. Forced conversion to Sunnism was common. For the Ottoman administrator, furthermore, resettlement was an accepted tool in the struggle to neutralise suspect groups, and this carried its own hazards.

Let us record what is, for our purposes, the most significant of these migrations, passed down by the oral histories and only recently committed to the page. In the first half of the seventeenth century there was a forced migration of certain Alevi clans to a rugged, sparsely populated district 100 miles to the south-east – to Varto.

Mehmet Serif Firat, amateur historian, foul-mouthed bully, sycophant, is before me now, on the table of a tea house in the upper bazaar. I have stapled his photograph to the photocopy I have of his book. Be-suited, glowering thickly with his crewcut and long sunburned nose, Mehmet Serif Firat looks like a bare-knuckle navvy stuffed into a sandbag.

Mehmet Serif Firat is a great man in these lands, a man who affected the course of history. It was Firat who defined the political boundary of Alevism here, a boundary that holds as true today, in the age of the PKK, as it did when he was writing in the late 1940s. Firat must have known that his *History of Varto and the Eastern Provinces* would make him one of the most reviled men in this region, for in that book he denied the existence of the Kurds and strove to bind his own Alevi community, once and for all, to the Kemalist establishment. Mehmet Serif Firat did not slink off to western Turkey after issuing his challenge. He stayed in his village, Kasman, in north-west Varto, and faced the music.

Picture Firat tapping away at his typewriter in Kasman. From here in the backward east he has done a remarkable thing. He has put himself at the service of a progressive effort, uninterrupted by Ataturk's death, to entrench the language and culture of the Turks across Anatolia. An inspiring campaign is under way to discredit the Armenians' and Kurds' separate – and, to an extent, competing – claims that eastern Anatolia is rightfully theirs. Patriotic scholars and amateurs have come together to denounce hostile inferences drawn from an ancient Persian inscription generally accepted as the oldest known reference to the Armenians, and again from Xenophon's *Anabasis* with its account of the Carduchians, a tribe whose homeland Xenophon and his men crossed, and to whom Kurdish nationalists claim kinship.

The new Turkish history joyfully rubbishes the supposed antiquity of the Armenians and the Kurds, and the related belief that the Turks arrived in Asia Minor embarrassingly late in the day. It's no easy job, uprooting these orthodoxies, but Firat and the 'scholars' whose work he admires, who include a retired colonel, are not put off. In Firat's *History* we find the Turks rolling into Anatolia from their Central Asian homeland 4,000 years before convention has it, and way in advance of the Armenians. We learn that the Parthian empire of the first century BC, hitherto considered an Iranian empire, was in fact a Turkish one. As for those so-called 'Kurdish' tongues, Zaza and Kurmanji, they apparently emerged when the Armenian emperor Tigran II (95–55 BC) forced his unhappy 'Turkish' subjects to forget their identity and debase their language. The result was two worthless alloys.

In the light of this information, it is advisable to look anew at the great westwards migration of Turkic tribes that climaxed with the defeat of the Byzantines at the hands of the Seljuk Turks, at Manzikert, east of Varto, in 1071 – and which, in turn, paved the way for the Turks' eventual domination of all of Asia Minor. It follows that these Turks, and other Turkic invaders that followed, including the Ottomans, were not taking someone else's land, as the anti-Turks like to claim, but repossessing property that had belonged to Turkic peoples at the dawn of recorded time.

Firat has an ally, I discover from the edition of the *History* that I am reading, in the form of President Cemal Gursel, the head of the military junta that seized power in Turkey in 1960.

Gursel had his hands full running the country, but he made time to write a glowing introduction to the 1961 reissue of Firat's *History of Varto and the Eastern Provinces*.

In this introduction Gursel praises Firat for showing, with recourse to 'irrefutable scientific evidence', that 'those citizens, living in eastern Anatolia, whose language, dissimilar to Turkish, has led us and them to suppose that they are not Turks, are in fact undiluted Turks' ... 'Upon the face of the earth,' he asserts, 'there is no independent race called the Kurds.' As for the 'Kurdishness' we have heard so much about – the Kurdish 'people' beloved of the foreign 'scholars' – this is the enemy's fabrication, whose aim is to destroy 'our national togetherness'.

'This work,' Gursel continues, 'demands to be read not only with care, but also with a view to instruction. This knowledgeable and idealistic schoolteacher took up his pen in order to save from darkness the history of the region where he was born and grew up; but he was unjustly martyred by those who feared the light cast by the beacon he lit ... the secret hands that carried out this bloody murder one week after the publication [of the *History*] were not content with the revenge they had exacted ... they seized copies from the shops and destroyed them. We do not even know in which corner of the homeland the unfortunate writer lies buried. Look at the degree of enmity! Like the book, they removed all trace of his grave ...'

Even now, reading this in a Varto tea house, before having met a single one of Mehmet Serif Firat's surviving relations, I know that this is not true. Firat was not 'martyred' by 'secret hands', but topped by an aggrieved uncle. He was killed not one week after the publication of his *History*, but a full year on. His grave is there in Kasman for all to see. Something in me finds it appropriate that a historian who improves reality should be embroidered in death. And from what I have heard of Mehmet Serif Firat – from his egoism and grandiloquence – he would have enjoyed being martyred in retrospect.

You and I know that the Kurds exist. We may argue over their alleged ancestral links to the Medes, the Carduchians and other ancient peoples, but we know that they have inhabited northern Mesopotamia and parts of the Iranian plateau for millennia. Mehmet Serif Firat knows what a Kurd is. He grew up in Kasman, in perpetual conflict with the Kurdish Sunni tribes who, with the complicity of the Ottomans, raided, raped and persecuted the Alevis. For him, and Alevis of his generation, that word, 'Kurd', has very precise and disagreeable connotations. So why does he write what he knows, emotionally and empirically, to be wrong?

The answer has to do with the weight of history and the irresistible appeal of great men. Firat is a leader in his community, painfully aware that since the time of Selim I his co-religionists, his tribespeople, have endured an unseemly existence as terrorised semi-troglodytes. In the Kemalist republic, by contrast, ethnically homogenising and studiously a-religious, led by a magnetic revolutionary, he sees a historic chance for the Alevis to change their destiny and achieve parity. Behind Firat's *History*, and the stress it lays on the Turkish ancestry of the Alevi tribes, lies a compelling appeal: that the Alevis of Varto declare which side of the boundary they are on – Turkish or Kurdish, republican or rebel. It's a question that has exercised the Alevis of Varto ever since.

Even today, if you walk through the villages of Varto, through mud that never seems to dry, you may come across an old man on a strip of pasture, bending down to toss away stones that the earth has brought up to its skin. The man has a flowery nose and ruined teeth and a rich grenadine complexion from the sun and snow. His clothes are dirty but expressive of a certain style, a European peasant style. He wears a jacket and a waistcoat strung with the chain of a fob watch, and a flat cloth cap.

He speaks the Turkish he remembers from military service, and conversation in that language, through the moustaches and the teeth, is slow, frustrating work. 'Uncle,' you say after a decent interval of small talk, 'are you a Turk or a Kurd?' He gestures with his old pink hand to the lapel of his filthy tweed, and there, small and red and glittering, there is a badge that shows the profile of Kemal Ataturk.

There are hundreds of men like him straining up the slopes in Varto. They are the children of Mehmet Serif Firat.

There were no Armenians living in Mehmet Serif Firat's village of Kasman, but there were about eighty, fifteen families' worth, in the neighbouring village, Emeran, which also contained many members of his Feron clan. The upper, richer part of Emeran, the Armenian part, had a church. Firat must have known those Armenians from Emeran; attending middle school in Varto town, he would have come across their sons, who attended the Fendukjian School there.

As a child Firat would have been aware of the Armenians' annual pilgrimage to Surp Karapet on the feast day of John the Baptist, and of the famous church of Akor Bab, in the neighbouring province of Harput, where ailing Armenians, as well as Sunnis and Alevis, sought cures. There would have been everyday commercial contacts with those Armenian artisans and salesmen – the costermongers, farriers and itinerant traders in linens and utensils – who held much of the Anatolian economy in their hands. The sound of church bells and of Armenian music at weddings; red Easter eggs; Greek crosses on stones in the cemeteries; some words of the Armenian, bright with Kurdish and Turkish loans, that was spoken in Mus; the Lent fast and the festival of Diarendas, when bonfires lit up the night – Firat knew all these things.

Something embarrassing must have happened, then, something needing to be forgotten, for Mehmet Serif Firat, in his *History*, to efface the Armenians. The Armenians are there in Tigran II's suppression of the 'Turkish' identity of the original inhabitants of eastern Anatolia. They are there in Firat's brief allusion to the ungrateful Armenian we know from the Turkish stereotypes, enjoying considerable rights and freedoms but 'betraying the homeland' without scruple whenever the Turks get into a tight spot. They are camp followers to the Tsar's army when it invades in 1916, looters of Alevi and Sunni property and wanton takers of lives in the brief interval between the Russian withdrawal and the arrival of Ottoman troops. And that, Firat would have us believe, is the sum Armenian contribution to the history of Varto and eastern Anatolia. As for the massacres, they are ridden over like a ditch.

If you read a little further around the subject you will see that there is nothing exceptional about this. You are looking into the same void. You broaden your search yet further, so it takes in histories and memoirs that have been written by historians and officials about Mus and its environs, with the same unsatisfactory results. Finally, a little desperately, you log on to the website of the Mus provincial governorate and click on 'Potted History'.

The official history starts with the Urartians and goes on, at breakneck speed through various Iranian, Arab and Hellenic dynasties: through the Medes, Achaemenids, Parthians and Sassanians, the Ummayids and Abbasids and Byzantines – headlong into the warm

Five generations of an Armenian family

Turkic embrace of the Seljuks and the triumph at Manzikert. The anonymous author of this history, an amplified version of which, you can be sure, is taught in local schools, deems the Armenians worthy of one mention during the ancient and medieval period. He or she counts them among the 'feudal chiefs' competing for control of Mus at the dawn of the Christian era.

From the official history, you would never know that Mus, known to the Armenians as Daron, was part of Tigran II's empire, which briefly extended from the Caspian to the Mediterranean. You would never know that it was dominated between the fourth and eighth centuries by one remarkable family, the Mamikonians, who acted as commanders-in-chief, regents, and kingmakers to various Armenian dynasties, and between the ninth and eleventh by a second family, equally remarkable, the Bagratunis. (The Mamikonians and the Bagratunis both endowed pious institutions in the district of Varto.) You would never know that the Armenians of the fourth century AD constituted the world's first Christian nation, or that the creator of the Armenian alphabet Mashtots was a local boy. You wouldn't know that, from the time of the Sassanians until the sixteenth century, the history of Armenia is one of constant flux, of regression and expansion, of fragmentation and coalescence and fragmentation again, and that the main preoccupation of magnates like the Mamikonians and Bagratunis was to balance two opposing pressures, from the Iranian east and the Graeco-Roman west. You'd be unaware that in the nineteenth century Archbishop Khrimian, travelling advocate for his people, was for a while abbot of Surp Karapet and there published the province's first periodical in any language. You would be in the dark about all this.

Victors' history, yes; for many Armenians in this and other provinces, as the Ottoman empire unravelled in the nineteenth and early twentieth centuries and the Greeks and Serbs and Macedonians and Bulgarians were reborn as independent peoples with the European Powers standing midwife – many Armenians did, indeed, dream of an independent Greater Armenia encompassing much of eastern Anatolia, and thousands plotted or took up arms to achieve this.

But there is a second aspect to this reticence, an aspect that reveals itself as I sidle up to people in Varto, speaking as casually as I can, trying to give the impression that I'm passing the time of day.

'How many Armenians were there in your village?'

Or, 'What happened here during the massacres?'

They reply, 'I don't know.'

Or, 'We had no Armenians.'

The people mumbling are different from the blond Turkish captain, who is in dudgeon because certain foreign countries have impertinently decreed that the Armenian massacres constitute genocide, and because they expect the Turks to acknowledge this and say sorry. That's an insult on a national scale and the captain shows the irritation that the Turkish republic, as inheritor state to the Ottoman empire, must logically feel.

Here in Varto the attitude is different. People are not hurt institutionally, at the level of a state with its armed forces and its collective pride, for they feel at best indifferently loyal to that state, and at worst treasonous towards it. Rather, the silence here comes from an absence of anything to say in response to the relentless drumming of politics and communications and the trajectory of apologies and human rights in the world – which come together and mean that this catastrophe, unlike so many before it, will not be forgotten.

In this silence, there is not the scowl and amnesia of an offended nation, but the cowering of individuals before a truth that has the ability to overwhelm them. This silence is a silence not of affront, but of fear.

Towards the end of my first visit to Varto, I was invited to spend the night in Emeran by someone who might become a friend. This man, Kamer Erdogan, was an Alevi, a member of the Feron tribe – he was a distant relation of Mehmet Serif Firat. He was in his thirties, but his manner was older, soft and tactful; his thick beard and weathered skin were older too. Kamer was a musician. He toured the weddings with his *baglama*, a kind of mandolin, and he went every so often to Istanbul to record his compositions, written in the Zaza tongue. But Kamer was first a farmer. His family had fields around Emeran, and several dozen sheep and goats. Kamer composed while driving the animals, while swinging a scythe, while labouring bareback through the snow after a lost ram. He had a girlfriend on the south coast; perhaps she would come and live with him in the house he was planning to build behind his parents' vegetable garden, looking on to the prairie below, and up, beyond that, towards Karliova.

Kamer's father was Huseyin, Huseyin with the ripe nose and rheumy eyes and a sack of gravel in his chest. Huseyin moved slowly, inviting comparisons with a few years ago, when he had moved faster, striding through snow a metre deep. He remembered a great deal, but not as much as last year. He rode, but more gingerly than before.

I spoke to Huseyin, recording his words. Kamer translated when his father's Turkish failed him and he lapsed into Zaza. Kamer sat deferentially on the floor in front of his father. When Kamer wanted to smoke, he crouched behind the stove, where his father couldn't see him properly. He helped his father and me to tea when he saw that our glasses were empty.

The door swung open and Kamer's mother brought in our lunch of mutton stock and bread that she had baked that morning. Again, the door swung open, and Kamer's younger sister Gulseren took her place with us. Having recently left school, Gulseren was occupied in weaving carpets on a loom that had been set up in the small primary school up the hill. We sat cross-legged on one of her creations, running from wall to rough wall, honest blocks of brown, black, grey, off-white. The same animals give us our breakfast, our milk and butter and a sour, chalky cheese that goes well on bread with honey, and the buttermilk we had with lunch.

Huseyin put down his cup. He exclaimed, 'Zeynel Efendi killed his own wife!'

I asked, 'Why?'

'You know Caneseran, just over the hill there?'

'Roughly.'

'Zeynel was a bandit. He was the Feron chief. He was on the run from the Ottomans. He found himself a hiding place at Caneseran. Zeynel was there with his wife Fatma and his son and his brother Veli. Fatma was heavily pregnant. Zeynel told Fatma to send word to her mother to come. But Fatma didn't trust her mother. Fatma's father was in jail and he knew that if he led the authorities to Zeynel he would be released. Fatma said to Zeynel, "*Efendi*! My mother can't be trusted. Don't summon her, don't let on where we are. Don't send word to her." But he insisted, "No! I'm going to send for my mother-in-law." And this is what happened, and she came and they made room for her. But Fatma's mother was thinking of her husband, and how to get him out of jail. One day she went to her son, a mere boy, and she said to him, "Go and tell the government where Zeynel is, and your father will get out of jail."

'The next morning Zeynel and the others woke up to discover that the house had been surrounded by soldiers who had come up from Ustukran. Fatma turned to Zeynel and said, "*Efendi*! Didn't I tell you that my mother couldn't be trusted?" The soldiers rushed in and found nothing and they shouted at the owner of the house, but he didn't speak Kurmanji, and they were just leaving when they saw a stone on the floor and they pushed the stone to one side and there was the trap door leading down to Zeynel's hiding place. The soldiers started firing down into the basement and Zeynel and Veli fired back. Zeynel said to Veli, "I'll keep them busy, you knock a hole through the back and escape with Fatma and the boy." Veli objected. "Brother! You look after Fatma!" Veli killed two gendarmes and then he took to the hills with Zeynel and the others.

'They reached a hamlet above Caneseran and rested there. The soldiers were pursuing them. Fatma couldn't go on any further. She was on the verge of giving birth. She turned to Zeynel and said, "*Efendi*! Don't let me fall into their hands. The soldiers ... kill me!" She was thinking of her honour. Zeynel wept. He said, "Fatma! I'll die alongside you." She said, "If you love me, take our son and get away. Kill me and flee." So Zeynel killed her with his own hand. Yes, he killed her with his own hand and he took the child and ran.'

Huseyin started coughing. Kamer got up to bring him water but the fit stopped. Huseyin shook his head. 'Zeynel was a good man.'

Early the following day Kamer and I went to several houses in the village with Kamer's two dogs, collecting sheep and goats from other people's pens until we had two or three hundred. Then we walked north out of the village. We passed the remains of an old village, further up, which was where the Armenians of Emeran had lived before 1915, where the church and mill had been. We walked over a mound where Kamer said the church had stood. Booty hunters looking for gold had dug up the place but found only fragments of worked stone. Then we went on, towards Karliova and the Bingol plateau, along the route that Zeynel Efendi had taken after killing his wife in 1912. It was the same route, in fact, that the people of Emeran and their beasts had used on countless occasions, to escape the Sunni tribes with their extortionate claims, and the tax officer, Ottoman or republican, with his.

We were climbing steadily through fine tufted grass, side by side for long periods, occasionally several hundred yards apart, according to the mood of the flock. We crossed the road that takes you to Karliova, and we passed the shell of a gendarmerie post that the Turks had started building in the 1980s, and which the PKK had firebombed before it was finished.

As recently as fifteen years ago, these higher reaches, fertile and well-watered spurs, were covered in tough, man-sized oaks. Then, in the 1990s, the valleys echoed to the sound of electric saws as the Turkish army, concerned to deny the PKK cover, cut them down. But the trees have a history here, they like the black lava beaches and the tireless wind thrilling their leaves. So now the oaks are coming back. They have grown as high as your thigh, thickening over the hills.

We stopped at a tea spot. There were stone windbreaks and a blackened pot containing tea leaves and matches and sugar cubes wrapped in plastic. The animals grazed on a knoll that was thick with celery-like cardoon, and dog rose shrubs – sacred to Alevis, home to djinns.

Sitting there, drinking our tea, we saw another figure approaching from lower down, driving another flock. It was Selim, Kamer told me, the elected headman of Emeran. Twenty minutes later Selim reached us, his animals straggling behind, and sat down. Kamer gave him a cigarette and a glass of tea and they spoke of this and that – the weather; someone's lost sheep; the death of a middle-aged woman in a neighbouring village. Then they mentioned the District Commissioner's Cup and I learned that this is a football competition open to village teams from everywhere in the district. A few years ago Emeran had a very strong team, which got to the final, where they were to face Republic, the Varto town team. The winner of that match would go to Mus to take part in the prestigious Governor's Cup, and the gendarmerie captain of the time was determined that Emeran, whose team contained several Kurdish nationalists, should not advance.

'The match was rigged!' Selim went on. 'Honest to God ... the referee and linesmen were army officers! We deserved to win. We scored a goal and the linesman raised his flag for offside and there was no way it was offside. No way! Anyway, a few of us went over to discuss the matter with the linesman and before we knew it one of the officers had come over to pull us away and there was a great big brawl. Everyone piled in.' Selim pulled on his cigarette and smiled fondly. 'We wasted them.'

'What about this year?'

'We won, but they didn't hold the Governor's Cup, so we didn't get to go to Mus.'

Selim stubbed out his cigarette and Kamer turned to me and said, 'We'd better move on before his animals get mixed up with ours.' We said goodbye to Selim and walked on.

A little further on Kamer pointed and said, 'You see those old pear trees? We still call these meadows after the Armenians who owned them. Those trees were in Hagop's meadow, and those ones in Khoren's.' He pointed in the opposite direction. 'This one is Asadur Efendi's meadow. Most of the land in Emeran was held by the Armenians. The Alevis worked for the Armenians.'

In the hierarchy of Ottoman Varto, the Sunni Kurds were on top, and the Armenians in the middle. Although they were spared the Armenians' fate, it was the Alevis, reviled as heretics, excluded from the plains, who were at the bottom.

We carried on climbing and Kamer told me that a few days from now the flocks would be taken up to the summer pastures. There, the men grazed the animals and the women made cheese and buttermilk and sold them to tradesmen jolting in bullock carts over the wind-blasted plateau, laying the cheese under gauze and taking it off for sale in Varto and beyond.

We had our lunch in the shade of a pear tree, bread and cheese and cold water from a tiny, rush-filled runnel. Kites circled above us, scouting for rabbits and snakes. A yellow-winged cuckoo, whose mournful call – 'Pepukh! Pepukh!'– gives it its name in both Kurdish languages spoken here, flew to the branch above us. In the 1970s, when everyone in Varto was a Leftist, you found shepherds in these hills, sitting in a rock, reading Das Kapital. But Kamer wanted to compose, to hum and declaim into an MP3 player. He just needed to make enough money to buy an MP3 player.

We turned back as the air started to cool. We walked an hour or two and then, from a long way off, I made out a Land Rover on the

Karliova road. A tall uniformed figure stood on the road. There was a shorter man next to him. The tall one seemed to stand across the land, his back straight, his hair resolutely blond – as distinctive and foreign, in this part of the world, as I.

'The captain,' I said. I turned to Kamer. 'The captain.' I walked heavily towards the road.

'Enjoying yourself with Kamer?' the captain asked genially when I reached him. 'A good place to talk, eh? Can't say I think much of the landscape around here. No trees.'

Then he asked, 'Learn anything interesting from Kamer?'

The captain was a busy man. He had onerous responsibilities and yet he had come all the way here, and parked by the side of the road, simply for the fun of it, to see Kamer and me, to make us feel uneasy.

Standing there, waiting for Kamer as he meandered down with the animals, the captain and I began to converse, and the captain's conversation drifted, as it was apt to do, to Sèvres and Lausanne. He cast an invigorating eye over Winston Churchill, T.E. Lawrence, Major Noel. Between them they had dismembered the Ottoman empire, gulled the Arabs, swindled the world.

'Tell me, Captain, are you happy with your Land Rover?'

The captain smiled broadly. 'Come!' He gestured for his driver to approach. The driver was grinning too. The captain asked him what he thought of the Land Rover.

'Crap, Sir.'

The captain turned back to me. 'You Brits won't even sell us decent vehicles. These heaps are always in the repair yard. Things keep dropping off them. Give me a Hummer any day.'

Who knows? The captain might not have this opportunity again, to speak freely and without constraint to an Englishman. He felt like telling me his thoughts about Iran. 'You live in Iran, no? The Americans won't dare attack. You don't just march into a civilisation thousands of years old! The Iranians draw them into the desert, into asymmetrical warfare, and the Americans stand no chance!' The captain reminded me that Iraq had been at peace under the Ottomans. Now, under the Americans … he laughed. We were both laughing, at different things, when Kamer appeared on the road before us.

'Good evening, Captain,' said Kamer. The captain stopped laughing and nodded curtly. The captain knew Kamer, but he didn't like him.

There was no point telling the captain that I had hated the invasion more than he, since it had been performed in my name. There was no point in lamenting the fact that its perpetrators – Bush and Blair and their accomplices, the editors and pundits who had trotted docilely behind them, in the manner of Kamer's sheep – would never be called to account. No point, for the captain would not trust in my sincerity.

One day, walking up the hill from the Teachers' Hostel, I heard a car behind me and turned to see the white Renault that had been intermittently following me since my arrival. I walked on and, to my surprise, the car drew alongside. The uniformed policeman sitting in the passenger seat wound down the window, and said, 'Get in. Ergun wants to see you.'

My initial fear was that Ergun had asked me in for one of the irksome 'chats' that he insisted we have from time to time. These meetings usually began with an insincere enquiry into how my work was going and with my responding that things could hardly be better, the people of Varto being exceptionally friendly, that I had learned a lot, etc, etc. Ergun would then try and draw me out on the Alevis, and the PKK, and the Armenians with their preposterous genocide claims, and the Armenian editor Hrant Dink, and I would fall in dutifully and we would sit for hours with the tall bald one chipping in and bringing tea and offering cigarettes though he knew full well I didn't smoke, and waste each other's time.

But this time was different. Ergun hadn't summoned me himself. He had recommended me to Varto's youthful police chief, whose pressed uniform and shaven cheeks made him look like a schoolboy next to the substantial Ergun, the autonomous Ergun with his stylish sandpaper moustache and superior leather jacket. I shook hands with the chief and he gestured at the bench behind him. Five people, two women, a man and two children, beamed at me. All were blond and blue eyed, the children – a boy and a girl, as I remember – stridently so. The passports of the five, the chief explained, showed that they were South Africans. They were here, drinking tea on a bench in Varto police station, because they had been discovered handing out Bibles shortly after they got off the minibus from Mus. (Ergun held one up by its spine, a neat volume printed in Istanbul, and let the pages flick open and shut.) Would I please translate for the chief so he could find out who these people were and decide what should be done with them? Certainly I would.

- Which organisation do you represent?
- None. We are private tourists who love the Lord and wish to share his message.
- Where are you going?
- Wherever the mood takes us. We love eastern Turkey. It's so … rugged.
- How would you like it if we came over to Africa and started trying to convert people to Islam?
- You would be most welcome. Such things are free in our country.
- The people here are serious in upholding Islam. You may find yourselves in danger.
- On the contrary. We feel ourselves to be in perfect safety among these wonderful people who have shown us nothing but kindness.
- Do you have any questions before you leave?
- Are there any old churches in Varto? We're interested in old churches.
- No, there are no old churches here, but there may be in Hinis.

The visitors were put on the next minibus to Hinis. The police chief thanked me. I turned to Ergun and said, 'It would be nice if your men would stop coming into the Teachers' Hostel and questioning people about me. The manager has said that I'm upsetting the teachers. If it goes on, he'll ask me to leave.'

Ergun shook his head. He looked perplexed and unhappy. 'That doesn't sound like our men. It must be one of the other outfits.' It was his way of saying, 'It must be military intelligence.' Then he said, 'Where are you going now?'

'To see Nazim Han.'

Nazim Han meets everyone. He invites Demir Celik for dinner one night, and Demir Celik's sworn rival, the former mayor, Abdulbari Han (no relation), the next. He's on good terms with the captain and the district governor but he also attends the funeral of a *Vartolu* militant whose body, full of Turkish bullets, has been retrieved by his parents from the morgue. Nazim Han is forever meeting people in Varto, at their offices or in a tea house or in the restaurant that his nephew owns. He attends marriages and funerals, both Alevi and Sunni. He spends a lot of time walking up and down the hill, to and from his house, spry and good with names, patting the passing heads of children. He has two mobile phones so he doesn't miss a call.

His house in the village of Kalcik, just up the hill from Varto town, is in an apple orchard. The pond he has dug next to the earthquake-proof summer house he sleeps in is full of trout that his wife deep fries and serves with rocket and radishes. When he receives guests in the summer house, he communicates with his wife through an intercom; that way, he can tell her what he wants and she can bring it. In the main house, a bungalow, there is tea on the stove and arrack in the fridge. His girls, his three daughters, young enough to suggest that this isn't his first marriage, smile from the wall.

He's a slight, elderly man. His spruce moustache and aquiline nose, and his equable, courteous manner, recall Bulent Ecevit, former leader of the Republican People's Party – Ataturk's party. Nazim Han's stint as mayor of Varto coincided with one of Ecevit's stints as prime minister, and Ecevit stayed with him when he visited Varto. But there can't have been much of a resemblance then. Nazim Han looks more like Ecevit the older he gets, the more his cheeks recede, the bonier he becomes. In middle age, he had a squarer face, quite unlike Ecevit's.

One of the things that distinguish Nazim Han from his fellow *Vartolu*s is the pleasure he takes from life. In general, *Vartolu*s never pass over an opportunity to say how unlucky they are. Even for this part of the world, with its huge modern patterns of migration – to cities in southern and western Turkey, to Europe and beyond – Varto is a place whose roads lead overwhelmingly out.

Nazim never left, except for military service in the late 1940s, facing the Russian divisions massed in the then Socialist Republic of Armenia, after which he returned to plant and farm. He was here for the earthquakes of 1946 and 1966, the 1980 coup and the beginnings of the PKK rebellion in 1984, events that, between them, convinced the majority of *Vartolu*s that their destiny lay elsewhere. He stayed in Kalcik, occupying the land he inherited from his grandfather, making his modest political career, meeting people, smiling, cracking jokes, unafraid to brandish his revolver when the need arose.

I've heard lots of people speak ill of Uncle Nazim, as he is known ironically, because he runs with the hares and hunts with the hounds. Two defences spring to my mind. The first is that Uncle Nazim is at least sincere in his hatred for the old conflict, between Alevis and Sunnis, that other local politicians have been known to exploit. The second defence is more personal. I cannot but feel gratitude to him because, at a time when people were slamming doors in my face, he kept his open.

Nazim Han is an Alevi. His ancestors came here from Dersim two centuries ago, fleeing a blood feud. They came to Varto because they knew that some fellow members of their Avdelan tribe were already here, and that they stood a chance of being safe. The Avdelans were less numerous and less powerful than the Ferons, Mehmet Serif Firat's clan, or the other main Alevi group, the Lolans, but they were good politicians. At the beginning of the twentieth century, when most Alevis lived high in the mountains, fearful of Sunni attacks, the Avdelans dwelt in safety near to Varto town. They were protected by the Cibrans, the biggest of the Sunni tribes, and the reason for this was that the Avdelans were an exception. They had taught themselves to farm, and this, among tribes that knew only how to herd and fight, made them valuable. Their grain was bread for the winter and their hay was fodder for the beasts. And so the Cibrans – horsemen, shepherds, cavalry to the Sultan – cherished them.

Nazim Han is the first person in Varto with whom I discussed history. It's from him that I learned the meaning of the past in a society whose members, until twenty or thirty years ago, had nothing to do at night except discuss the exploits of ancestors, to regale and sing. The fractures running through this society mean that dramatically different versions of history are being recounted in neighbouring valleys, even next-door houses. Occasionally in Varto, or among the *Vartolu*s of the diaspora, you will meet a man or a woman who confesses that a close relative – a grandfather, say – committed an appalling crime. But this is the exception. In general, *Vartolu*s use the past to acquit their ancestors and string up their enemies.

Sometimes I get infuriated and say to myself that these people must take me for a fool, starting their assassinations with weasel words: 'I'm not one to rake up the past, but you know so-and-so's great-grandfather ...' Perhaps they don't expect me to believe everything they say, or at least to be aware that this is a ritual demonstration of loyalty to the tribe.

But loyalty here is never simply a ritual. If your brother suffers a rush of blood to the head and starts a futile tribal feud, you must fall in with him and be prepared to kill or be killed for a cause that part of you, your conscience, knows to be wrong. This loyalty respects no borders. In Germany there is a *Vartolu* living in perfect accord with the rationalist spirit of the times, a model immigrant, but when he is reminded of a second *Vartolu*, a man he last met thirty years ago, he exclaims, 'A traitor, just like his father.'

I'm interested in this because I come from a country where the past is preserved only in the façades of buildings and the Queen's profile on coppers; in fact, the past has been forgotten and eyes are locked greedily on the future, and something in me finds this a meagre way to view the world, an unsalted way, conducting us to an existence without depth and art. Here, in eastern Turkey, there is no such clean break. The past and the future compete with each other in people's hearts and we can call that the present.

History lives and bleeds here, but the version one hears is a disinfected one. No self-respecting *Vartolu*, being questioned by an outsider, is going to admit to the failings and aberrations of his ancestors; that would be betrayal. This tendency is widespread among Sunnis and Alevis alike. In his *History*, in the course of a tediously long homily to his ancestors, Mehmet Serif Firat omits to mention that they made a living as bandits and highwaymen. He portrays a certain club-wielding forebear, a very Neanderthal, as a Galahad *sans pareil*, and another distant uncle, a brigand, as a man who 'set himself against injustice and oppression'.

The period of Varto's history that is available for inspection is the period that people either remember or remember other people remembering. One of the features of this history is that quite often the person telling it finds it hard, or superfluous, to link what is happening in Varto to the bigger events that we know from the history books. But no one mixes up the personalities and their foibles and weaknesses, and whether they were good or bad.

Among the national personalities, a few are distinct. The first is Abdulhamit II, sultan and caliph, self-described father of the Kurds and author of the anti-Armenian pogroms of the 1890s. There is not one but three Ataturks, the first two laudable and the third – for the Kurdish nationalists, at least – a grave disappointment. The first Ataturk, as an Ottoman officer, performed a service by helping to prevent the Armenians from gaining control of eastern Anatolia – for part of 1916, Mustafa Kemal, as he was then called, commanded the Sixteenth Army Corps, which helped hold up the advance of the Russians and their Armenian allies, and temporarily liberated Mus. The second Ataturk, a nation-builder after the Ottoman collapse, is also a good fellow; his nationalist government promised the Kurds substantial autonomy. The third Ataturk is a backstabber. He betrayed the Kurds at the Treaty of Lausanne, which did not recognise them. Not once did he mention the Kurds by name in his public speeches after the republic's proclamation. He set in train decades of oppression and denial.

The last of these national personalities is still alive. He is Apo, the PKK leader, and he has been living on a prison island in the Sea of Marmora, off Istanbul, since his capture by Turkish special forces in 1999. Millions of Kurds adore him. A great many *Vartolu*s have died and suffered in his name.

None of these men came to Varto. Few *Vartolu*s saw them in the flesh. The urgent history is local. It involves my uncle and your great-aunt. The personalities are not distant. They loom larger.

In the early nineteenth century, the Ottomans tried to centralise their rule, especially in Anatolia, and this led to the eclipse of Kurdish emirates that had enjoyed much autonomy. But the Ottomans were not strong enough to replace the emirs with an efficient civil administration, and much power and prestige passed to Kurdish men of religion, the sheikhs. In the late 1870s a sheikh called Ubaydallah launched what is thought to be the first Kurdish revolt to have had as its aim an independent Kurdistan. In particular, Ubaydallah was spurred by fears that the empire would succumb to pressure from the European Powers, Britain in particular, and grant the Armenians autonomy in south-eastern Anatolia – a territory that Kurdish nationalists and others in the Ottoman bureaucracy had long referred to as Kurdistan.

Abdulhamit II wanted to reduce the power of the sheikhs, blunt Armenian irredentism, discourage Russian interference and bind the Kurdish tribes to his Sunni, pan-Islamist orthodoxy. The scheme he hit on was to invite leading Kurdish tribal families to form auxiliary cavalry regiments, called Hamidiye after their founder, and to exempt their members from paying tax and performing military service in the regular army. By mobilising tens of thousands of Sunni Kurdish tribesmen, the sultan tipped the balance of power in eastern Anatolia further away from the Armenians and other minorities. During the 1890s these Hamidiye regiments committed atrocities against the Armenians in Sassun, south of Mus, and other places.

In Varto, the government deputed the Sunni Cibran tribe to raise two Hamidiye regiments. Originally from near Cizre, further south, the Cibrans had spread north during the nineteenth century and become the overlords of new territories, presumably with the blessing of the Ottoman authorities. In the middle of the century, the then Cibran chief ordered his son Ali to take control of Varto, and the Sunni tribes and clans of the district, some of which were in any case Cibrans, were gradually brought under his sway.

Mahmut, Ali's grandson, was the first Cibran chief to raise a Hamidiye regiment, in 1891, the year the scheme was implemented. Two years later, Mahmut and other regional Hamidiye commanders went to Istanbul and were brought before the sultan, to whom they swore allegiance in return for ceremonial sabres and money. While he was in Istanbul, it is likely that Mahmut visited his son Halit, who was studying at Abdulhamit II's newly opened School for Nomadic Tribes, on the European bank of the Bosporus.

Here was another imperial innovation, an educational establishment for the sons of tribal leaders from the sultan's Arab and Kurdish dominions. The plan was to turn these uncouth and mostly illiterate boys, many of them of dubious loyalty and character, into model Ottomans, acquainted with the languages and sciences of the day, and equipped to transmit Abdulhamit II's message of pan-Islamic Ottomanism to their followers at the edges of the empire.

One can well imagine the astonishment and trepidation with which Halit and his cousin Kasim, both members of the school's first intake, arrived at the Ottoman capital and the seat of the caliph of Islam. Istanbul in the 1890s was in jarring motion, destination unknown. It was a first stop for migrants, many of them Muslim refugees from the war-ravaged Balkans, speaking a great array of languages. It was also a nursery for the politics of the future. There was an incipient Turkish nationalism, and the more secretive Armenian and Kurdish varieties. Many subversives, whatever their ethnic background, were united in their hatred for the sultan, whom they regarded as a reactionary despot. Secret meetings took place, tracts were distributed. All this and the city's cosmopolitanism, its Jewish, Greek and Levantine minorities, the European bankers and merchants, the sultan's Art Nouveau kiosks and neo-Gothic mosques – these must have had a profound and perhaps unsettling effect on the new arrivals, masters over apparently static tracts of the Middle East, novices in the dynamic politics and culture of the world.

Amid the groans of a sinking empire, besieged by devious European Powers, there were signs of the future. The Germans threw down railways; the British introduced a postal service; the French extended the telegraph network; global financiers bought Ottoman bonds. Native compradors, many of them non-Muslims, got rich and the Bosporus was lined with fabulous villas. And then there was the sultan

A Hamidiye regiment, c. 1900

himself, rarely visible to the public, fearful of assassination, living in isolation and splendour. Abdulhamit II took a personal interest in the School for Nomadic Tribes, which was not far from his Yildiz Palace. Halit and Kasim may have glimpsed the sovereign during his weekly excursion to the imperial mosque in the palace grounds.

Halit and Kasim received instruction in Qoranic Studies, Ottoman Turkish, Arabic, Persian, French, geography and history. The school was housed in a former palace but the dormitories were freezing and the food bad enough to provoke riots. Discipline was severe but not always effective. A fight broke out between the school's Arab and Kurdish pupils after an Arab boy criticised one of the Kurds' pronunciation of an Arabic prayer. The authorities intervened savagely, injuring several boys. To escape further chastisement some of them took refuge in the grounds of the Yildiz.

There is a formal photograph of Halit and twelve fellow Kurds, immaculate in braid and epaulettes, which must have been taken shortly after their admission to the Military Academy in 1897. Seven of the boys, Halit among them, have the embroidered fez, rapier and white gloves of an Ottoman officer. Halit, who must have been fifteen or sixteen at the time, is slighter and more boyish than the others, and his upper lip is bare.

Not long after that, moustaches now grown, he was in Ottoman-governed Palestine, where he performed well enough to be promoted lieutenant-colonel. He was probably away from Varto for both of Lynch's visits, but he was certainly back by 1901.

Mehmet Serif Firat alludes to Halit's return in his *History*; it is described in a chapter titled *Eastern Provinces in the Age of Despotism*. As you might expect from an Alevi and a Kemalist, Firat loathes Abdulhamit II. The sultan, he scoffs, calls himself 'Father of the Kurds' even though he knows that 'our eastern provinces are not Kurdistan and the tribes there are not Kurds'. Firat goes on to list the cruelties and indignities that the Hamidiye regiments, under the pretext of maintaining law and order, inflicted on the other tribes of Varto, and the despotic powers that each chief enjoyed within his own tribe. In cases of protracted inter-tribal fighting, Firat notes, the government might send a pasha to investigate, but the pasha would inevitably take the side of any tribe that was associated with a Hamidiye regiment, and perhaps even send a battalion of soldiers to reinforce the mounted irregulars.

The Cibran goal was to turn the towns and fields of Varto into the 'personal farms' of the Hamidiye, and it is a shame that Firat makes this point so cursorily. Some things, at least, can be gleaned by comparing the brief account of Varto by Brant, the British consul at Erzurum, who passed through in 1838, with those of Lynch half a century later.

The Varto town seen by Brant was a 'village' of thirty Kurdish and fifteen Armenian households. The chief was a sheikh, the head of a 'sect of dervishes'. Thanks to their links to the sect and the religious endowment it maintained, the townspeople were exempt from paying the 'annuity' that people were bound to pay the pasha of Mus, and from supplying men for the army.

By the time of Lynch's visits in the 1890s, the district had gained Kurdish migrants and lost some Armenians, who had settled in the Russian Caucasus. The Ottoman government had awarded two formerly Armenian villages to Caucasian Muslims who had come the other way. Lynch's Gumgum was twice as big as Brant's and it had new shops; the new arrivals were Kurds and the town's Armenian population had probably fallen. The sheikh was nowhere to be seen. The character of the place was no longer religious, but military. The Cibrans and the Hamidiye regiments had become the overwhelming features of Varto life.

In Brant's time, the main complaint made by villagers in this region concerned their obligation to provide board and lodging for Kurdish tribesmen in the winter. This burden had increased considerably by the 1890s, when the district was headquarters to two Hamidiye regiments of at least 600 horse apiece. The Cibrans, whose stronghold in Varto consisted of three villages that were close to the provincial centre, did not have much land, certainly not enough to provide for the 'vast flocks', in Lynch's words, that they maintained. But they had rifles and sabres, and good connections with the standing army, and the district governor was usually a friend and ally. In this way they were able to shift the burden on to the local non-Cibran population.

In the case of tribes like Nazim Han's Avdelan tribe, living in close proximity to the town, there cannot have been much choice but to comply with the Cibrans' demands. In Nazim Han's telling, his family did well, putting large numbers of men to work in the fields, taking Sunni wives and getting rich. Lynch also mentions that the Cibran tribesmen from one of the regiments would spend the summer on the pastures of the Bingol Mountains, where the Alevis also took their own livestock. In the summers many Alevis would come and work in the Sunni fields, and some of them would tend the Sunnis' livestock. But not all Alevis were willing to act as bailiffs to the Cibrans, and this led to prolonged and bloody exchanges between the two communities.

The Alevis, at least, were the beneficiaries of the Young Turk revolution, which climaxed in 1909 when officers and bureaucrats from a reformist political organisation called the Committee of Union and Progress forced Abdulhamit II to abdicate in favour of his brother. As part of a wider process of reforms, the Hamidiye regiments were each assigned a regular army colonel, introducing a new and welcome degree of discipline and oversight. 'Now,' Firat writes, 'the Hamidiye regiments were unable to attack Alevis or lay waste to villages.'

The Committee of Union and Progress pardoned several Alevi fugitives. Mehmet Serif Firat was one of several Alevi boys who took up places at the new government middle school in Varto town, boarding with Sunni or Armenian families. In Firat's words, 'Although all the Hamidiye regiments seemed on the surface to be bound to the constitutional administration, they harboured a hatred for it. Under these conditions, they lived quietly and at peace with the big wages and high ranks they received. For two years, all the peoples of the east lived securely and comfortably.'

It was summer now. The days were hot, though not oppressively so, and the harvest had started in leisurely fashion on the valley floor. I had been away from Varto, for ten days in Ankara and Istanbul, and then I had come back again. I had spent more than four weeks in Varto. Soon I would go away and mull over what I had learned. As I got ready to leave, I was admitted to the last of Varto's boxes.

I had seen but never met the district governor. His youthful appearance and his manner, one of precarious nail-bitten superiority, detracted from the aura of his office. The district governor was the son of a businessman from the Black Sea region. He was in his late twenties but he looked nineteen. He wore a dark blue suit and a white shirt and a blue tie with a big knot. The district governor may have been feared but he was not respected. I am not sure he was even feared.

Ergun stayed at the door when I entered the district governor's office with Ismail Han, Nazim Han's nephew. Ismail was in charge of the local branch of the Pir Sultan Association. Pir Sultan had been an Alevi holy man, a sixteenth-century poet who raised a rebellion against the Ottomans. Now, in Pir Sultan's name, Alevis around the country were agitating for the government to recognise the Alevis, make room for their beliefs in the school curriculum and offer incentives for the building of *cem* houses. Ismail had accompanied me to invite the district governor to an evening of Alevi music, but without much hope of success; the district governor had recently refused the Pir Sultan Association's request that they be granted land in the upper bazaar for the building of a *cem* house.

I'm not sure if the district governor knew that Ismail had spent time in jail on suspicion of helping the PKK, but his distant manner suggested that I had erred in befriending him. As we talked awkwardly of this and that, the district governor's phone rang. He spoke at length about which of his colleagues had been appointed to which provinces. 'Yes, I heard he got Isparta ... yes, it's hard, difficult ... we'll see what happens when the next transfers come around.'

The district governor told me about the state's efforts to improve the local economy. He had personally distributed twenty-five rams to different villages; it was a way of replenishing stock that had been depleted when the conflict with the PKK was at its most intense. Private sector incentives were also in place. But the district governor did not seem hopeful. The tribal system, he told me, is very strong in Kurdish society. 'All the same, they expect the state to do everything for them.' He smiled one of his unpredictable smiles, a smile that said: you see what we have to put up with here?

'And what is being done to satisfy the demands of minorities – for example, the . . .?'

He cut in quickly. 'We have no minorities in Turkey. A lot of people talk about minorities, but we don't have them. It's out of the question to have minorities. There is no discrimination in Turkey.'

We sat dully. Ismail had crossed his arms and was looking intently at the floor.

I asked what proportion of the local population had moved abroad. 'I'm not sure we have those figures to hand, but I'll get them for you. It will be something for our statistics department to work on.' (Again, that unpredictable smile.) The district governor pressed a buzzer.

A man came in and the district governor asked for the population statistics. 'I want ages and place of residence.' The man looked puzzled. The district governor repeated what he had said and the man left the room. He turned back to us and picked up the thread of his thoughts. 'As I was saying, we have no minorities.' He looked at Ismail. 'Isn't that the case, my friend?'

Ismail nodded sagely. 'Of course, Mr District Governor.'

A different man appeared holding a piece of paper, but it contained the wrong information. Eventually, after more buzzing and toing and froing, the first man came back with the statistics that the district governor wanted. According to these figures, the district had several people in their mid-140s. The district governor saw nothing amusing in this. 'Some people must have died without informing us.'

That evening, the district governor invited me to his house so that he might practise his English. He had spent a year on a language course in England's west country, apparently to little effect. His English was poor. He would utter the first two or three words of the sentence in English, finish it in Turkish and get me to translate what he had said. Then, he would repeat my translation.

I remarked on the music stand next to his sofa. The district governor removed a violin from its case. 'I shall play,' he said, 'if you ...'

He said the rest in Turkish.

'Don't mind.'

'Don't mind?'

'Don't mind!'

He smiled. 'I shall play if you don't mind.'

The district governor played a piece by Zeki Muren, a composer who used to appear in drag on state TV at new year. When he had finished, he lamented that, what with his duties, he rarely found time to practise. His teacher would be cross.

He laid down his bow and began to tell me about himself. I learned that every civil servant must spend at least five years in the south-east.

'How long have you been in the south-east?'

'Three years. But I do not know how more ...' He ended the sentence in Turkish.

'How much longer I can take it.'

'Yes! Take it for two years more.'

The district governor wanted to invite girls home, for tea and Zeki Muren. He wanted to stroll down clean streets, watch a film, eat lamb kebab without a bodyguard. He wanted to be liked, respected. But he was handicapped because he wasn't interested in what was going on around him. It seemed rather to scare him. He clicked his tongue when he heard that I planned to put my life in the hands of an Alevi from Xelefan and make a visit to the summer pastures up on Bingol.

I left his house at ten p.m. and found Ismail and his friends sitting on stools in a small shop that sold beer. Ismail introduced me to a dapper man in a suit: Abdullah, the town jailer.

Abdullah gestured towards Ismail. 'I locked him up. I've locked up most of my friends at one time or another. You get used to it. Of course you long to hand over the key and say, "Get out," but the authorities aren't going to like that. Ismail knows the score.' He raised the can to his lips.

We walked up out of Xelefan, over hills and ridges and giant steps created from lava flows, towards the Bingol plateau. Above Kovike we joined a path following a gentle meridional course, between young dwarf oaks. We crossed a brook but my companion stayed me in favour of a spring further up, and its water was indeed a revelation – soft, cold, perfectly refreshing. The vale of Varto was brushed with black strokes where the Bingol Water and its affluent, the Serafettin Water, flowed into curvaceous oxbows, thence to swill lazily, profligately, into the Murat. The sumptuously variegated floor was studded with golden stooks and men moving scythes across the earth, revealing a damper, greener layer. A haze in the distance indicated the Serafettin Mountains where they are cleft by the Murat, and beyond that the busy, populous plain of Mus.

It took an hour and a half to attain the surface of the plateau. A furious wind announced a dramatically different world, as remote and heavenly as the valley was tamed. The plateau spread before us like a troubled ocean, squalled here and there into a barren knoll, plunging again as hollows and basins. Again, the wind – pushing us back towards Varto, irritating the richly perfumed yellow mullein at our feet, thrilling the purple thistles and mint clumps along tiny cavorting runnels. In the distance lay Bingol Mountain itself, a sickle's recumbent blade, strewn with loose tile-like lava.

It's up here on Bingol that Lynch, having scoured all of Armenia for the source of the grandeur of the Christian scriptures, found what he was looking for. My fulfilment was more secular. I felt not so much at the origin of things, but on the other side, spinning away from the fragile edifices of knowledge that man has raised in his cities, marking time not in the life span of a personality, or even a parliament, but in the passage of a cloud across the sky. If I were to see a patrol of Turkish troops up here, or a group of PKK guerrillas, I would feel amused by their presumption. Perhaps, it occurred to me, the reason I had given for coming to Varto was fraudulent, and I had come here to escape history, not to record it.

On we walked, my companion and I, until Varto had sunk from view behind us and we were alone under a brilliant blue tarpaulin, dabbed in movement by the unrelenting wind. We came to the first of the carcasses, elderly goats and kids that died cowering at the bank of the river during a freak snowstorm. The carcasses lay untouched by bears or wolves; it could only mean, my companion surmised, that a greater feast lay strewn along the higher slopes.

We reached the summer camp after midday. There was no 'goat-hair canvas', as in Lynch's account, 'divided up into compartments by screens of osier' and having the appearance of 'a roof with many gables', but a rude collection of pens of boulders with plastic sheeting for a roof. Inside, a large chimney emitted some heat, most of which escaped through cracks between the boulders. There was a thick, pervasive smell of goat and the slightly astringent aroma of a dry, brittle bush that the goats feed on in summer inflected the buttermilk and cheese that we were offered.

Our host was an old woman, my companion's stepmother, her head richly hennaed against headaches, her neck garlanded with red mountain ash seeds. She was occupied in skimming milk using a hand-wound centrifuge, and draining curds to make cottage cheese. Her varied produce lay in containers all around her. A man entered and lamented the carnage of the storm. He had been out again last night, watching over the survivors in his felt cloak; the mastiffs had seen off a grubbing bear.

On our way back, using a different route, we passed the martyr's resting place, though no one remembers who he was or why he was martyred. We paddled in a stream. Then we turned and climbed a steep slope to what resembled, from this distance, the hull of an upturned warship, iron-clad and foreboding. The closer we approached, the harder was the going; the warship was made out of ungainly black boulders the size of a man. At the summit we found an enclosure of stones and, within that enclosure, a dog rose shrub. Earlier pilgrims had fixed hundreds of bright scraps of cloth to the dog rose, each one attesting to pain or desire, flags for the inexactitude of life.

This eyrie is called Hazir Baba. Hazir Baba was an Alevi holy man, and it was in his honour that God manufactured this remarkable massif. At our feet lay Varto, flattened by the altitude. Further along the cliff, to the south-east, we made out a cone, exclamatory against the sky, burial place of the Prophet's cobbler. Due east rose the massive Kog peak, at Varto's eastern extremity. I turned from one wonder to the next, then down to the magnificent valley, and felt, once again, thankful awe: that I had been brought here, and not to some other place.

I was to leave Varto the next morning. I had called on Ergun for protestations of mutual esteem: 'You must let me know when you come back; we haven't seen enough of you!' I had kissed Ismail Han on both cheeks. Everyone seemed delighted I was going.

'Did you hear about Gulseren?' someone asked in the street.

'Kamer's sister?' I replied. 'The carpet weaver? What happened?'

'They kidnapped her.'

That phrase, 'They kidnapped her', is not unusual here. 'They' are a suitor and his family. In many cases, the girl is a willing accomplice in what amounts to an elopement – an elopement that, in the past, often led to violent reprisals and the beginning of a blood feud. Now, increasingly, a mullah or a village headman, or a senior tribal member, acts as a mediator between the two families. A dowry is fixed, the wedding is held and everyone is reconciled.

But that wasn't the case here. The boy who kidnapped Gulseren Erdogan was a Feron from Kaynaksu, a village in the neighbouring district of Karliova. He'd recently been in jail for theft. He and his family had visited the Erdogans a few days before, to ask for Gulseren's hand, but Gulseren had turned him down and the two families had parted on chilly terms. Now, he had come with his brothers, across the hills, to claim what he had decided should be his. They had gone off with the terrified Gulseren, over the hills and into Karliova. That was four days ago. They would hold on to Gulseren until all parties, including her family, consented to the match.

If this had happened in western Turkey, the police would have treated it as a serious crime. They would be out in force now, combing the hills, knocking on doors. There is every chance that the police's interest would have been matched by the press and TV stations. The lost carpet weaver might have become a cause célèbre, and her abduction a national scandal.

But things here are different. Girl-napping, as the usual phrase might be translated, is a common occurrence, as old as the hills, and the occupying force prefers to stand at a discreet distance from the barbarous rites of a backward people.

There is a more personal gripe. Take this fellow Kamer, brother of the kidnapped girl. He is no friend of the Republic of Turkey. Come election time, he campaigns hard for the Kurdish nationalists. He works against the state and then, when his sister gets into trouble, expects the state to help him out!

Such thoughts may have run through the mind of the gendarmerie commander whom the Erdogans approached following Gulseren's abduction. Rather than send a team to the scene of the crime, the commander requested witnesses. When Kamer asked him why no one had been dispatched in pursuit of the kidnappers, who were on foot and might possibly have been apprehended, the commander replied that, since no one had been wounded or killed, the incident could not be considered important. He told the family that Gulseren would be sought the length and breadth of the district, but his tone, of boredom and revulsion, suggested otherwise.

That evening Kamer happened to be in Varto town, drafting a press release, for dispatch to the national newspapers and women's rights associations, in the offices of the local newspaper, the *Gimgim News*. According to this document, after visiting the gendarmerie post, Kamer had pursued Gulseren to Karliova. There, Kamer had been able to speak to his sister on the telephone. She had told him, 'I have to stay here now,' and then the telephone had gone dead.

'On the third day after the incident,' ran Kamer's account, 'we learned by telephone that the girl together with the armed men were in the house of Cemile Surmeli ... in the village of Kaynaksu. We duly went to the Karliova prosecutor and requested his help. The prosecutor stated that he would not intervene because he had not received any communication from the Varto prosecutor about the case, and he said this in an extremely impolite fashion. Upon our saying that we knew the location of a girl who had been kidnapped at gunpoint, and that he had no right to react with indifference, he called the police and had us thrown out.

'We stood no chance of recovering my sister, except through our own endeavours. We went by vehicle to Kaynaksu, where she was being held. We spoke to Cemile Surmeli and said that we wanted to see our sister and Cemile Surmeli replied that our sister had not been brought to her house and that she was in the dark over the affair. But her neighbours contradicted her and said that the girl had been held in her house, but that, on hearing that we had come to Karliova, the kidnappers had taken her to another village.'

That was a few days ago. The trail was cold now. The gendarmerie had done nothing. Kamer was tired and angry, chainsmoking in the offices of the *Gimgim News*. He wanted to embarrass the state into action. Among some of his kinsmen, there had been support for the idea of raising a force of armed men and abducting a girl from Kaynaksu in response. Kamer has resisted this. He had spoken to a prominent local lawyer, but the lawyer had not offered to help; his cold response had angered Kamer as much as the state's indifference.

It wasn't just a question of Gulseren, Kamer told me. It was about the subordination, the enslavement, of women. He seemed alone, this gnarled, woody farmer – his brave voice lost in one of Varto's anthill houses.

I went north, following the route taken by Xenophon's 10,000, through Hinis and up high again and finally down to the Camel's Neck, a broad corridor leading to the scowling garrison town of Erzurum.

'After the Russian withdrawal from Erzurum during the First World War,' the driver told me, 'a blind man asked a companion to guide him to a spot in the Camel's Neck. When they reached the spot, the blind man put out his hands and said, "Where are the trees?" His companion replied, "They were all cut down by the Russians." The blind man said, "There is a fine treasure buried here, but I can only find it using the trees." So they returned to Erzurum empty handed.'

Erzurum should be a cosmopolitan town, a humming place where traders from the Republic of Armenia, 100 miles to the east, mix with Turkish-speaking wholesalers and Kurdish porters. But the Turks closed the border in 1993, in response to Armenia's annexation of a territory that had been held by another Turkic people, the Azerbaijanis. To that dispute has been added the recent juggernaut of parliamentary resolutions recognising the events of 1915 as a genocide, each one received with satisfaction in Armenia. The border is unlikely to reopen soon. There are no visiting Armenians in Erzurum, and the Kurds, a sour, vulnerable minority, skulk in their ghettoes. Here, on the southern side of an enormous plain, entrance to central Anatolia, the wind screams and fist-like mosques push stubby thumb minarets into the sky.

Coming north from Varto, Erzurum marks the beginning of Turkish nationalism. The Turks here cling fanatically to their Turkishness, and for this they are applauded by the state. But the state, being secular, is less keen on their Islamist leanings, and this leads to interesting tensions.

I watched enraptured as two female students in headscarves approached the entrance to Ataturk University, in the outskirts of the town. Turkey is famous for banning headscarves in public universities. In *Snow*, Orhan Pamuk makes a novel out of this policy and the vengeful Islamism it engenders. Islam is famous for banning the exposure of women's hair. In *Snow*, the result is a rash of suicides and murders. What would be the result here, at the gates to Ataturk University?

The girls entered a kiosk before the entrance. They emerged looking dramatically different. The taller of the two now had a magnificent cascade of brown tresses. Her friend was platinum blonde; she would not have been out of place in the Copacabana. They entered Ataturk University unmolested.

Somewhere, some doctor of Islamic law, a local or national authority, had ruled that these preposterous wigs, whose effect was not to kill the sexuality of these two women but to accentuate it and even to turn them into objects of fantasy, constituted an acceptable Islamic head covering.

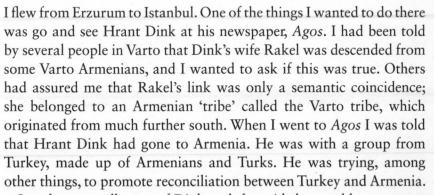

I flew from Erzurum to Istanbul. One of the things I wanted to do there was go and see Hrant Dink at his newspaper, *Agos*. I had been told by several people in Varto that Dink's wife Rakel was descended from some Varto Armenians, and I wanted to ask if this was true. Others had assured me that Rakel's link was only a semantic coincidence; she belonged to an Armenian 'tribe' called the Varto tribe, which originated from much further south. When I went to *Agos* I was told that Hrant Dink had gone to Armenia. He was with a group from Turkey, made up of Armenians and Turks. He was trying, among other things, to promote reconciliation between Turkey and Armenia.

I spoke to a colleague of Dink and she said she would pass on my enquiry. She didn't advise my contacting Rakel Dink directly; it would be best, she said, to go through Hrant. We drank tea and chatted. We spoke of Istanbul's small, beleaguered Armenian community and of Orhan Pamuk's impending trial. Pamuk, I remarked, could not have had much idea of the reaction his comments about the deaths of Kurds and Armenians would provoke – *Das Magazin*, after all, is hardly the *New Yorker*, and Turkey's judicial authorities are far from consistent in their reaction to comments made in the public domain about the Armenians and the Kurds. Then we spoke of the decision by the Swiss judiciary to launch an investigation into Professor Yusuf Halacoglu, the head of the Turkish Historical Society, a public research body set up by Ataturk, on the grounds that his denial of the Armenian genocide during a speech in Switzerland may have constituted illegal racism.

I remembered Halacoglu from the 1990s, long before the international debate over the fate of the Ottoman Armenians reached anything like today's pitch. I remembered sitting in his office in Ankara as he told me that the number of Armenians who died during the deportations had not exceeded 30,000 – a very long way from the figure, of between one and one and a half million, that is more commonly advanced. And here was Dink, and other Armenians in Turkey, deploring the Swiss position, defending Halacoglu's right to express his views.

Dink referred publicly to the massacres of 1915 as a genocide, but he didn't insist that everyone else do so, and this distinguished him from the maximalists on both sides. His humane, pluralist instincts upset Armenians outside Turkey who had campaigned for genocide recognition in the world's parliaments; and he had criticised legislation approved by French deputies outlawing genocide denial. From what I knew of him, I liked this man. I liked his small poky offices, at once at the centre of the Armenian world and, somehow, at its remotest extreme. And I felt hot embarrassment for the Turkish state, and its legion of barrel-chested defenders, for calling him a threat.

That afternoon I went to Istiklal Street, to the bookshops I had visited idly as an Istanbul resident, and which I would now go to again and again – with new urgency. I went to Simurg, Pamuk's haunt till he got too famous, where the cat rests on the computer monitor and tea is served and the management maintains its tact and urbanity in the face of the customer's spiralling demands.

'*The Waking: A Handbook for Turkish Socialists*?'

'Got that.'

'Besikci's *Structure of the South-east*?'

'1967 edition. Very rare. But I think we have it.'

'Mehmet Can Yuce's *The Sun that rises in the East*?'

'You'll have trouble finding that. It's banned.'

Further down Istiklal Street, beyond the Galatasaray Lycée, deep in the Alhambra Arcade, I visited Medya for current titles on Kurdish subjects. I went to the Armenian publisher Aras, where I found the memoir of the Armenian military leader Andranik, and got the telephone number of the venerable Parisian Samuelian, who would surely have a copy of the Armenian nationalist hero Roupen Pasha's memoirs in its French distillation. In another, non-specialist bookshop, I bought Pamuk's *Snow* and Halacoglu's *Armenian Deportation*.

I stopped at the top of Faik Pasha Street, admiring the gorgeous Italianate first bend, but advanced no further. Passing the shops where I used to do my shopping, recognising familiar figures leaning in the doorways or standing behind the counters, I put my head down and walked. I would have gone in and saluted these men and women, who had been friendly and kind to me, but they would have asked me what I was doing now, and I would have been ashamed to answer with the truth.

The following morning, labouring under all the new books, endless back copies of Varto's local newspaper, the *Gimgim News,* and photocopies in sheaves, I boarded the bus for Ataturk Airport. The Iranians returning from their holidays put on their headscarves in the departure lounge and the captain said a short prayer for the martyrs of the Iranian revolution and I was no longer in Turkey. Next time, I decided, I would arrange things so I could return overland from Varto to Tehran. I would take a bus or minibus to Van and from there go on to Dogubeyazit and the land border.

Dogubeyazit is where I got engaged. It's where I wrote a letter to my prospective father-in-law, asking for his daughter's hand, and she crossed the border back into Iran, passing under Ataturk and Khomeini, holding my letter.

We had travelled during that sojourn full of promise, our emotions accelerating, from the palace of Ishak Pasha near Dogubeyazit up to Kars, where we ate Kars cheddar and were surprised by the Russian prostitutes, and thence to the ancient Armenian capital of Ani, on the Turkish side of the closed border with modern Armenia, where there was a French-speaking conscript from Izmir, seeing out his military service, surprised by his own enthusiasm for the history of the Armenian kings. We drove through the modest roadstead of Caldiran, where Selim I smashed Shah Ismail, and we went to Van, whose lake loops like a noose. And everywhere we were caught in the skirts of Mount Ararat.

'Take your time, my love,' she says down the crackling line, 'we're fine without you. I can manage; just a little tired …'

I said I'd be away three weeks, I know, and it was closer to six. This time will be the last, I promise. Next time I will rely on my imagination, and sit in a library near to home.

I wrote this in a cream-coloured bribe purchased from the handbag department of the brand new Harvey Nichols in Istanbul, in its lissom straps and the credit card slip in my wallet, and in its brand name, almost invisible against the blushing leather.

I went every day to our cottage just outside Tehran, and looked at the books and papers and transcriptions lying around me. I had dozens of hours of interviews, with *Vartolus* in Varto and elsewhere. Many of these hours were worthless except as an illustration of history's imprecision – not science at all, really, but the landscaping of churned ground so it looks nice.

We are not in the realm of historical interpretation. Under discussion are the bare facts. I had heard diametrically opposed accounts of things that happened 100 years before or last week. Concerning a single event dividing families or communities, I might be told three or four versions. Sometimes I sensed that all sides were lying or deliberately omitting things and I would be convinced that even on so simple a question as who started a riot, I would be unable to work out what happened. 'It does not follow,' the Cambridge historian E.H. Carr once wrote, 'that because a mountain appears to take on different shapes from different angles of vision, it has objectively either no shape at all or an infinity of shapes.' And yet that is what I saw: an infinity of shapes.

Here in the reserve store, rummaging through facts that no researcher had yet privileged with his attention, far less threaded into a coherent narrative, I got a new impression of the past: as a chaotic series of emotions, of outrage and guilt, scornful of chronology and very often founded on gossip, hagiography or slander. A second obstacle was the tendency of my interviewees to dramatise things and turn them into a pageant; they shamelessly versified the most prosaic people and events. Every story had its 'hero', but often I found that the hero was spotted with villainy.

In Varto it is commonly held that the PKK leader Apo is a great man, and that I am a spy. These views are wrong, but that doesn't prevent people from cherishing and loving them. The point of no return comes when such things are written down, for everyone knows how hard it is to refute the written word. How on earth did one of my Varto informants, a voracious but spasmodic reader, get it into his head that Major Noel, a British intelligence officer notorious among the Turks for his pro-Kurdish views, visited Varto in 1919, and that he was killed by a patriotic Turkish officer? (Noel did not get as far as Varto, and he was not murdered in Turkey. He died in England in 1974, at the ripe old age of eighty-eight.) But it hardly matters. These are the facts as he stated them and since he is one of the top men in his village, and is known as a writer and a scholar, they have grown a crust of truth.

From the second half of the nineteenth century until the beginning of the First World War, and then from the suppression of the Kurdish rebellion of 1925 to the present day, things are relatively straightforward. The first period is a heyday of cooperation between the Sunni Cibran tribe and the Ottoman government, and the persecution of the Alevis – and, to a lesser extent, the Armenians. With the Kemalist triumph over the Kurds of 1925, and the gradual fall from prominence of the Cibrans in favour of the Alevis, there begins a period of political ferment, and rearranging hierarchies, that will climax with the emergence of the PKK. But there is a bottleneck, from 1914 to 1925, where pressure builds from the sheer agglomeration of suffering and atrocities, a steaming decade of war, massacre, famine, invasion, liberation, rebellion and reaction. We find such bottlenecks in other places: in the Poland of the Second World War, for instance, ravaged by German and Russian invasion, a scene for the Jews' extermination. They furnish proof after proof of the beastliness of humanity, and, less frequently, of its exquisite nobility.

Such periods of compressed history tend to define the long unpressured decades and centuries that follow, but there is a tendency among those who lived through them, those whose features became distorted and ugly, to forget what they saw and did. And then, by the time a generation or two has passed, the historical landscaping has begun: the mass graves are planted with trees, a pleasant park grows over the bones. Briars conceal the rusting barbed wire and the syringes of a ghastly ideology.

I am here, with my notes and my books and my enquiries to helpful scholars, to hack through the briars. I stand now at the edge of the thickest part, to which no researcher or historian has been admitted. If there is no coherent account of the fate of the Armenians of Varto, there are two explanations. The first is that the evidence for what happened has been substantially hidden, and the second is that the events themselves, the evils perpetrated, are shockingly banal. Varto is not an Erzurum or a Mus, with their numerous eyewitness accounts and the prominence they enjoy in the oral libraries. Varto is a small place and it speaks in its smallness of those hundreds or thousands of other small places across the rebel land, where the atrocities happened far from prying eyes, and where the cover-up is already so advanced that, if not now, then certainly in a generation, the people will be able to say: 'Armenians? What Armenians?'

I am here to prevent the people of Varto from being able to say this. It will be my contribution.

'Tell me about the Armenians,' I asked a Varto Alevi one day, and he replied in an unexpected way, with a story about the *pepukh*, the yellow-winged cuckoo whose mournful call echoes over the slopes in spring.

'There were once a sister and a brother. Their mother had died and their father had married again. The stepmother was wicked and she was cruel to the children, who were scared of her. When spring came, and the cardoon started to sprout across the meadows, the stepmother gave the children a saddlebag and told them to fill it with cardoon. When they had filled it, they set out for home, the little boy carrying the saddlebag over his back. As they approached home, the girl noticed that the saddlebag was empty and she accused her brother of eating the cardoon. "It's almost dark! What will our stepmother do to us now?" Her brother was distraught. "I didn't eat the cardoon. I only took one stalk, and that was with your permission. Open up my stomach and look; you'll find one stalk inside." So the girl split open her brother's stomach and saw that he was telling the truth; there was only one cardoon stalk inside. Then she was filled with remorse, for her brother would never rise again, and after washing and burying him she prayed: "God! Turn me into a bird that will forever mourn my brother." And this is what God did. And she sang:

> "*Pepukh*! Oh woe!
> Who slew him? I slew him!
> Who washed him? I washed him!
> Who buried him? I buried him!"

'We and the Armenians were like brother and sister,' the Alevi smiled sadly. 'Only we didn't have the decency to bury them.'

Rebel Land

On the plain of Mus the Kurdish chief Mirza Bey honoured the Armenian saints and spoke Armenian. They tell that on one occasion, visiting an important monastery, his son Halil, an obnoxious boy of twelve, mounted the beautiful but unbroken horse of the Father Superior; doing so, he shouted, 'I'm riding the horse! I'm riding the monastery! I'm riding the Father Superior!' Upon which the horse went berserk and bolted, returning several hours later, dragging the boy's lifeless body behind him. Mirza Bey attributed his son's death to the sacred power of the place, and retired with his head bowed.

SOON AFTER THE OUTBREAK of the First World War, writes Mehmet Serif Firat, 'to the beating of drums', the Alevis of Varto 'were inducted into the army and sent off to defend the homeland'. This does not sound like the Alevis of old, and a straw poll of the elderly in Varto today, people whose fathers and uncles were young men at the time, suggests that things happened differently. A great many Alevis in Varto responded to the mobilisation not in the manner described by Firat, but in time-honoured fashion, by taking to the hills.

The leading Ottomans of the time were supporters of the Committee of Union and Progress – the officer-dominated party that had engineered Sultan Abdulhamit II's abdication, and which endeavoured after that, under the guidance of three ministers, each of them committed Turkish nationalists, Enver (War), Talat (Interior) and Cemal (Marine), to prepare the empire for war.

These men had local cronies. There was the prefect of Mus, a friend of Talat Pasha. Then there were the Sunni Kurdish lords, such as Halit of the Cibrans; despite their nostalgia for the days of Abdulhamit II, such men remained the empire's regional pillars.

The Armenians were now the biggest Christian minority in an

empire whose other Christian subjects, predominantly in the Balkans, had mostly achieved independence. To the Armenians, independence seemed distant. They inhabited lands that the Ottomans rightly deemed vital to the empire's survival, and they shared this land with others – Turks, Kurds, Circassians, Jews. According to their own figures, the Armenians constituted well under half the population in the core Armenian area. And the Armenians themselves were not united. Many viewed with scepticism the aspirations to an independent, Socialist Armenia, that had been articulated by the Hunchak Socialist revolutionary movement. Opinion was divided on the wisdom of those patriotic groups who had, prior to Abdulhamit II's unseating, roamed the countryside assassinating Ottoman officials, Kurdish lords, and sundry collaborators, inviting reprisals by the authorities.

Briefly, on the eve of the Serbian crisis that heralded war, there was a new element: hope. In February 1914 the Ottomans acceded to European pressure and enacted comprehensive administrative reforms in eastern Anatolia. According to these reforms, the Armenian-inhabited areas were to be formed into two super-provinces enjoying much administrative autonomy and overseen by Europeans.

With the outbreak of war, which Ottoman Turkey entered on the side of Germany and the Axis Powers, the reforms were shelved. But even then, a large number of Armenians continued to express their loyalty to the empire, even if desertion rates were high. The biggest of the legal Armenian political organisations, the Dashnaks, had refused a demand from the Committee of Union and Progress to send volunteer groups into the Russian Caucasus, but they declared their support for the Ottoman war aims.

In Mus, while a number of revolutionaries readied themselves for hostilities against the Ottomans, prominent local Armenians tried to moderate the often brutal implementation of official measures, sometimes aimed at the whole population but usually much more rigorously applied to the Armenians, such as the requisitioning of food and provisions for the front. They did not have much success, as this account by Alma Johansson, a Swede working for the Deutscher Hilfsbund, a missionary and charitable organisation in Mus, shows.

'[The Armenians'] goods, their money, all was confiscated … only a tenth perhaps was really for the war, the rest was pure robbery. It was necessary to have food ... carried to the front, on the Caucasian frontier. For this purpose the government sent out more than 300 Armenian men, many cripples among them, and boys not more than twelve years old, to carry the goods – a three-week journey from Mus to the Russian frontier. As every individual Armenian was robbed of everything he ever had, these poor people soon died of hunger and cold on the way. If out of these 300 Armenians thirty or forty returned, it was a marvel; the rest were either beaten to death or died from the causes stated above.'

Docility; terror-struck torpor; an unwillingness to look lethal reality in the eye; these are the conditions of mind that the Armenian revolutionary Garo Sassuni, in his *History of the World of Daron*, written years later, associated with his fellow-Armenians in the first months of war. But there was another, more urgent sense among the hot-blooded, that amid the clash of arms lay an opportunity. For all the hardships that Russia had inflicted on the inhabitants of Caucasian Armenia, many Armenians living in Anatolia believed that they stood a good chance of attaining autonomy or independence if the Russians defeated the Ottomans. Convening abroad, the Hunchaks pledged defiance of the Sultan. Having slipped across the border to Tiblisi, Erzurum's Armenian parliamentary deputy Pasdermajian organised partisan units for operations against Turkey; he and other revolutionary leaders were joined by groups of young Ottoman Armenians. And numerous Armenian agitations in Anatolia, generally precipitated by the Ottoman policies of conscription and confiscation, often acquired a revolutionary character.

Would it be fair to characterise these instances of defiance, as a prominent pro-Turkish historian has done, as the stirrings of a 'large-scale rebellion'? I don't think so. Relentlessly monitored, intermittently terrorised, the vast majority of Armenians, even in the politically literate towns, were in no state to launch a rebellion. As for the dirt-poor rural majority, subsisting in villages that were constantly threatened by Kurdish raiding parties, for them, all nuance was flattened by a single readily comprehensible reality, that to leave home, to abandon one's four walls, one's hearth and one's vegetable garden, probably meant death.

Enver, the war minister, was a foolish man. His fantasy was to unite the Turkic peoples of Anatolia with their distant cousins in the Caucasus and Central Asia. To that end, soon after the beginning of hostilities, he moved east against the Russians, with catastrophic results. In December 1914, at the battle of Sarikamis in north-eastern Anatolia, the Ottomans were routed, losing 70,000 men to the Russians and the cold. Armenians, fighting for the Russians, played a prominent role in the battle; Ottoman opinion turned decisively against all Armenians, loyalist or not. The following month all Armenians in the Ottoman army were disarmed and assigned to labour battalions. At a meeting of Muslims in Erzurum, the Armenians were denounced as 'traitors', and 'dangerous to the empire'. In Mus, the Armenian revolutionary Roupen Pasha, then a schools inspector, prepared for conflict.

It is possible to describe the first months of 1915, as the Russians prepared for their offensive, as a time of sizing up, of forced smiles and concealed intentions. What, the Ottoman Muslim thinks to himself, is going on inside the head of my Armenian neighbour? He professes loyalty to the sultan, but what will he do when the Russians start to advance? Will he slit my throat? Hadn't I better slit his first?

Let us turn to Professor Halacoglu of the Turkish Historical Society, and his book, *Armenian Deportation*, for an idea of what the Turkish establishment says about the 'so-called genocide'.

The front cover of *Armenian Deportation* shows a troop of people – Armenian deportees, it must be presumed – as they make orderly progress across a bridge. Their mules are loaded with possessions; some of the people are on horseback. The road is serviceable. The impression given by this photograph is that the deportation of Anatolia's Armenians was a calm, well-organised business, blander than the Armenians' histrionics, their stories of slaughter and pillage, would lead us to believe. The cover, it turns out, accurately reflects the book's content.

Although he doesn't explain himself this way, it is clear that Halacoglu is concerned to answer the hottest Armenian claims, the claims on which today's controversy turns. The first is the assertion by Armenian and pro-Armenian historians that around 1.5 million Armenians died during the deportations – tens or perhaps hundreds of thousands in appalling massacres, and the remainder from lethal conditions, of hunger, disease and exhaustion, that the Turks deliberately created. The second claim is that the deaths were secretly orchestrated by the leaders of the Committe of Union and Progress, in other words, that they amount to state-sponsored genocide. The third Armenian claim is that, before they were wiped out, the Ottoman Armenians were loyal subjects and not preparing to revolt or go over to the Russian side. This, if true, would deny the Turks the slightest extenuating circumstance.

Halacoglu starts by briefly describing the Armenians' experiences under various Turkish dynasties. Remarkably for a historian who reads no Armenian and has entered no Armenian archive, he feels able to assure us that there exists not a single document indicating dissatisfaction on the part of Ottoman Armenians with their Turkish rulers. Drawing on sixteenth-century Ottoman records, he argues that Ottoman Armenians made up a far smaller proportion of the population than is often supposed. Finally, he blames foreign powers who, 'in line with their own religious, political and economic interests, began to provoke and use this community' in the nineteenth century. Leaving aside this unfortunate manipulation, there was 'no pressure whatsoever from the authorities that might have impelled them to rise'.

Halacoglu's Armenians are well fed and well administered and it is a source of sadness and bafflement to him that they should have succumbed to European blandishments and agitated against the state that had protected them for so long. It is hard to find in *Armenian Deportation* a single instance of an Ottoman official behaving cruelly or negligently towards the Armenians. The Ottomans are often imprudently generous. There are some references to 'disturbances' in two dozen places across Anatolia in 1895 and 1896, when Armenians, incited by the Hunchaks, set fire to Muslim-owned houses and businesses and massacred Muslims. This is a neat inversion of the version of events that is generally accepted outside Turkey, according to which Muslims carried out pogroms against Armenians in the same two dozen places – helped or directed, in many cases, by the authorities.

Halacoglu writes of the Ottomans' 'understanding and tolerance' towards minorities, and it is true that the authorities placed few bars

on the enrichment and advancement of Christians and Jews. Many
became rich indeed, and others held high office under the Ottomans.
There is even an argument that life for the ordinary Muslim subject of
an empire beset with corruption and iniquity was no better than it was
for his non-Muslim equivalent, but this is to disregard the contempt
and prejudice that Christians and Jews often suffered at the hands of
the Muslim majority. At best, this argument is admissible for parts
of central or western Anatolia. It does not apply to the Kurdish east.

The lot of Armenians in the eastern provinces can be illustrated
by the story of Gulizar, a comely, high-spirited Armenian girl from
Bulanik, just across the Serafettin Mountains from Varto, who
achieved unsolicited celebrity during the reign of Abdulhamit II. One
spring night in 1889, Gulizar was abducted by the followers of a local
chief, the notorious brigand Musa Bey. The authorities in Mus, where
Musa had influential friends, reacted feebly, but the perturbation
generated among local Armenians, and the concern raised by
European diplomats in the region, ensured that Gulizar's case came
to the attention of the government and foreign legations. Gulizar was
moved from village to village; she was forcibly converted to Islam
and married to Musa's younger brother. But the young hostage, while
acting the part of a woman resigned to her fate, had the pluck and
presence of mind to make secret contact with her family. She later took
the exceedingly dangerous step of asserting her Armenian identity in
a court in Bitlis – making her, in the eyes of many Kurds, an apostate
deserving execution.

Gulizar was restored to her family and moved to Istanbul for her
own protection. She was famous – you could buy her postcard in
London – and the Turkish government was forced to bring Musa Bey
to trial. But the trial was a fiasco. Musa Bey's friendly relations with
the imperial court ensured that he was first acquitted and then, upon
appeal by the plaintiff, given an absurdly light sentence, one year's
exile to Mecca. Musa Bey went on to participate energetically in the
carnage of 1915, which Gulizar narrowly escaped.

The story of Gulizar shows the importance that both communities
attached to religious honour, and the disgrace, personal and collective,
that a loss of religious identity was seen to entail. Gulizar's mother
felt as much pain at her daughter's conversion to Islam as she did at
her abduction. Sectarian revulsion was widespread on both sides. It

was widespread among Ottoman Muslims and, due to the peculiar circumstances of the Ottoman empire, vast but alone, conducive not to a feeling of strength, but vulnerability.

This insecurity can be traced to the independence movements that spread among the sultan's Christian subjects during the nineteenth century, culminating in the Balkan Wars of 1912 and 1913, which had the cumulative effect of robbing the Ottomans of almost all their European possessions. The Ottomans committed atrocities during these wars, but so did their Christian foes; Balkan Muslims suffered greatly and many of those who did not die in massacres, or while fleeing the violence, ended up in Ottoman Thrace and Anatolia. The refugees brought reports of Christian brutality, and a burgeoning resentment towards those western powers supportive of Christian irredentism.

Turkish fears were fed by a subtler, more invidious enemy, the mainly Protestant missionaries, whose efforts to uplift distressed Anatolian Christians by setting up schools and hospitals elicited much suspicion. The missionaries were sometimes insensitive to local sentiment, stirring up hostility to Islam and blithely exposing converts to mortal danger as apostates. Later, as Turkish treatment of the Armenians got harsher, so the tendency of some missionaries to paint the Turks in lurid and malicious colours grew, with a commensurate effect on western public opinion.

It's here that one feels most keenly the absence of a group of truly impartial scholars, conversant with the languages, methodically sifting through relations between the Ottoman authorities and the Armenians prior to and during 1915. Clearly, the task is beyond the official Turkish school, of which Halacoglu may be considered the dean. Halacoglu assures us that he wrote *Armenian Deportation* 'at a distance from ideological thinking, and according to entirely scientific and objective criteria', but his work is less one of history than of modern neurosis. Halacoglu can hardly bring himself to tap out the word 'Kurd', unless it is to accuse 'Kurdish tribesmen' of carrying out an unsanctioned massacre of Armenians, and to draw a straight line between the Armenian question of the turn of the last century and the Kurdish question at the beginning of ours. 'By supporting a certain terrorist organisation,' he writes, 'trying to set up a Kurdish state ... what was, in the past, demanded under the rubric "Armenian reform", is now being demanded for the Kurds.'

While deploring Halacoglu's history and his indifference to Armenian suffering, it is important to understand where he and others like him are coming from. In the memory of these people – the official memory, shared by millions of Turks – the cards in the late nineteenth and early twentieth century were stacked not against the Armenians, but against the Ottoman empire. The Ottomans were the victims of the machinations of the European Powers, and of the intrigues of sly minorities, and modern Turkey has inherited these curses.

It was such a mentality, scared and scabrous in turn, that fathered those fateful memoranda of May 1915, ordering the deportation of Ottoman Armenians from potential war zones and the vicinity of sensitive installations, and their dispersal to Syria, far from the front line. As Halacoglu points out, the government ordered administrators to protect the lives and possessions of the displaced Armenians. The government envisaged a mass return of Armenians after the war was won. That, at any rate, was the official story.

Here in the east: the Kurdish cavalrymen, the bands of deserters from the regular army, the Armenian caravans, a flotsam of terrified Muslim civilians – a tide of humanity washing westwards.

The stage well set.

The Massacre of Newala Ask

There was once a man, the servant of a big aga, who was up on the plateau, observing a lame bear. The bear dragged itself to one of the tarns on the plateau's surface, and heaved itself in. When it emerged, the bear was quite recovered. The man resolved to bring the lame daughter of his master to the same place, but when he did so, he could not find the miraculous healing lake. 'There are a thousand lakes,' he said, 'how should I know which is the one?' And this is how Bingol, which means one thousand lakes, got its name.

SOME 5,200 ARMENIANS WERE living in the district of Varto in 1914, including 600 in Varto town. Eight churches, three monasteries and five schools catered to them. Gundemir in the south-west of the district was the biggest and most important of the Armenian villages, and it was the administrative centre for two other Armenian villages, Dodan and Baskan. All three exist today, bearing Turkish names that no one uses; they lie on the valley floor, close to where the Bingol and Serafettin ranges meet, and are watered by two brooks that feed the Murat. On the eve of the First World War, these three Armenian villages, and several Kurdish villages besides, were overseen by the Cibran chief Ahmet Bey in neighbouring Kulan. Ahmet had a son living in each of the three, and he had taken a wife from the leading Armenian family of Gundemir, the Sarukhanians.

When he visited Varto in 1895, Lynch described Gundemir as 'an Armenian village of considerable size', and 'better built than is usually the case. It possesses an ancient church, and the houses cluster round it, rising up the slope of a little eminence from the plain. The place is evidently as old as the hills. Several groves of lofty poplars spring from the surface of the level ground, which extends in all directions except in the north. One will enclose a field of cabbage, another the fringes of a tobacco plantation, with its large and luscious leaves. Most of the male inhabitants were absent in their (summer pasture); the headman was present, one Avedis Efendi; and he supplied all our wants with the utmost zeal.' Lynch has a photograph of the threshing floor at Gundemir, with the Armenians' troglodyte houses behind.

Avedis Efendi was a member of the Sarukhanian family. Today, people in Varto remember the leading member of the family as Sarukhan Aga. One Asadur Sarukhanian had come to prominence as a teacher, trader and judicial official towards the end of the nineteenth century. When in 1913 the authorities seized some guns that were being transported by mule to an Armenian revolutionary in Dodan, and the man was arrested and put in Varto jail, it took Asadur Sarukhanian, who knew perfect Turkish, to persuade the authorities to release him.

Back in 1895, according to Lynch, there were no Muslims in Gundemir. Between then and the First World War, therefore, the place must have received a number of Cibran Kurds from Kulan; their presence underscored the village's status as a feudal possession. There was the usual round of abominations. An Armenian girl was raped several times by a Kurd and his brother, on one occasion in

The Armenian village of Gundemir, c. 1900

the presence of members of her family. Christianity was the object of hilarity and derision. One Easter communion, the Kurd Ghawaz entered the church in Gundemir and mischievously began distributing the communion bread and wine; his companions lifted the veils of the women in the congregation and commented on their looks. On another occasion the same Ghawaz, along with two friends, forced the Armenian girls of Gundemir to dance for them in the village square. From each absentee they levied a sheep.

Garo Sassuni, in his *History of the World of Daron*, presents the Turkish administrators at the time of the outbreak of the First World War as not merely incapable, but actively malevolent in their negligence. This is a hard point to prove, for the empire was so sick in these, its final years, that Ottoman rule at the extremities was a polite fiction. Sassuni records an attack by brigands on the gendarmerie chief in Varto, and another on pilgrims to an Armenian cathedral outside the district. A Kurdish scoundrel made off with a whole winter's collection money from the church at Gundemir. Written complaints against the Cibrans, brought by Varto Armenians before the court at Mus, were 'lost'. A Gundemir Armenian declared in the presence of the pasha of Mus, 'The Kurds are not the government, but they govern us. They are not priests but they hand out religious strictures. They are not leaders but they lead.' The pasha sat on his hands.

If there was revolutionary activity among the Armenians of Varto, as suggested by the case of the Dodan revolutionary, it seems not to have been particularly widespread. From the Armenians' timid reactions to their worsening predicament, and their faith in the government's intent and ability to administer justice, one has the impression of a people both timid and naive – an impression that Sassuni unhappily confirms.

'The Russians advanced [in 1915],' a venerable Cibran told me, 'and the Sunnis of Varto began to flee. Our family took forty Armenians under their wing – old women, young men and children – and took them all the way to Harput. One morning my mother came downstairs and opened the door and saw the room was full of people.

She immediately ran upstairs to her mother-in-law and said, "Who are all these people?" The lady replied, "Daughter, they are Armenians. They've taken refuge with us." So when the flight started everyone went as far as Harput, the Armenians under our protection, and, after staying there awhile, the Armenians set off to go to Syria.'

Another *Vartolu*, an Alevi, told me: 'One of the Armenians came to my grandfather with two young children and said, "We're going off. I want you to look after my children." My grandfather looked after the children until they were about fifteen years old. He did this secretly. If the authorities had found out, the children would have been taken away and my grandfather would have been in big trouble, for it was forbidden to harbour Armenians.'

A third *Vartolu*, a descendant of Ahmet Aga of Kulan, lord over three Armenian villages, told me: 'Ahmet Aga had a pool in Kulan. Everyone used to gather around the pool and talk. One day an Armenian came to Ahmet Aga at the pool and said, "Ahmet Aga! What is the use of salting meat?" Ahmet Aga replied, "It's to protect the meat from rotting." The Armenian went on: "So what's to be done if the salt itself is rotten?" His point was that Ahmet Aga's kinsmen, who proclaimed themselves the protectors of the Armenians, were not in fact protecting them at all. After that Ahmet Aga made enquiries and found out that one of his relations had treated the Armenian in question very badly. Ahmet Aga had his relation brought before him. The man was thrown into the pool, and then beaten with a hook. What I mean to say is that our relations were warm. The majority of Armenians living in Varto today owe their lives to Ahmet Aga.'

If you go around Varto and ask people about the deportations, you will only hear accounts such as these. You may be tempted to conclude that Varto is singular for the generosity and selflessness that its Sunni Kurdish and Alevi inhabitants displayed in their dealings with the Armenians. But there is something odd about these vicarious affidavits – they seem almost too good to be true. And then you learn how the deportations happened in the areas adjacent to Varto – on the Mus Plain, in Hinis, up at Erzurum – and you realise that, yes, they are too good to be true.

For the Armenians living in the district of Hinis, the agony began during the second week of May 1915. The government ordered the emptying of some thirty-seven Armenian villages in the district, and a fury of bloodletting and pillaging, noteworthy even by local standards, ensued. Several thousand Armenians were killed by a combination of local tribesmen and Kurdish cavalrymen who had deserted and fled the Russian advance. A large number of Armenians, presumably the inhabitants of Hinis town, were formed into a convoy that was moved into neighbouring Varto, from where, they were assured, they would be escorted in safety to the Syrian border.

In Mus, home to a strong and well-armed revolutionary movement, an Armenian revolt had begun with the slaying of some seventy Turkish gendarmes who had been sent to capture or kill leading partisans. Faced with the possibility of a general insurrection, the government suspended its process of enforced disarmament of Armenians and assured the Armenians that the gendarmes and Kurdish tribesmen, whose brutality was legion, would henceforth be restrained. Towards the end of May, Armenian villages in the plain were again pillaged, on at least one occasion with gendarmes on hand. The Armenian insurgents moved down from the hills around Surp Karapet, but they were too few to even attempt an assault on the city. On 29 May, the government gave Kurdish and Circassian cut-throats carte blanche. By the following evening, the Armenian neighbourhoods in the town of Mus had been lain waste. The female prisoners were distributed as spoils and many unarmed Armenians taken off and burned to death in neighbouring barns. 'The number of Armenian victims is very large,' the Armenian revolutionary Roupen Pasha later reported in affidavits that appeared in the British government's *The Treatment of the Armenians in the Ottoman Empire* (1916): 'In the town of Mus alone, out of 15,000 Armenian inhabitants there are only 200 survivors; out of the 59,000 inhabitants of the plain hardly 9,000 have escaped.'

In contrast to Hinis and Mus, where the majority of Armenians were murdered *in situ*, in Erzurum the deportation order was largely implemented. The village clearances started in May and intensified in June and July. The thrust was to be westwards, past Erzincan and then south to Syria, but the majority of Erzurum's 65,000 Armenians fell on the way. Apart from the usual victims of exhaustion, hunger and dehydration, thousands were slaughtered by tribesmen and government troops in and beyond the Erzincan plain.

Elsewhere, among the Armenians, among the foreign observers, we read of charred flesh, the torn women saucer-eyed, gleeful Kurds carrying belts, purses, crosses. Shoes no longer carry a price; everyone has several pairs. Something is absent at midday: the bells! They will never ring again. This is the scene across Anatolia, at points hundreds of miles from the hostilities, nowhere near sensitive facilities.

Professor Halacoglu of the Turkish Historical Society concedes that there was a massacre of Armenians from Erzurum. He allows that a total of six massacres took place during the deportations. He does not think that the sum of casualties from massacres across the nation amounted to more than 10,000. This figure is so far removed from the most parsimonious of conventional estimates, so shabby in its smallness, that one is obliged to impute malice, rather than eccentricity, to its author.

The big historical question is not whether very large numbers of Anatolian Armenians met with a violent end in the spring and summer of 1915, but whether or not the killings took place by fiat. The Armenian argument lost lustre in the 1980s when two Turkish scholars demonstrated that a famous telegram by Talat Pasha, minister for the interior, ordering the elimination of Anatolia's Armenians, was probably a forgery, but the absence of written evidence in the public domain hardly amounts to acquittal. First, whatever evidence exists is in the hands of the party that has most to lose from its dissemination. (Or existed; there have been plenty of claims of spring cleaning in the Turkish archives.) Second, the killing of Armenians was not part of a declared national ideology, celebrated by theorists and enshrined in bills and edicts, but a crime on the sly. If, as the Armenian historians say, there was a general order for the killing of Armenians, it was issued in secret and at variance to those ordinances, documented by Halacoglu, which urged concern for the deportees' well-being.

The innumerable eyewitness and survivor accounts that have reached us suggest that the mechanism of deportation, and the extent to which it became a mechanism of extermination, was subject to local vagaries such as the disposition and character of the local tribes, administrators and military commanders. In Dersim, for instance, we find several Alevi tribes protecting the Armenians, and there are reports elsewhere of humane Turkish officials doing all in their power to help the deportees to safety. In the east of Anatolia, at least, most of the massacres were committed by tribesmen and at a discreet distance from the towns, and this has facilitated a favoured Turkish argument: that the killings happened at the behest of rogue gendarmes or unruly Kurds. But this argument, as events in Varto demonstrate, is a flawed one.

Over several weeks in the spring of 1915, the Armenians of Varto town, having been partially disarmed by the government, were subjected to nightly raids by tribesmen from the surrounding villages. On at least one occasion, some Armenians were locked in a barn with a crazed buffalo that had been doused in kerosene and set on fire. This would become a common practice during a period of severe ammunition shortages.

At around this time the Armenian village of Gundemir received a visit from a police officer named Sukri, and his men. Sukri was angry because those Gundemir Armenians who had been drafted into the Ottoman labour battalions had deserted; he demanded that they come out of hiding, threatening to burn the village if they did not. Some of the villagers fled, including fifteen-year-old Meguerditch Darbinian, whose handwritten memoir, seen by Garo Sassuni, is our main source of information about events at Gundemir. Others formed a caravan of around 100 people; it is not clear whether this was composed of deserters, normal villagers, or a combination of both. The caravan moved off towards Varto town and all raised obedient encomiums to the sultan, except for one Boghos, who remained doggedly silent, for which act of rebellion Sukri broke his ribs.

This is Sassuni's last mention of the 100, from which we may infer that they were killed on the way to Varto town or, more likely, pressed into one of the two caravans that set off south from Varto town. One caravan was composed of bureaucrats and army deserters, and the other of ordinary people. The first group was driven south to the neighbourhood of Diyarbakir, and there annihilated. The second meandered south, picking up Armenians from various villages: Hirbakub and Tepe in Varto itself, and a further six on the plain of Mus. Having cleared Mus, the caravan climbed into the Taurus Mountains, where a second massacre took place.

Meguerditch Darbinian came out of hiding and returned to Gundemir to work the land. Word spread that Gundemir was defenceless and Kurdish tribesmen from the neighbouring villages began their ravages. Out in the fields, Meguerditch and another man were ambushed by two Kurds, but ran back to Gundemir under fire to help the others defend it against yet another raid, in which three villagers were killed and many animals stolen. One of the Armenian defenders suggested pursuing the thieves but a friendly Kurd named Mahmut dissuaded him. 'I have eaten from your table many times,' he said, 'and I am telling you that the government has ordered the massacre of Armenians and the looting of their goods. Save yourselves!'

This is the first that we hear of the edict – *firman* was the word, Persian in origin, used by Ottomans – which, in the memories of the people of Varto, connotes a death sentence emanating from Istanbul. Since no such edict was issued, certainly not openly, the *firman* of popular memory must have been a locally generated deportation order. According to a senior member of the Cibran tribe I spoke to in Varto, an earlier *firman* had been issued, only to be revoked – perhaps on the intercession of pro-Armenians in Varto town. It is now, at the time of the second *firman*, that the deportations started from Varto town, while in the surrounding villages, according to my Cibran informant, the authorities gave the people three days' carte blanche. 'The government killed,' he told me, 'and the Kurds killed, and the Armenians, or those of them that could, fled.'

At some point during these events the remaining inhabitants of Gundemir had felt safe enough to depute a delegation of boys, Meguerditch Darbinian among them, to go to the district commissioner in Varto town and complain about the behaviour of the tribesmen. Some of the stolen animals were returned, the district commissioner and gendarmerie commander chose a few for themselves, and compensation was paid for any unrecovered beasts. When the boys got back to Gundemir – walking across country to avoid the tribesmen – they found it even emptier than before. Most of the villagers, Meguerditch's aunt told them, had gathered their possessions and sought refuge with friendly Kurds, leaving orders that the boys defend the village and land. 'It may be,' writes Sassuni, 'that other villages in Varto witnessed small scale defences, but no accounts remain of them … some of the Kurds genuinely wanted to harbour their friends, and to become the owners of their possessions.'

The inhabitants of Gundemir threw themselves on the mercy of Ahmet Aga and his clansmen. The price they paid was measurable in material wealth and religious and sexual honour. Lives were bought; virgins hastily converted and married off. As for the unfortunate ones, those women with neither gold nor a male guardian, they were the victims of a frenzy that is said to have revolted even Ahmet Aga. 'The Kurds were taking the Armenian women off to their beds,' my Cibran informant told me, 'and Ahmet Aga came and saw what was going on and he said, "Even if God accepts this, I cannot accept it." '

Across the district, history was raising its stench. At the northern end of Varto, in the mixed Armenian/Sunni village of Karakoy, the people were dying from hunger. The previous autumn, forty-five Cibran horsemen had raided the village, emptying the winter stores. Now, after the *firman*, they returned. They gathered the village's emaciated Armenians, built a high wall of dried grasses around them, and burned them to death.

The ragged remnants of a once-proud race limped in a north-westerly direction towards the friendly Russian advance. They cowered stupefied in caves. In the spurs above the Alevi village of Rakasan a certain Hasan chanced upon an Armenian and her child. He accepted the gold she offered him but reneged on his own pledge, to care for them both. He strapped child to mother and – triumph of economy! – did for the pair with a single bullet. We find a high caste Feron murdering his Armenian blood brother out of lust for the man's wife. (He had her, of course; what choice did she have?) Hungry young men formed gangs that roamed the hills and searched the caves for shivering Armenians to rob and kill. On the road a deportee collapsed in a ditch to give birth and a gendarme beat the life out of her with his rifle butt.

Examples of nobility shine like jewels in the dung. In the village of Caneseran the Alevi Haco protected his Armenian adopted son until the boy was denounced. Rather than give him up to death or deportation, Haco accompanied him as far as the Russian lines and sent him off with a prayer. A band of women saved some Armenian fugitives by raining stones and abuse on a gang attacking them. For two tense weeks an Alevi woman secretly fed an Armenian and her child, only for the authorities to find and slaughter them.

It is now, in the spring and summer of 1915, that we find the
modern district of Varto, like the rest of this guilt-ridden land, come
bawling, bloodily, obscenely into the world.

After well over two millennia it is time to kill off the Armenians of
Varto and Hinis, and that privilege lies with Meguerditch Darbinian,
whose diary of events, relayed by Garo Sassuni, is our most complete
account of how it happened.

Following the implementation of the Varto *firman*, it seems that the
few Armenians remaining in Gundemir were not molested – which
confirms the supposition that the authorities allowed three days'
looting before calling the district to order. Orderly, indeed, was the
subsequent arrival of a very big caravan of Armenians, led by the
Gregorian primate of Hinis, on the high ground above Gundemir.
This caravan was composed of the surviving Armenians of the district
centre of Hinis and it seems, from Meguerditch's description and the
recollections of today's *Vartolus*, to have numbered several thousand
people driving dozens of carts – and supplemented by Varto Armenians
who had so far evaded deportation. Meguerditch reports that the
caravan was escorted by twenty gendarmes under the command of a
man of unusually dark complexion – a 'black man' in Meguerditch's
unworldly fifteen-year-old eyes – suggesting that he was an Ottoman
subject of Arab or North African origin.

The impression Meguerditch gives us is that the Hinis Armenians
were unaware of the fate that had befallen their massacred co-
religionists, and jovially convinced that they would be escorted safely
into Syria. Their faith was not disturbed by the warnings of a local
Kurd to whom Meguerditch refers by what may be a nickname,
Huspi, one of several local Kurdish auxiliaries who had been deputed
to accompany the gendarmes – a 'good man', Sassuni tells us, and
a close acquaintance of the Darbinian family. Huspi had discovered
from the gendarmes that the caravan's destination would not be Syria,
but the nearby Newala Ask, which means 'dry valley' in Kurmanji,
and he instructed Meguerditch, who was on good terms with the
Hinis Armenians, to warn them of the looming danger. But the Hinis

party rejected Meguerditch's words. 'Boy!' one member of the caravan exclaimed. 'We have twenty gendarmes with us and we have set out on the order of the government with all our possessions and animals. Who can do anything to us?' Indeed, on the third and final night of the Armenians' stay in Gundemir, when a few Kurdish tribesmen approached the caravan with aggressive intent, the gendarmes sent them packing and calmed the situation.

Clearly, Meguerditch was affected by the optimism of the Hinis party, and he decided to join the caravan, without, however, telling his aunt. The date was 11 June 1915. They set off at midday. First the caravan crossed the Gundemir river, with Meguerditch and a Hinis boy leading the way, singing and playing, followed by the carts and animals and then the bulk of the deportees. Presently they crossed a second bridge and arrived at Baskan. Then, at the head of the valley of Newala Ask, the gendarmerie commander ordered the boys to stop. A few minutes later, once the rest of the carts had caught up, the commander brought ten of his men to the head of the caravan and, in Meguerditch's account, 'began shooting ... suddenly, we saw a multitude come upon us'. The 'multitude' was made up of local tribesmen, the horsemen carrying guns and those on foot axes and hatchets.

Thus began the massacre of Newala Ask, and if Meguerditch's account is threadbare and rudimentary, we may attribute this to the amnesia of a traumatised teenager. Some hellish images reach us: the primate of Hinis, pulled off his horse and beheaded; the ground covered with corpses; Sunnis and Alevis fighting over the carts, loaded with possessions, that the Armenians had been driving before them. Among the survivors was a woman who hid in the nearby woods and later strangled her baby for fear that it would give her away with its crying. Meguerditch Darbinian, after watching the beginning of the massacre with his friend, finally came to his senses. 'We screamed and ran.'

After the worst was over and the scavengers had moved in, Meguerditch chanced upon the Kurdish auxiliary Huspi. 'May God ruin your house!' Huspi exclaimed. 'What are you doing here?' Huspi offered Meguerditch sweet *gata* bread, cooked meats and various types of fruit that he had found among the looted possessions, but Meguerditch, although weak from hunger, 'couldn't eat anything ... at every step I saw women and children who had been massacred'. He was particularly disturbed by the sight of five or six youths who had been shot and were convulsing 'like chickens'.

Huspi gave Meguerditch his fez and a donkey and the two set off for Huspi's home, several miles distant, where it happened that the uncles of Meguerditch had earlier found refuge. Hiding with them in a barn, Meguerditch told one of his uncles what he had seen, upon which he received a slap so hard, 'I remember it to this day.'

Meguerditch's uncle was unable to believe what he was hearing. 'I'll believe that they killed the men,' he said, 'but not the massacre of women and children.' All this, Sassuni concludes sadly, goes to show 'how naive the Armenians were'.

In the behaviour of many Armenians in Varto and elsewhere during the deportations, we do indeed find evidence for a slackening of the senses, a dereliction of the human duty of self-preservation. From a historical perspective this is useful to know, for it undercuts the Turkish depiction of the Armenians as implacably united around the goals of rebellion and betrayal, and the corollary view of the deportations as an indispensable security measure. Having lived through, or heard about, the pogroms of the past, it would have taken uncommon clarity of vision to judge that this time would be decisively different, and uncommon initiative to act on that judgement. Denied their breadwinner and guardian, very often unaware of what was happening in the next district, many Armenians buried their heads in the warm sands of optimism and denial; it was unconscionable that the Ottoman government, whether by commission or omission, intended their destruction.

As for the Kurds, Sassuni writes, those outside the government 'had no idea of the scope' of the deportations and massacres. According to people I spoke to in Varto, the Kurdish response to the *firman* was founded on expectations of pillage – a mainstay of the Kurds' economy and culture – and not on sectarian hatred, for the Sunni Kurds did not generally hate the Armenians, certainly not as intensely as they hated the Alevis. For all that, the killings required moral legitimation, and this came in the form of rulings issued by local sheikhs. The primate's monstrous death at Newala Ask and numerous reports of atrocities being carried out amid cries of 'God is Great!'; these indicate that essentially mercenary instincts were now robed in religion – and refined by fear, for the possibility of an Armenian dictatorship under Russian auspices had seemed, to some, close indeed.

Primary responsibility for the massacre of Newala Ask lies with the dark-skinned gendarmerie commander. But Meguerditch's account contains a reference to ten armed auxiliaries taking aim as if to defend the Armenians, which suggests that not all government forces took part. The commander's shots acted as a signal for the marauders; they, not the government, did the bloodletting. The participants in the massacre and the looting that followed came not only from Varto but also from other neighbouring districts.

It is possible to identify certain direct beneficiaries of the massacre, particularly the Cibrans of Kulan and their chief, Ahmet Aga. It was Ahmet Aga's clansmen who had controlled the Armenian villages of Gundemir, Baskan and Dodan before the massacres, and it was they who got much of the booty, even if certain prominent members of the family, such as one man I spoke to in 2007, claim that Ahmet Aga piously refused his share.

'The local sheikhs had put out a ruling authorising people to kill the Armenians and take their possessions … The villagers brought some of their booty to Kulan. They said to Ahmet Aga, "Aga, we've brought this for you." Ahmet Aga said, "What did you do?" And they replied, "We killed the Armenians and this is our war booty and we've brought these carts for you." And that's when Ahmet came out with a famous line: "If God is God of all the world, he will not forgive you for this." And he sent them on their way.'

'My father,' the Varto Armenian Violet Mooradian told me on the telephone from America, 'was a Sarukhanian and my mother an Igidian. They were mill owners so they had a good position in Gundemir. They had one son and then my father left for the United States in 1914, when the Ottoman army started calling people up, to avoid the draft. He ended up in Richmond, Virginia, and the Carolinas, working the mines. Many others did the same. They all intended to return.

'When the massacres started my mother was with her parents-in-law and their fifteen-year-old daughter Manoushag. Manoushag had typhoid. Everyone was fleeing. A friendly Kurd told them to get out. But how could they, with Manoushag? The friendly Kurd kept coming and telling them to leave, but they feared that the girl would be raped if they left her. Eventually Manoushag's mother gave her something to drink but she realised it was poison and said to her father, "She's trying to poison me!" In the end they got her out of bed and handed her over to some friendly Kurds and said, "Look after her until we come back." They learned later that the Kurds had choked her to death because they feared that the government would punish them for harbouring her.

'My mother was one of five girls. She had one brother, Murat. Everyone adored Murat. He had just got married. During the massacres my mother went on foot towards Harput. She worked in a Kurd's house as a maid. She had her son, my elder brother, with her. One day, when she was working in this house, a gang of Kurds came to the door and shouted, "You're from Gundemir, aren't you? Come out and have a look! Come and see whose head we cut off!" Eventually my mother went out and saw it was Murat whose head they had cut off. My mother saw Murat's wife after that but she had gone insane. In the end she died of hunger.

'The hunger was terrible. My mother was so hungry she went from house to house, begging for bread, and everyone kept slamming the door and saying, "We don't have enough food for you." Eventually, someone gave her a bit of bread and my brother wanted it and she shooed him away, and then she felt so bad and she gave him a little bit. That was how bad the hunger was.

'My mother ended up in a camp in Syria. She learned where my father was through an Armenian newspaper that people used in order to track each other down. They would come into the camp and read out the names and addresses. One day my mother heard my father's name being read out. She went to America, and she found him.'

The massacre of Newala Ask took place in June 1915, but there was to be a coda, violent and abrupt. At the beginning of February 1916, having turned the Turkish flank in the Bingol Mountains, the Russians occupied Varto. Within a few days Mus would be theirs. The Russians were accompanied by camp followers and irregulars – Armenians, for the most part, thirsty for restitution, justice and revenge.

Most of Varto's Sunnis had fled westwards, some of them, in the case of the Cibrans, taking possession of former Armenian homes. Varto was ruined. The end of the Armenians had robbed the district of most of its farmers and artisans. The misery brought by a severe famine, exacerbated by the war conditions and requisitions, was compounded, in the summer of 1915, by a severe outbreak of typhus. When the Russians entered Varto town on 3 February, they found the place half-deserted and the people ill and emaciated.

Why did the Sunnis flee the Russians, but the Alevis remain? It is likely that the Sunnis, having fought against the Russians and massacred the Armenians, feared retribution. It also seems that the Alevis, while nervous about Russian intentions, felt safer on their uplands than on the open road to Harput. Most of them stayed.

From the pages of an invaluable local history written by a resident of the Alevi village of Tatan, Ali Kemal Sarikas, and the recollections of elderly *Vartolu*s, we get a picture of the Russians as considerate and courteous during their twenty-month occupation. I have heard of *Vartolu*s who learned good Russian, and of Varto women who married Russian soldiers. It is remarkable how frank, even now, the Alevis remain in their Russophilia – an indication, also, of their remembered loathing for the Ottomans.

Sarikas's initial account of the occupiers, who included Azeri Cossacks and white Russian infantrymen, features a rapt description of Russian uniforms (much pelt and fox skins to keep out the cold), food (millet porridge and pork stock soup) and horses (enormous 'Hungarian' steeds effortlessly dragging the heavy guns through snow and mud). The favourable impression created by the Russians' 'red-bearded, just and honourable' unit commander, a man who averted his eyes whenever a village woman passed, was enhanced by his impatience with the Armenian 'gangs' who, Sarikas writes, lost no time in attacking and looting the Alevis. It was not long, however, before the commander was replaced. The new man was more sympathetic to the Armenians and they responded by 'raining down on [him] bogus claims to property in the hands of the Muslim populace'. Relations further deteriorated when the Alevis retrieved the guns they had buried and began defending themselves. It is interesting, however, that even in Sarikas's biased and incomplete account the Armenians present themselves as even-handed, assuring the Alevis that 'in the Armenian government that would be set up, Muslims would have right to free abode and expression'.

Sarikas tells us of a man called Huseyin, whom the Russians had appointed village headman of Tatan. Huseyin was no friend of the Armenians, and they had it in for him. According to Sarikas, the Armenians bribed a local man to accuse Huseyin of murdering Armenians before 1915, and seizing their property, and now of spying on the Russians. Huseyin's second enemy was an Armenian woman from Gundemir called Lale. She was the daughter of a rich man whom Huseyin had surrendered to the Ottoman authorities in 1915. Sarikas leaves us in no doubt that Lale survived the massacres because she was a 'beautiful, young, attractive, vivacious coquette'. Intent on avenging her father, she filled the Russian commander, whose 'tent and bed' she knew intimately, with accounts of Huseyin's perfidy, with the result that he and several others were arrested and taken off by the Russians. Trudging to the command post a few miles away, the party was attacked by a band of Armenian 'gangsters', including one Armenian from Gundemir. All eight were killed in a spray of Russian and Armenian bullets.

It is possible to detect in the Russian interregnum a mood of equivocation. The proximity of the Ottoman army, regrouping to the west, must have contributed to the atmosphere of danger and opportunity. Those most in doubt, the Alevis with blood on their hands, kept their heads down and willed a swift liberation.

Few were more notorious than Hasan of Rakasan – the Hasan who had bound an Armenian woman to her child and shot them both with a single bullet. Twice during the occupation, Armenians who had heard about Hasan came looking for him. On the second occasion, he was intercepted by a group of armed Armenians while on his way to a neighbouring village to winnow grain. 'Where is Hasan?' one of the Armenians asked him. 'Do you know Hasan?' Hasan pointed over his shoulder to a young man called Huseyin who was walking a few hundred yards behind him, and said, 'That is Hasan!' The Armenians shot Huseyin and wounded him, but he cried out, 'Why are you killing me? I'm not Hasan!' and they left him. Hasan lived to a ripe old age.

Justice, of a kind, caught up with a Sunni sheikh from the village of Kers in northern Varto. He had participated in the massacres of the Armenians. Then, during the occupation, he disappeared. His body was discovered boiled in a cauldron.

There was a more cheering encounter between Haco of Caneseran and the Armenian adopted son he had conducted to the Russian lines during the deportations. During the Russian occupation, Haco had been pressed into a chain gang that built a road from Varto to Hinis. Haco found himself being eyed by one of the guards, who eventually approached him and enquired who he was. When Haco told him, the Russian burst into tears. 'Don't you know me?' he cried. 'I am your son!'

Haco also sobbed. 'I didn't recognise you. You have become a man.'

'And you have got thin!'

The boy helped Haco escape from the chain gang and sent him back to Caneseran laden with food.

Nowadays, if you ask a young person in Varto about the Russian occupation, they will tell you two things. The first is that the Russians distributed sugar lumps to the hungry Alevi children. The second is that, as they prepared to leave in 1917, the Russians advised the Alevis to be careful of the Armenians who would take over from them. 'Until now,' they said, 'we have kept the Armenians from taking revenge. Once we are gone, there will nothing to stop them from cutting your throats.'

In the memories that Varto's Alevis have of the twenty-month Russian occupation and the five-month period of direct Armenian domination that followed, the Armenians loom larger than the Russians. Until the Russian front collapsed when troops deserted after the October revolution, the Armenians who roamed around Varto were mostly irregulars and camp followers, including Varto Armenians who had survived the massacres, and the Russians sometimes had difficulty controlling them. After the Russian withdrawal, the district came under the sway of the Armenian army. Briefly united with the Georgians and Azerbaijanis in a Transcaucasian federation, the Armenians hoped to force the Ottomans to at least grant autonomy to Turkish Armenia. It was a forlorn hope, as the lightning Turkish counter-offensive of early 1918 showed, when the Armenians were pushed back.

Whichever Armenians governed Varto in the wake of the Russians' departure – and the sources I have seen, and the accounts I have heard from contemporary *Vartolus*, are silent on the subject – it seems that their intent was not murderous. According to Mehmet Serif Firat, who was a teenager at the time, the Armenians set up a 'strong centre of government and administration' in Varto and other places; there was a national fiction to maintain, after all, that these lands would remain Armenian. From the beginning of 1918, however, as the Ottomans advanced and the Armenian army was pushed back in the north, the fiction was exposed. In retreat the Armenians adopted a scorched earth policy. This was expressed, in Varto as elsewhere, in acts of wanton destruction.

The killings seem to have been carried out indiscriminately, in a hurry, by people who felt that they had little to lose and plenty to avenge. Perhaps the first victims, some three days before the Ottoman entry to Varto, were thirty-four men from the village of Kalcik – Nazim Han's village. According to Nazim Han, these men had been ordered by the Armenians to come down and help open the snow-bound roads; upon reaching Varto town, they were forced into a barn, where many were run through with bayonets, 'after which the Armenians put two buffaloes in the barn, doused them in petrol and set them alight'.

Was this a punitive massacre? Had the people of Kalcik been found to have been in contact with the Ottoman forces? Had they perpetrated some appalling act during the deportations? Nazim Han says not, and certainly there is little indication, if one follows the Armenians' trail as they went east, into Hinis and on towards their feeble republic, of any guiding precept save fury and hatred.

The withdrawal does not seem to have been orderly: a series of Armenian groups, low on ammunition, heading eastwards on horseback and on foot. The inhabitants of the Alevi village of Baltas, on the route, pluckily resisted one party of Armenians, only for a bigger group to massacre all who had not fled the village – fifty people, according to my informant – and raze the place. The fate of those who had fled, their numbers depleted during one freezing night in the open, would surely have been similar were it not for the fortuitous cutting of the Varto–Hinis telegraph line on which the

Armenians depended for communication. This threw the Armenians into a panic. The withdrawal was accelerated.

Baltas, in its spirited defence, was the exception. In Dirba, further east, there was a massacre, although the local beauty Elif achieved saintlike status by killing her Armenian would-be ravisher and committing suicide rather than surrendering to his comrades. In Keranlix the Armenians drove forty people on to a roof before burning the building to the ground. In nearby Sercuge, the men were shot. The Armenians' final stop in the district of Varto was the grandest of all. From here, in the shadow of the basalt citadel of Eskender, on the banks of the magnificent Lake Hamurpet, the Armenians drove forty men six miles into the district of Hinis, and there, mimicking the Ottomans, slaughtered them.

Following those Armenian footsteps, wandering through villages whose sole fault was to lie on the Varto–Hinis road, speaking to the elderly and the talkative, one meets recurring images. The first is the ignorant and naive villager: ignorant of a massacre in the next valley, ignorant of the Ottomans' imminent arrival, crediting the Armenians' promises of privilege and preferment. (In Sercuge, for example, I spoke to a man whose grandfather had been promised the position of district administrator, only to be killed when he left to take up his non-existent post.) Then there is the image of the Armenians' Muslim informants and collaborators. They were sent ahead to impress on each village the Armenians' friendly intentions and, in Eskender, they carefully learned which household had arms, before triggering the horror. The third is the image of the survivor, recovered, half-dead, from the mass of dead bodies. In Baltas he was a three-year-old, Hasan Gul, and he carried the scars on his forehead until his death in 2005.

Perhaps the most unsettling image of all is one we already know, from the massacre of Newala Ask, that of the docile victim. The men of Eskender, very cattle as they allowed themselves to be bound together, were forty strong. So were the people in Keranlix, huddling on the roof as the flames began to lick. Could these people not have resisted, hurled themselves on their executioners – lived, or died as heroes? There is something in death that speaks with a numbing authority to its congregation.

The events of 1915 flung the Armenians on to shores across the world – from Beirut to LA, from Marseille to Buenos Aires. The diaspora Armenians were free to swim in their rage and grief, though it was a while before they did. In the 1960s and 1970s young Armenians started asking their grandparents about the past. These grandparents, spurred by intimations of mortality, broke a long-standing taboo. They recalled the spring of 1915 and that was the start of today's well-oiled locomotive of remembrance: the published memoirs, oral libraries, internet forums and parliamentary lobby groups. Some young Armenians honoured the dead by assassinating Turkish diplomats and their families, and more than a dozen Turks, including women and children, lost their lives to these wanton, useless acts of vengeance.

In 1965, after a long, politically expedient silence, the Russians let the Armenians of Yerevan, capital of the then Soviet Republic of Armenia, have their genocide memorial. It stands today, a concrete artichoke on a hill, the first port of call for any official visitor, and it testifies, with its long list of eliminated Armenian communities, to the completeness of Armenia's defeat. The view from the memorial is further confirmation. Across the valley lies the drab accessible present: Yerevan, undistinguished capital of the small, poor Republic of Armenia. To the west, on the other side of the Turkish border, there rises the glowing, incandescent, inaccessible past: Mount Ararat, Armenia's eternal symbol, in enemy hands.

It is hard to take issue with much of the detail that one finds in the Armenian accounts of the events of 1915. For the Armenian diaspora, flung around the world, speaking different languages, it would require a stupendous concert of deceit to fabricate the descriptions of massacre, to dream up the reminiscences. Such a conspiracy would be without precedent. The massacres did indeed take place, many hundreds of them, big and small, and the victims' bones slowly entered the soil.

Nearly 100 years after the event we find ourselves in an absurd situation: two sides have drawn themselves up, those who work night and day to prove that this was genocide, and those who strive equally hard to prove that it was not. This is a travesty of history and memory.

What is needed is a vaguer designation for the events of 1915, avoiding the G-word but clearly connoting criminal acts of slaughter, to which reasonable scholars can subscribe and which a child might be taught. By raising knowledge about this great wrong, a way might be opened to a cultural and historical meeting between today's Turks, Kurds and Armenians, for they were not alive in 1915, and need not live in its shadow.

But no; this is the prattle of a *naïf*, laughable, unemployable.

The reality is Professor Yusuf Halacoglu of the Turkish Historical Society and his belief, clearly expressed in his books and public pronouncements, that history is politics fitted to the past. Is Yusuf Halacoglu concerned by the truth or is he actuated by modern fears: that the Turks, by admitting to the crimes of their forebears, would expose themselves to territorial and pecuniary claims, as well as to other more abstract forfeits – penitence lasting long into the future; the whole life-sapping pantomime of wreath-laying and apologies? No one in the Turkish Historical Society, you may be sure, envies those lesser, effeminate nations, forever saying sorry for this and expressing regret for that.

And the reality is the Armenian historical institutes, in Armenia, Europe and the United States, which nowadays address the barbarism of the Turk in holistic fashion, drawing no line between the atrocities of the Ottomans and those that have been committed, in the modern-day Caucasus, by the state of Azerbaijan – a Turkic state, warmly supported by its cousins in Ankara – against the tiny, virtuous Republic of Armenia. In the archives of these institutes, the 1915 massacres and the Azeris' modern desecration of ornate stone crosses are on the same evil continuum. Their perpetrators are the very image, in their medieval wickedness, of those unspeakable Turks who, in the baroque imagination of a prominent Hapsburg bishop, 'spare no age or sex and mercilessly cut down young and old alike and pluck unripe fruit from the wombs of mothers'.

The dead waters of Turkish history writing have their plankton of state historians – limited linguistically, *parti pris*, salaried advocates. And on the Armenian side, although the history is more reliable, it is often undermined by a tendency to subordinate all to the genocide fixation, and also, when it is convenient, to leave things out. There are some in between, prepared to think in terms of grey, and to allow that the sinned against also sinned, but they are few.

It is well known that during the Tsarist advance into eastern Anatolia, in 1915, Armenian irregulars massacred Muslims in and around Van. Equally, it is well known that following the Russian withdrawal at the end of 1917, more atrocities took place, in Anatolia and later in the Caucasus, where Turk and Armenian continued until 1921 to dispute the bloodied carcass of the Tsarist empire. Did not the Americans Niles and Sutherland, exploring parts of eastern Anatolia in 1919 on behalf of the American Committee for Near East Relief, observe that the Armenians, fleeing the Turkish advance of 1918, had 'massacred Musulmans on a large scale with many refinements of cruelty', leaving behind them 'a country completely ruined'? One cannot easily brand Lord Curzon a Turcophile, and yet he, addressing the House of Lords as foreign secretary in March 1920, felt 'bound in truth to admit – speaking as severely as I have done about Turkish action and Turkish complicity in massacres – that the Armenians in that part of the world have not even, in the last few weeks, been such innocent lambs … I have at the moment in my possession papers relating to a series of very savage and bloodthirsty attacks made by them, conceivably under provocation, in those parts of the world.'

If, as seems irrefutable, many thousands of Muslims were slaughtered by the Armenians during and after the First World War, it is odd that so erudite an Armenian authority as Vahakn Dadrian should skip the subject in his exhaustive *History of the Armenian Genocide*, perhaps the most widely consulted book on the period written in English. Is this because the Turks and Kurds killed more abundantly? Or would it be awkward for Dadrian, who painstakingly builds up a picture of Armenian agony, to concede that his countrymen inflicted agony of their own? Why, again, in his *Armenian People from Ancient to Modern Times*, does the respected Armenian historian Richard Hovanissian refer parsimoniously to Turkish claims that 'Armenian bands had perpetrated atrocities against Muslims in the occupied eastern provinces' without examining these claims or commenting on their veracity? The suffering of the Alevis of Varto, under Armenian occupation and then during the Armenian flight, was not unique. Far from it; their agony, like the massacres that came before, was horribly commonplace.

The Armenian lobby is strong in countries where the massacres of 1915 are the subject of scrutiny and debate, and where well-defined communities, like the Armenian-Americans or the French Armenians, live in safety and prosperity. And the lobby is strong, for obvious reasons, in the tiny, envious Republic of Armenia. There is no doubt that this lobby, rich, active and extremely attentive, has influenced the nature of Armenian history writing.

There is not much of a lobby among the Armenian community of Istanbul, which is made up of some 40,000 people whose forebears avoided death and foreign exile, surviving the horrors of 1915 with their faith and identity intact. The 40,000 are one of Turkey's recognised religious minorities, and enjoy some rights and privileges, but they remain timorous and withdrawn, and do their best not to be noticed.

There is no lobby among the Armenians, a few dozen in number, who survive in the district of Varto. For them, and for the tens or hundreds of thousands like them, descendants of Armenians who converted rather than die in 1915, there can be no settlement without identity. And this is what they lack.

Some, at least, know what they want to be. Varto's king of white goods is of Armenian stock, but he has embraced Sunnism and Kurdishness with an obliterating zeal. Of a certain taxi driver, a man who spent the journey from Hinis to Varto expounding the virtues of an exceptionally dry interpretation of Islamic law, I was later told, 'He's an Armenian.' But he isn't; not really. For such people, zealous Muslims, vigorous exponents of a Turkish or a Kurdish identity, the only thing that makes them Armenian is the badge of apartness that others have slapped on their forehead. And that, with the passage of time, will wear off. When the next conflict comes, they will surely be on the winning side.

There are others, scattered across Anatolia, who cannot bring themselves to adopt wholeheartedly the identity that was imposed on them. Although they know little of their parents' language and beliefs, they are aware of the irony of adopting Sunnism, or Alevism, as if it was their own. So they live in a cultural vacuum, unable to love the symbols of others, having none of their own.

In the summer of 2006, in the verdant dormitory town of Wuppertal, in western Germany, I found a married couple from Varto; he, grizzled

and a little downcast, she, bustling, a model homemaker. Salahettin
Cakar and his wife Sukran had four skins. They were Armenian by
origin. They grew up as Kurds but the state said they were Turks.
They now lived as Germans. They were exemplary immigrants, proud
of their nice house and their polite, friendly children.

The Armenian-ness of Salahettin and Sukran Cakar was a memory.
They were not observant of any religion. Turkish; German; Kurmanji
– I heard all of these in the Cakar household, but hardly a word of
Armenian. Salahettin and Sukran were content to savour the names
and nicknames of dead ancestors: Sano; Melkon; Vartan; Zeka; Sene;
Sinjar; Kefo. Their background gave them little choice but to be
eclectic. Sukran baked her flat bread in a Kurdish oven in the garden,
and her kitchen table sagged from wholesome Turkish dishes. I was
astonished to hear that Salahettin was a Kurdish nationalist. 'It was
the Kurds who killed the Armenians!' I wanted to explode. 'It was
they who did the dirty on you! And now you identify with them!'

This identification, I would discover, is quite common among
Armenians. In Yerevan in the Republic of Armenia the following year,
I would meet an Armenian from Turkey who had joined the PKK,
got captured and spent several years in a Turkish prison, before being
freed and emigrating to Armenia. I once regarded the Turks' claims
of widespread cooperation between the PKK and the Armenians as
dubious propaganda. No longer. That cooperation exists, though I
suspect it is superficial and opportunistic. If Turkey were wiped off
the map, and the field left to the Armenians and the Kurds, the killing
would start all over again.

Talking in the Cakars' sitting room in Wuppertal, having supper
around their table, I didn't get a general picture of the deportations,
but fragments. Here was Salahettin's grandmother fleeing her village
of Dodan with her infant, following the family's incineration at the
hands of the mob, only to abandon the bawling mite by a brook.
Twenty members of Sukran's family fell in the massacre at Newala
Ask. Her grandfather and some of his relations were saved by the
Cibrans and taken to Harput. There the grandfather met and married
Sukran's grandmother. After the war, newly converted to Islam, the
couple settled in Varto.

From the Cakars I learned something of what it was like to grow
up an Islamised Armenian after the massacres. Barely ten families

had survived, and everyone knew who they were. Sukran beat up the postman's son when he taunted her, 'Armenian girl! Armenian girl!' The older generation, the survivors, secretly continued their Christian prayers – a grandmother slyly making the sign of the cross, or substituting Christ for Mohammad in the Muslim prayer. The Sunnis refused to marry their daughters to the sons of converts and the Armenians became a self-perpetuating subset. The Armenian sent away to do military service, his identity card marked 'convert', was marked from the outset as a potential traitor. 'Do I still,' he wondered, 'in my pathetic and ragged state, represent a threat? Isn't it enough that you have killed me and trampled my dignity?'

This is what the ambivalent survivors lacked: dignity. I realised it while speaking to the Cakars, and in remembering snatches of other conversations with Armenians who had lived; there was no pride in this survival. The qualities that enabled one to escape death and carry on living in Anatolia were not heroic ones: guile; mendacity; opportunism; selfishness. Gold and a pretty daughter helped. So the eyes of the survivor do not sparkle as he recounts the story of his ancestors' escape.

Salahettin Cakar told me that his great-grandfather had successfully sought sanctuary, along with his children, with the Cibrans. Were it not for this stroke of luck, I remarked tritely, Salahettin would not be sitting before me now.

To my surprise, Salahettin sighed and shook his head. 'They say they harboured my great-grandfather and his family because they loved him, but that's not true; it's because he was rich.' There was a pause, and I pictured money passing hands, and the trauma of a religious conversion. 'If you're truly an Armenian,' he resumed, 'and the others were resisting – dying or fleeing, but in any case not falling underfoot – it seems to me that death is better than that sort of escape.'

Selahattin Cakar was not 'truly' an Armenian, and he knew it.

On I went, south from Wuppertal in my hire car, and two of the Varto Armenians who had agreed to see me cried off. One left my messages unanswered. The wife of the second told me that her husband would be on night shift when I aimed to pass through. 'In any case,' she added, 'he doesn't see much point in speaking to you.' I had got used to rejection. I didn't take it personally. But I saw that even now, nearly 100 years on, even here, hundreds of miles from Turkey, no Armenian felt free of the ancestral fear. It was a fear that the Turks might be searching for a pretext to resume the rounding up and the killing. More immediately, it was a fear that simply by opening your mouth you might endanger a family member back home.

The following day: whizzing past the spires of Coblenz to broad boring Wiesbaden. Here was my contact Simon, small-voiced Simon, standing diffidently where we had arranged to meet. Simon was a young man from Varto. He had come to Germany, abandoned his old Turkish name, and been baptised. But he was not yet Armenian – not by a long shot. The Armenian community in Wiesbaden had not made him welcome, he told me. He spoke vaguely of finding a wife in Armenia, but his Armenian was not good. He seemed to gravitate to other young men who shared his background. A good friend was an Alevi Armenian, a cake maker called Tigran; Tigran's mother's family was also from Varto.

Simon and Tigran promised to introduce me to two brothers in Wiesbaden who could tell me about the deportations in Emeran, the mixed Alevi and Armenian village where I had stayed with my friend Kamer. We fixed a time to talk to the elder of the two brothers, but he disappeared from view after work. The younger brother kept his mobile phone off. It transpired that the wife of one of the brothers had warned them against speaking to me. 'They have relations in Turkey,' said Tigran. 'They are scared.'

My heart bleeds for those Armenians who are citizens of the Republic of Turkey. In a state that forbids open debate of the events of 1915, it becomes doubly impossible to discuss their ramifications, and the unique people, hybrids with weird overlapping labels, that inhabit the vacuum. It is these people who are forgotten amid the learned mudslinging and parliamentary bills and letters to the editor. Their priorities differ from those of Professor Russell of Harvard University; their objective is not to slam the word 'genocide' down on the flat-backed head of the unrepentant Turk, to slam it down and slam it down again, but to live with dignity, and gradually to explore their past – in a state that regards them as full and complete citizens. There must be in them – shivering in the rags of their identity while the Armenians scream 'Genocide!' and the Turks retort 'No Genocide!' – a terrible sense that they no longer count for anything at all.

During a subsequent trip to Varto I stayed a night in the house of a man in a Sunni village overlooking the formerly Armenian village of Baskan. My host was a village notable, a religiously observant Sunni, and he was interested to hear about Shiism as it is practised in Iran. When I had finished answering his questions, he remarked with satisfaction that what he had heard was right; the Iranians had been led astray. Then we went to bed.

My host rose early the next morning to say his prayers and then he went and attended to his sheep and goats. I got up and came outside. The air was cold and watery. There had been heavy rain over the previous few days, but then the sun started rising decisively and I walked away from the valley, over the scree and black rocks with their gorgeous electric blue lichen. I was in high spirits, but when I turned around and looked down the valley I spotted my host climbing hurriedly towards me and pawing the air with his hand, in a gesture that could only mean, 'Stop!'

I had been enjoying this moment of solitude. I pretended that I hadn't seen my host, and turned up the hill. To my right, bearing down on me with a dog, I saw another man, also intent on catching me. This second man was walking in a straight line across the hillside. He hailed me and I was forced to stop.

'What is your business?' he asked.

'My business?' I told him whose guest I was, and added that I was going for a walk.

'You'll get lost,' the man said.

'No I won't,' I replied, but the man gestured down the hillside at my fast-approaching host. 'It looks as though he has something to say to you. Let's sit down on this rock and wait for him.' We made difficult small talk and a few minutes later my host reached us. 'It would be better if you didn't go on,' he said. So we went down the hillside again.

It was only later on, when I knew more about the massacre, and learned where it had taken place – and where, it is said, the soil remains ashen from the bones of the dead – that I realised I had been heading into the valley of Newala Ask.

Great Man

Years ago there was a young man in Varto, the scion of a powerful Alevi house. He was a mere boy when his mother told him to go and inform on his brother-in-law, the great Zeynel, who was then a fugitive from the Ottoman authorities, and this is what he did.

Later on, during the Armenian massacres, the same man went out to ambush and kill Armenians who were fleeing.

Much later, he fell for a married woman, a beautiful woman, and he gave his teenage son a gun and told him to kill the woman's husband, which the boy did, by shooting him in the back.

The murdered man's relations were fearful of picking a fight. Only his sister reacted. She took the exceptional and dangerous step of walking to Mus, engaging a lawyer and lodging a complaint against the killer, who was apprehended and jailed.

When this woman died, in 1993, they opened her kofi, or head covering, and found a man's shirt, bloody and holed, wrapped tightly around her head. It was her brother's shirt, and she had worn it since his death, decades before.

IN HIS ORDER OF *Eastern Anatolia,* Ismail Besikci displays an un-Turkish dislike for rhetorical sunbursts. There is a curt integrity in the tables and diagrams in this book, and in his methodical, defiantly utilitarian phrasing. Besikci has changed over the years, as every old Lefty has changed, but his contrarian instinct has stayed. Years in jail have soldered and riveted his opposition, making him, if anything, a more formidable vessel.

He is well known for his work on the Kurds, but Besikci is in fact a Turk from north central Anatolia. Back in the 1960s, when he was researching *Order of Eastern Anatolia,* he was a teaching assistant in the Department of Sociology at Ataturk University in Erzurum, which cannot have been easy, for Besikci, even then, was a positivist

Kurdophile revolutionary, and Erzurum, even then, was dominated by religious extremists and Turkish supremacists. The doctoral thesis Besikci wrote during his Erzurum years, on a nomadic tribe called the Alikans, showed more concern for the lot of the Kurds and their treatment at the hands of the government than was considered proper. He was dismissed from his post after the *coup d'état* of 1971, saw thirty-two of his books banned, and went on to spend more than fifteen years behind bars.

Order of Eastern Anatolia remains essential reading for any student of the east. Like the Kemalists, those subscribers to Ataturk's rigorous philosophy of technological and social modernisation, the author argues that the east is backward, and partially pins the blame on the agas and sheikhs. Again, like the Kemalists, those enemies of obscurantism and superstition, Besikci concentrates on religion's structural penetration into society, and in particularly the relationship between the agas and sheikhs, somewhat in the nature of medieval princes and bishops.

Where Besikci most strikingly differs from your average, left-leaning Kemalist is in his criticism of official attitudes towards the Kurds. He ranges over economic neglect to forced cultural assimilation, persecution and even murder. 'In the course of my research [in the Kurdish region]', he writes, 'I showed a picture of a big, multi-storeyed block of flats to a boy of between ten and twelve. I asked, "What's this?" His response: "Army post." Then I showed him a picture of a two- or three-floor house and asked him what it was. Again, he answered, "Army post." Then I showed him photographs of a sentry box and a school, and again he answered, "Army post."' In Turkish Kurdistan, Besikci is saying, a region under occupation, everything seems to be coloured khaki.

Part of the trouble, of course, is that many Turks' stated commitment to equality and integration is a fiction. These Turks are the first to concede, through unguarded expressions of superiority, the existence of a regrettable subspecies, the Kurds. Once, as Besikci sat in the office of a publisher in Istanbul, 'a translator entered, a woman charged with translating a novel from the English. The action takes place in Spain. There is a Turkish character, the sort of character who incarnates all that is bad about human nature. Theft, fraud, drug smuggling, murder, prostitution; he's involved in the lot. "He's guilty of every bad thing under the sun. He's a very bad man. I thought at length about this," the translator said, "and I decided to turn the word 'Turk' into 'Kurd', because I couldn't impute to a Turk so much ill." '

Besikci is one of the very few Turkish public figures to have learned Kurmanji, and there is something admirably counter-intuitive about his choice. At a time when his academic colleagues were counting their invitations to universities in France or Germany, Besikci was traipsing around Turkish Kurdistan with the Alikans.

This links Besikci back to Evliya, the old Ottoman traveller and writer, but it also puts him in the company of a select band of modern Turks, divided by discipline and ideology, but united in their conviction that somewhere in the primitive semi-colonised east lies an elusive prize.

Take, for instance, the journalist Fikret Otyam, whose series of 1950s travel books, being informed by Mustafa Kemal's *mission civilatrice*, and spiced with anecdotes about the quaintly barbaric people he meets, deserves inclusion in any orientalist library. Going about the east and genially recounting his experiences for people in Ankara and Istanbul, Otyam was performing a patriotic service. He was contributing, quite consciously, to the republic's cohesion.

There is a handful of other writers and journalists who operated in this vein. Then there were others with a more specific mission, such as the musicologists who went around eastern Anatolia purloining Kurdish and Armenian songs for adaptation and absorption into a new, official 'Turkish' canon.

In 1999, the ranks of Turks in the east were bolstered by an intimidating presence, Orhan Pamuk. Imagine the reaction of Pamuk's friends and associates when, in that year, he made the first of several visits to the city of Kars, to research *Snow*, his seventh novel.

Even then Pamuk was a famous man, the country's tutor in history and art, and going to Kars was not at all like going to Izmir. There was the PKK to consider, and the Islamists, and the cold and the lack of a decent hotel. How many times was Pamuk warned to be careful – 'The east can be dangerous, my friend!' – by people who had never set foot east of Ankara? I liked the fact of Pamuk's going, his giving creative flesh to the much abused vision of national unity.

I read *Snow* after finishing Besikci, and I found that I knew much of the plot from the reviews – this love story of Ka, an expatriate Turkish poet, and Ipek, the daughter of the owner of Kars's Snow Palace Hotel, guttering and dying against a backdrop of political murder and unrelenting, muffling snow. I found myself looking down the byways of this book and admiring Pamuk's depiction of a forgotten little town embarrassed by its own wrathful cosmopolitanism – a 'border town' whose nearest border, with Armenia, happens to be closed.

Reading about Ka through the eyes of Pamuk's narrator, I also found myself looking for me. Like Ka – and like Pamuk, who misleadingly carried a press card while researching in Kars – I describe myself as a journalist when I go to the east, though more truthfully. Like them, I know what it is to be monitored at every turn, and to be asked, again and again, 'Why are you here?' I too have sat in tiny newspaper offices, attended pathetic little ceremonies, and felt the intensity and insignificance of all that is going on around me.

I returned to Varto that same autumn, in the early hours of a national holiday. I hurried to Government House. There, before Ataturk's bust, stood the army captain, the district commissioner, the mayor, the elected headmen and the local representatives of the utility companies, postal service and national political parties. Each of these dignitaries – the men in suit and tie, the women in a white blouse and a sober jacket and skirt – was accompanied by a flunkey holding a wreath of artificial flowers. Prompted by a young woman speaking into a microphone, recorded by a photographer from the *Gimgim News*, the sombre wreath layers came forward, many of them bitter opponents of the Turkish state, and paid their homage.

I had come to the east with an idea that I should get to know not only the natives, but also the men and women who had been posted there by the state. I would draw the latter out of their reticence, and they would tell me about their lives. But this, I came to realise, was a fantasy. However hard I tried, however sweetly I talked, I found no chink in the armour of hostility that the policeman, the army officer and the civilian bureaucrat wore while speaking to me. My opponent was not merely the man before me. It was a political philosophy that killed creativity and imagination. And this, in a way, was also the opponent of the civil servant himself. How is one to instil in a young district administrator a sense of destiny and ambition, if he (or, less often, she) has been drilled to distrust new visions and stick to the well-trodden path, to perpetuate the stalemate?

What would happen if one day it got around that the district commissioner or the police chief was learning Kurmanji; what if he tried out his new skills in the bazaar? The people would be delighted and it would do wonders for community relations. For the state, on the other hand, it would be a worrying development. How long before the linguist was reported to his superiors for displaying Kurdophile tendencies, for being – despite himself, despite the system that had reared and protected him – a splittist?

I was, I realised with dismay, under even closer surveillance than I had been during my first visit. The men from military intelligence made themselves known to me. One of them, a slight, toothy fellow who called himself Ozgur and claimed to be from Diyarbakir, insisted that we have lunch in the Berlin Restaurant. I was to phone him, he advised, whenever I wished to set foot out of Varto town. It was for my own protection.

As a reporter back in the 1990s, I had found it amusing to be followed on my trips to the south-east; I once spent an hour playing hide and seek in a mosque with a confused plain-clothes cop. But these fond memories were now crowded out. I felt the effects of being followed and monitored, and of knowing that everyone I approached ran the risk of being questioned by the authorities, in subtle ways. I was taut from annoyance and frustration – and guilt, for implicating those people who did agree to speak to me. I found myself once again comparing this Turkey with the old Turkey I had once known. I had only myself to blame. Turkey was not one but two countries, and I had willingly strayed from the soft one to the hard one.

I nurtured a strong dislike for three young teachers who lived in the Teachers' Hostel. In the morning I would see them in their suits and ties, breakfasting on lentil soup and pastries in a restaurant owned by Nazim Han's nephew, sizing me up as I passed. In the evening they congregated in front of the hostel TV, lounging in their tracksuit bottoms on dirty sofas, eating sunflower seeds. They reserved their arch comments for the commercial breaks. 'What will your book be about?' (The very question he asked yesterday.) 'It seems unlikely that anyone will be interested in reading about a place like this.'

They were successors to the teachers who, in the childhood of the mayor, Demir Celik, had beaten children for speaking languages other than Turkish. They were the republic's eyes and ears. They would be expected to inform the authorities of a spike in nationalist sentiment here, a nocturnal visit by a PKK guerrilla there. They taught the national anthem and Ataturk's speeches and the ingratitude of the Armenians to kids whose fathers were PKK guerrillas. I am not sure they appreciated the irony of their situation.

I began to explore again. I went with a local man to see the Urartian citadel of Kayalidere, high above the Murat. I discussed politics and drank tea around the stove in the Karinca stationery shop. I spent an uneasy Saturday evening watching the big match, Galatasary versus Fenerbahce, in the policemen's club, a smoke-filled establishment frequented by my three teacher friends; they winced superciliously over their dominoes. I went out to the village of Tatan to see a prominent government loyalist. He spoke pointedly of the British intelligence officer Major Noel, and his attempts to stir up the Kurds after the First World War. And I heard some good news. Kamer Erdogan, my host at Emeran, had succeeded in recovering his kidnapped sister Gulseren, and he had taken her to the coast.

I visited the Kurdish bard Selahattin out in Baskan and recorded his rendition of some famous Kurdish laments and epics. Then Selahattin and I went outside and I took photographs of him standing in the mud with his pinstripe suit and his one eye, and he showed me the new village mosque, on the site of the Armenian church.

I saw Demir Celik about the place. We had tea a couple of times; he was cordial but more distant. I learned that he was being pursued in the courts, along with more than fifty other Kurdish nationalist mayors who had urged the prime minister of Denmark to resist Turkish pressure to close down a pro-PKK TV channel broadcasting from Copenhagen. Celik remained well liked, but some people suggested he was too soft and bookish, and perhaps too accessible, to be a really effective mayor. The previous winter the snow had stayed on the roads because the municipal snow plough lacked spare parts. It was a scandal. Then there was a second charge, levelled by Celik's predecessor as mayor, Abdulbari Han. Abdulbari Han accused Celik of behaving like a Kurdish nationalist leader when he should be concentrating on collecting the rubbish.

It unsettled me to hear this criticism of Celik. I liked the mayor for his habit of wandering about the town centre, accessible to all, rather than surrounding himself with minders as Han had done. It struck me that Celik's position inside the Democratic Society Party, with its close but informal links to the PKK, might be an invidious one. On the one hand, it had guaranteed him election in Varto, where he had united to a sufficient degree the Kurdish nationalist and the Alevi votes. Once elected, however, he could not rely on the goodwill of the Islamist national government, or of the district administrator and gendarmerie captain, even on so minor a subject as the provision of parts for a snow plough. It also meant that Celik would have to toe the party line, refraining from any criticism of Apo and biting his lip when the PKK murdered its Kurdish opponents. I had a hunch that, were he free to do so, Celik would criticise some of the PKK's less likeable practices; he seemed to be the most instinctively democratic person I had come across in Varto. But I didn't know this for sure. It was only a hunch.

On quiet days I would go to the offices of the *Gimgim News* and read back copies to find out what had happened over the past few months.

A Sunni official had caused consternation by observing, after flooding hit Alevi areas, that 'they are paying the price for their sins'. In the Hurriyet neighbourhood of Varto town, a feed store belonging to fifteen families had been deliberately burned to the ground. The mayor had been in Berlin as guest of honour at the fourth Varto Culture and Solidarity Evening, a jamboree of live music and speeches held in the Prestige Wedding Lounge, punctuated by pro-Apo slogans and attended by 600 people. Addressing the estimated 4,000 *Vartolu*s living in Berlin, Celik had said, 'We may be physically apart, but when it comes to history, culture and values, we must be able to achieve unity.' '*Ez taz e me*', the new single by the singer Nilufer Akbal, a Varto Alevi, had reached number two in a chart compiled by WDR Funkhaus Europa.

I cherished my sole friendship, with Ismail Han, nephew of Nazim Han. Ismail went around the place with me, despite the white Renault, despite the questions that the police and military intelligence put to him when I wasn't around. Who does he work for? How much money does he have? He may have felt protected by his membership of a national organisation, the Pir Sultan Association. In his heart, though,

Ismail was a cautious man, a man who had seen the inside of a cell and had no desire to do so again.

Ismail took me to the tomb of Seyit Neseme, an Alevi holy man, in the village of Rakasan. He procured the key to the white building where the Seyit had been buried with his wife and son. We gazed at the pictures on the wall, of the twelve Shia imams. Ismail told me of the Seyit's celebrity as a clairvoyant. He told me that the Seyit had once placed a curse on a bad man and the man had abruptly died. There was another story about how a Sunni had asked the Seyit whether Sunnis or Alevis were more worthy, and he had replied, 'The good are good.' This axiom had become famous among members of both communities. It was up there on the wall of the Seyit's tomb.

Ismail told me that the Seyit, who died in 1949, had grandchildren in Germany but that there was no longer the old longing in each Alevi community for a spiritual leader, let alone a hereditary one – Rakasan, probably for the first time in its history, had no such guide. Then we came out of the tomb and gazed for a while across the valley.

Ismail, I now know, was only moderately informative about Rakasan and Seyit Neseme. He didn't tell me that the local man who endowed the Seyit's tomb, whose own grave lies just outside the door, was the father of Mehmet Can Yuce, who rose to membership of the PKK's central committee. He didn't tell me that, in the run-up to the *coup d'état* of 1980, Rakasan was among the most fractured of Varto's villages, and that different left-wing groups fought each other here regularly.

Ismail didn't tell me this because he was cautious, because the white Renault was just a little way off, and because he didn't trust me.

Varto looked bare in November, the sky unimpeded and the earth sleepy and black, the leaves in drifts and the flocks huddling in the pens. We had forty-eight hours of freezing rain driving off the Bingol Mountains and then, after a glorious sunlit pause when the wind died and the robins gossiped, the skies grew black and the snow began to fall.

The following day, the snow still falling, the town of Varto folding in on itself: another summons to the police station. What now? A visitor, they told me at the door. It was the policeman Vedat Bey, all the way from Mus. I stamped the snow off my boots and was escorted down a corridor into an untidy little office belonging to one of the plain-clothes cops.

Three men entered. One of them, Erkan, I knew. There was another fellow, tall and raven-haired, and a third, to whom the other two deferred in spite of his relative youth. Erkan and the tall one grinned skittishly at the younger man, and glared at me. I was in the presence of a clever man, they wished me to understand, a man of the world.

Vedat Bey threw off his overcoat, loosened his collar and smiled through thin lips. His lifeless hair and the gleam on his forehead and his slack unattended midriff attested to fatigue and boyish eating habits. But the most important features of Vedat Bey's round face were his eyes, beady and alert, and his sharp, inquisitive nose. There was a tangy self-regard about him, the ammonic aura of a young man of whom it has been said, 'Expect great things.'

Vedat Bey was grinning. Ah, here was the tea. Good man, Erkan. Did I smoke? I did not? Would I mind? Splendid! He had expected someone older. So had I? How amusing. Now, where should we begin?

In this way Vedat Bey, the policeman from Mus, a man whose name was certainly not Vedat and who was not a policeman and not from Mus, began his interrogation.

Vedat Bey leaned back in his chair and smoked his cigarette and announced that he would now be very frank. It was our privilege, here in Varto while the snow fell, to be frank with one another, and Vedat Bey wanted to inform me that while he was obliged by his position to observe the official policies of the state, he personally had no time for the West. 'I don't feel an iota of trust for a single European,' he said. 'I am the sort of man who is attuned more to Central Asia than to Europe. However much the English shouldered an imperial responsibility, to the same degree I endeavour to further the interests of Turkey's colonial mission.'

Vedat Bey warned me that on these and other subjects, I would find him an unconventional man. He had been informed that I was a correspondent of long standing in Iran. There was much to discuss, he told me. He was, for instance, full of admiration for Iran's resistance to the American hegemony, and also for Iranian democracy. 'By the way,' he said abruptly, stubbing out his cigarette in the ashtray in front of him, 'Ayatollah Meshkini has been the head of the Assembly of Experts for ever. Isn't it time he stood down?'

This is how Vedat Bey initiated a most unexpected conversation, about the structure of power in the Islamic Republic of Iran, while Erkan and the tall dark one looked on dumbfounded. The Assembly of Experts; the Council of Guardians; the Expediency Council; Vedat Bey knew all of these exotic organs. 'What about Montazeri? Do you think he still has any influence?' His questions were not meant to be answered. 'I don't think for a minute that Iran resembles Iraq in the way that the Americans and the British think it does. What we're talking about here is a state being run according to Islamic law. But which Islamic law? That's the key ...' He lit another cigarette and said to Erkan, 'Can we have these teas changed? Mine has gone cold.'

The fresh tea arrived and, refuelled, Vedat Bey powered on. He soared over Iraq. 'What are Sistani's relations like with Khamenei?' He skimmed the rooftops in Beirut. 'Just imagine, Christopher Bey, if Musa Sadr had survived; how things might have turned out differently!' We were friends and colleagues now, adepts in the same arcane art, delighted to sit together in the same small room in a police station in eastern Turkey. Then quite suddenly Vedat Bey changed course, and landed in Varto.

'Tell me, Christopher Bey, what are your thoughts on the Alevis? I'd be interested to know what you think of them. It seems you've been spending a lot of time with them.' He lit another cigarette.

'Vedat Bey,' I said, 'when Major Noel was in Turkey in 1919, he observed that the *Kizilbas* he ran into considered themselves to be Kurds. The interesting thing is that, certainly in Varto, by the time of the Sheikh Sait Rebellion we find the *Kizilbas* of Varto fighting on the side of Turkish government against the Kurdish nationalists. Later still, we find large numbers of Alevis joining a Kurdish nationalist group, the PKK. And now, at the turn of the twenty-first century, if you ask an Alevi here what he or she is, the answer is very often, "Neither a Kurd nor a Turk, simply an Alevi." That's a remarkably fluid sense of identity, don't you think?'

A shadow fell across Vedat Bey's face. He leaned forward and his voice dropped. 'Doesn't the constantly changing position of the Alevis, from one generation to the next, strike you as a little suspicious? Don't you think that outside manipulators might be to blame?' The tall dark one grinned wolfishly. Yes, Vedat Bey continued, fixing me with a poached eye, it had been suggested – he would be frank here, if I permitted it, painfully frank – it had been suggested in certain quarters that I was part of such a scheme, a scheme of outside manipulation, just as my Major Noel had been.

The tall dark one could contain himself no longer. 'Are you here on a commission from your government?' Vedat Bey exhaled jubilantly.

I replied, 'I admire people like you, patriotic people working for your country. But I am too selfish to subordinate myself in this way. I'm here for myself. You have seen my references.'

Vedat Bey smiled and his fat hand slapped against the air. 'Yes, yes – a friendly write-up from our ambassador in Tehran. Personally,' he went on soothingly, 'I never believed these suggestions.' I smiled gratefully.

'Let us be clear, Christopher Bey,' Vedat Bey declaimed. 'The question of ethnicity is a debatable one. The problem begins with this question: How do you define ethnicity? As Barthes does? As Marx does? Perhaps you are a Weberian? Certain quarters wish to make of the Alevis a separate ethnic group, and that has nothing to do with identity. It has to do with politics.'

Gradually Vedat Bey let himself become overwrought. 'You know what angers me? In the midst of all this hoo-ha about the so-called Armenian genocide, who will be called to account for the death of my grandfather, whom the Armenians killed?' Again, the hand rose, the voice hardened. 'Who will be called to account for the murder of my Muslim cousin in Srebrenica? Oh yes,' he swept on, 'you lecture us on opening the Ottoman archives, but it's the British and the French and the Italians who have closed their archives.'

This, finally, was a barefaced lie. I sat silent.

The tall dark one waded in gratefully. 'If you are interested in ethnic conflict, why aren't you investigating Corsica? If you are a journalist interested in social issues, why don't you go to Tokat, in western Turkey, and investigate the status of women there?'

I replied, 'Thank you for these suggestions. Once I have finished my current project I will propose both of them to my editors, and I am sure they will be welcomed.'

He said, 'I have been told that Hrant Dink's wife is from Varto. What have you heard?'

I shrugged. 'Nothing.'

Vedat Bey rose impatiently. He extended his hand. 'You have given us much valuable time, Christopher Bey, and for this I thank you. And I note,' he smiled again, 'that the West has decided to reward its faithful servant.'

I stood for a moment, puzzled by Vedat Bey's parting comment, which had prompted a shout of derisive laughter from his subordinates, but he was already striding from the room.

I strolled to the upper bazaar to buy a newspaper. The headline read: 'Orhan Pamuk Awarded Nobel Prize for Literature.'

The *Diary of Major E.M. Noel, CIE, DSO, on Special Duty in Kurdistan*, printed and engraved by the Government Press in Basra, is a modest unbound publication, coming apart in my hands. It describes Noel's journey, which he made between June and September 1919, from Diyarbakir up to Harput. Major Noel of the Indian Political Department was a fluent Persianist who also knew decent Kurdish. Much admired by Sir Arnold Wilson, the British administrator in the Persian Gulf, Noel's exploits during the First World War, which included a period of imprisonment in a verminous dungeon in northern Persia, would have filled, in Wilson's words, 'a good-sized volume', but it is to Noel the romantic Kurdophile, rather than the adventurer, that we must turn.

Eastern Anatolia had been transformed by the war, and not only because the Armenians had been liquidated. Huge numbers of Kurds and other Muslims had also been killed in the fighting, as well as by famine and disease. Anatolia lay defeated and prone, its destiny to be decided in far-away cabinets. The post-war conferences; the chandeliers and the bureaucratic constellations beneath them; an under-secretary improvising with genius on the back of a dinner menu; the Fourteen Points and other morsels; this was the genesis of a new Middle East, and here in the territories being divided up by the winners, where rumours and proposals – Greater Armenia! Greater

Kurdistan! an American Mandate! – came and went like mercury, the people watched, entranced.

It was the time when your energetic political officer, operating on the ground with verve and a sound command of the languages, could have a discernible influence over imperial policy. Noel was such a man. In 1919 the new Republic of Armenia, occupying but a portion of what had been Tsarist Armenia to the east, was busy diplomatically, pressing its claim for more chunks of Anatolia. But it was Noel's ardent Kurdophilia, and his belief that the establishment of a Kurdish state, or at least an autonomous entity under a British aegis, would delay the revival of Turkey to the north and help Britain subjugate Iraq to the south, that initially found support in Whitehall. At Sèvres in 1920, the year after Noel's mission, the Kurds were promised 'a scheme of local autonomy' for the area lying 'east of the Euphrates, south of the southern boundary of Armenia ... and north of the frontier of Turkey with Syria and Mesopotamia'. Rarely in their history had the Kurds been so close to achieving an independent national home.

'Both the Armenian and the Turk,' Noel writes midway through his diary, 'are against the Kurd for the same reason, namely that a recognition of the Kurd as a people would interfere with their individual claims to sovereignty. Up to now the Armenians and the Turks have thought that they were the only competitors in the ring and both had their hopes of victory. The Armenians relied on the sympathy of Europe, the Turks on the overwhelming majority of the Muslim population. The Kurd was looked upon by both sides as nothing more than a pawn in the game ... that the hitherto despised Kurd should now enter the ring and point out that he is numerically by far the strongest element in the country, cannot be anything but intensely galling to the original competitors.'

Picturesque and evocative, Noel's account is helpful for the description it gives of the uncertainty, bordering on chaos, that prevailed in post-war eastern Anatolia. Many of the people he meets are grimly convinced that the Allies are determined to press the Armenian case. The Ottoman government, chafing under Allied supervision in occupied Istanbul, is trying to rally the Kurds in the name of pan-Islamic unity against the Armenian claims, and also to counter the new threat of Kurdish nationalism. Noel's progress, naturally, is regarded with the greatest suspicion by the Turkish authorities, who denounce his 'evil designs on our fatherland … Turks and Kurds are brothers, the sole mainstay of Islam'.

If Noel's report is of limited use as a historical document, this is down to the author's infatuation with the Kurds and his contempt for the other 'original competitors'. Noel isn't the first westerner to go gaga over the noble, excitable, pitiable Kurd, and he won't be the last. The more one reads of his ride north through Diyarbakir, Maras and Malatya to Harput, while he enjoys the hospitality of the regional agas and evades as best he can the attentions of hostile local officials, the more one is inclined to question the judgement of a man so obviously enchanted.

Noel's Kurds are a people of boundless charm, hospitality and ignorance, good at falconry, proverbs and a pastime which 'consists in one man prancing and dancing a length of thirty to forty yards with his hands above his head' while 'another Kurd with a … thong belabours him across his back'. Among the Kurds, Noel uncritically records, 'the chief complaint against the Turk is on account of his stupidity, his contempt for everything that is not Turkish, and his uselessness'. Nor does Noel shed tears for the Armenians. They are remembered as timid, avaricious and deceitful. This is reporting of a most partisan kind.

Noel does not fail to exonerate the Kurds of systemic involvement in the elimination of the Armenians, even though his informants are the Kurds themselves. 'It will be found,' he writes, without foundation, 'that the Kurds most implicated in the massacres were the townsmen, who from long contact with the Turks had acquired all the bad habits and characteristics of the Stamboul *Efendi*. Such men have lost their sense of Kurdish identity; they are in the swim of the [Committee of Union and Progress] current, and dread a change which might interfere with their present sources of graft. It is this type of Kurd who is produced by the Turk for the edification of chance European visitors.'

Noel's most significant determination concerns the fitness of the Kurds for revolt. He finds everywhere 'a very lively sense of Kurdish nationality, antipathy to the Turk, and a great hatred of the government. There is a general disposition to revolt against the government, but at present it is held in check by the fact that the tribesmen have been thoroughly cowed during the war. It would not, however, require a great stimulus from the outside to start an insurrectionary movement.'

For all the support they generated at the time, Noel's findings did not in the end swing the British behind Kurdish irredentism. In 1925, south-east Anatolia was to experience a major Kurdish rebellion, engineered by Halit Bey of the Cibrans, but it would not enjoy active British support.

In part, Britain's change of heart can be ascribed to the opposition of British administrators in Iraq to a separate Kurdish entity, on the grounds that it would undermine the Baghdad government. But the main reason was the stunning success of a former Ottoman officer who, at the time of Noel's journey, was soliciting support for an administration to supplant the current government in Istanbul: Mustafa Kemal, later known as Ataturk.

The Cibrans are the leading tribe of Varto. Back then, when the tribes mattered, they held the people down using their arms, their flocks and the favour of the sheikhs and the government. When you sit and talk about tribal history with an elderly, courteous member of the Cibran tribe, you may expect, from the authoritative clearing of his throat and the correctness of his bearing, to receive a decorous official version of events.

So it proves when I speak to Selim Kilicoglu. Selim Kilicoglu is a patrician Kurd. He lives with his wife in a modest but comfortable development near Istanbul airport. His father was Halil Efendi, a kinsman and brother in arms of Halit Bey, and Selim speaks with uniform reverence of his forebears, whose family tree he knows by heart, lest the slightest criticism spot his account of virtue and achievement.

There is one way to depict the history of the Cibrans as one of virtue and achievement, and that is to bleed it white. Selim's account of the Cibrans' gradual annexation of Varto, including his father's seizure of several villages in the east of the district, is a lifeless slab. Halit Bey's grandfather 'bound all the region's chiefs to us ... a series of lesser Kurdish chiefs pledged fealty of their own accord; they came to us and said, "Please protect us." ' Selim's account does not allow that the process of Cibran expansion was brutal and violent, or that the inhabitants of the villages that his father seized nowadays recall Cibran sovereignty as a bleak, arbitrary despotism. And he insists, in the face of voluminous evidence to the contrary, that the Cibrans played no part in the Sunni-Alevi warfare that almost tore Varto apart.

Kurdish Hamidiye fighters, c. 1900

In Selim's telling Halit Bey and his cousin Halil are exponents of an oriental *noblesse oblige*. They show generosity and fairness to the villagers whose lives they run, allied to a lively intolerance of any abuse of power. The tribe owes its prestige to the court's favour and to prowess in the saddle. 'There were seven gazetted officers in our family,' says Selim, and this brings him to the outstanding manifestation of Cibran achievement: the Hamidiye regiments.

At the beginning of the First World War, Halit was in overall command of no fewer than four regiments. 'Assuredly God is great,' sighs Selim, 'but by goodness Halit Bey was a great man.' Selim puts Halit and his men at a safe distance from the rout of the Ottomans by the Russians at Sarikamis. The Cibran cavalrymen were successfully defending the fabled Sabre Pass, and only withdrew after their flanks, manned by Ottoman regulars, collapsed. Indeed, 'wherever Halit fought, he won magnificent victories'.

Halit Bey's finest hour was another stirring defeat, on Varto's eastern border, in January 1916 – the upshot, again, of soft flanks and feeble regulars. Russian infantrymen had got in behind Halit's men via Hinis and a desperate battle ensued as the Kurds tried to break through the enemy lines and regain the Varto valley. Halit Bey's ostler saved his master from capture, picking off two Russian soldiers who were trying to pull him off his horse. 'We left behind 300 martyrs,' says Selim. 'That place is a graveyard.'

Selim Kilicoglu has left me in the dark as to how Halit Bey and his men spent 1915 – that awful year, between Sarikamis and their return to Varto, when the Armenians were being deported and the Kurdish cavalry brigades, in Mehmet Serif Firat's words, 'gave themselves over once more to robbery and brigandage'. This is Firat's polite, ethnically imprecise way of saying that the Sunni Kurds ran the Armenians ragged. Selim Kilicoglu is adamant that the Cibrans did not participate in the massacres and that Halit Bey 'gave express orders that the Armenians shouldn't be touched'.

I am not convinced by this. Even if Halit and his men were not in Varto when the Armenians were being deported and massacred, that does not exonerate them of maltreating Armenians further east. If Halit's Hamidiye regiments did, indeed, remain indifferent to the opportunities for murder and pillage, this would be exceptional, even aberrant, for eastern Anatolia was a free-for-all. Nor am I convinced by Selim's depiction of Halit and his men as doughty and successful fighters. Turkish commanders regarded the Kurdish cavalry regiments as all but useless, and military historians have described them as showing scant enthusiasm for serious military activity except when looting opportunities arose.

These doubts of mine are unsettling, for Halit of the Cibrans is the second of Varto's great men, and I am not sure whether I should admire him or not. The photographs show him to be handsome and clear-eyed. From the respect he continues to arouse, and his audacity as a soldier, it is clear that he was a brave leader. To Halit is even ascribed a prescient aphorism, following the defeat of the Armenian army in 1918 and the securing of Turkey's eastern borders. Brooding in his tent after the fray, Halit was asked by a comrade why he was not celebrating like everyone else. 'We have whetted,' he replied, 'the sword that will cut our own throats.'

None of the Armenians I have spoken to can tell me anything about Halit's attitude towards them, but it is notable that, among the Alevis of Varto, who might be expected to revile and detest him, there is grudging admiration. That he was not personally motivated by sectarianism is confirmed by his later, conciliatory behaviour towards the Alevis. Even Mehmet Serif Firat's *History* is restrained in its treatment of Halit of the Cibrans.

I suspect that Halit Bey will remain a great man for longer than his Alevi counterpart Mehmet Serif Firat, for Halit owes his status not to the state, but to the people and their memories of the past. Perhaps the aura that clings to him comes from his espousing a tragic cause, his death at the hands of an ungentlemanly Turkish jailer, and the romance that surrounds noble failure.

Halit Bey's active engagement with the Kurdish nationalist movement can probably be dated to the latter part of the First World War, when he was sent to Dersim to pacify some troublesome tribes there. Remarkably, given his family's history of conflict with the Alevis, he won a reputation as a skilful administrator, and many Alevi friends. In 1921, after Halit had left Dersim, the province was the scene of a major Kurdish rebellion.

In 1921 or shortly thereafter, Halit established *Azadi*, or Freedom, in Erzurum, with the aim of launching revolution and making an independent Kurdistan.

From our perspective, looking back at more than three quarters of a century of republican hostility to Kurdish nationalism, it seems logical that Halit's loyalty to the Turks should have ended with the transition from empire to nation state in 1923. But Halit became an active nationalist before many other leading Kurds, who continued to trust in Mustafa Kemal's generally pro-Kurdish rhetoric. Halit and several of his fellow Kurdish officers had been exposed to imperial Istanbul, with its various nationalisms, at an impressionable age. Thanks to their familiarity with the military establishment from which Ataturk came, they were able to foresee a hardening of the government's Turkish character – and, as regional leaders accustomed to considerable autonomy, the threat that Ataturk's centralising tendencies posed to their own pre-eminence. As Halit's successful public relations in Dersim show, he was now convinced of the need to draw the Alevi tribes into his nationalist plans. For the moment, at least, his cousin and former schoolfellow Major Kasim of Kulan (as he now was), who had become Varto's district administrator, agreed.

This is the context for a meeting that took place in northern Varto, probably in 1920, the only recorded meeting of the major Sunni and Alevi chiefs in the region's history. Two eyewitness accounts remain, one of them, inevitably, by Mehmet Serif Firat. In this version, Halit urges the Alevis to join him in a heroic endeavour to put an end to 600 years of 'servitude' under the Turks and 'win Kurdish independence'. In a second account, Halit is absent from the meeting and it is Major Kasim who makes the appeal. Both accounts have the Alevi tribes rejecting the appeal and Mehmet Serif Firat's uncle Halo, Varto's most powerful Feron, replying as follows:

'Let us speak like men. We are not Kurds ... we have no faith in you. You had the Hamidiye regiments and for years we fought each other. Now you want to be the sultan; we will not be your slaves.'

'After the government found out about this meeting,' Mehmet Serif Firat writes, '[Halit Bey] was regarded with suspicion ... it was decided that he should be distanced from the tribes in the region ... thus he was kept in Erzurum, his rank frozen, and placed in charge of of the Army Corps accounts commission.'

The suspicions against Halit Bey did not prevent him from building up *Azadi* in Erzurum, propagandising against Mustafa Kemal and preparing for a rebellion. The government was monitoring *Azadi*, but may not have been aware of its size or precise intentions. Rather than make wholesale arrests of Kurdish nationalists, risking what support it enjoyed among the Kurds, the government preferred to isolate, bribe or otherwise neutralise potential troublemakers. The first sign of open confrontation came in September 1924, when the Turks foiled a mutiny of *Azadi* officers and their followers, some of whom fled into British-controlled Iraqi Kurdistan. The government responded by court-martialling several suspects and arresting and interrogating Halit's confederate Ziya Yusuf, who had sent a cipher telegram that was intended to spark off the mutiny. So it was in an atmosphere of shared trepidation and mutual suspicion that Halit accepted a dinner invitation from the commander of Erzurum's Eighth Army Corps, in October 1924, to meet the new president, Mustafa Kemal.

Erzurum had not been on Mustafa Kemal's itinerary during this, the latest in a series of provincial tours, but the town had been badly shaken in a recent earthquake and he went to give assurances of help. In Erzurum, as elsewhere, he defended the most radical of his recent reforms, the abolition of the caliphate and the sending into exile of all surviving members of the Ottoman dynasty. Other steps, including the abolition of pious foundations and the standardisation of education, pointed no less forcefully to the transformation that Mustafa Kemal was envisaging, a transformation that dismayed and angered many traditionalists. The opposition cells in Ankara; the foot-dragging in the provinces; the Allies with their arrogant conviction that no Turk could be truly modern – these obstacles seem only to have stiffened Mustafa Kemal's resolve, that modern champion slashing through coils of inertia and sloth. As he declared on this same tour, 'For everything in the world – for civilization, for life, for success – the truest guide is knowledge and science. To seek a guide other than knowledge and science [is a mark of] heedlessness, ignorance and aberration.'

Imagine Mustafa Kemal seated in the senior officers' mess of the Eighth Army Corps, flanked by the corps commander, the mayor of Erzurum and other notables. Mustafa Kemal had not dressed for dinner. He was got up like a country squire, in plus fours and thick stockings and inappropriate patent leather shoes. He was not yet paunchy from the booze, and he smoked his monogrammed cigarettes with élan. Upon entering the mess, Colonel Halit of the Cibrans and Resit, his cousin and fellow officer, immaculate in their uniforms and clipped moustaches, were startled to discover that the president of the new republic was accompanied by his young wife Latife. She, unveiled, prettily extended her hand to Halit, who begged her pardon for not taking it; his religion did not permit it. Mustafa Kemal, that enemy of ignorance and aberration, was visibly angered and a chill descended on the evening.

It's tempting to speculate that, had they met twenty years before, as young Ottoman officers, the two men might have got on. But the world had changed and Mustafa Kemal was leading Turkey in a new direction. The new geography books made no mention of Kurdistan; the secular courts and schools did not admit the use of any language other than Turkish. Mustafa Kemal's civil servants practised a bias against Kurds and a new law, promulgated by his parliament, allowed the government to seize the land of Kurdish families and give it to Turkish-speaking settlers.

Then there was the cultural divide that had opened between Mustafa Kemal and Halit Bey – now that they no longer shared the old composite Ottoman identity, now that one had reverted to being a feudal Kurd and the other had become a free-thinking European. It would have been unthinkable for Halit to bring his demure, veiled wife to such a gathering. But there was Latife, daughter of a family of merchants in Izmir, a permissive city. Latife had studied in France, where she must have learned her famous obduracy. In Tokat, on the way to Erzurum – everyone was talking about it – she had the gall to argue with her husband in full public view. There was also Mustafa Kemal's drinking to consider, his repeal of the old law banning alcohol. No, there seemed little chance of an accommodation.

Mustafa Kemal hardly addressed a word to Halit. The important conversation took place between Halit and the corps commander. The commander enquired why Halit had repeatedly tendered his resignation, to which Halit replied, 'I want to go back to my corner.' The commander said, 'So it's true what they say, that you are preparing to betray the homeland.' Halit replied bitterly, 'Does someone living on land that has been thickened by the blood of his forefathers, of his entire family – does such a man commit treason against his own land?'

He glanced in Mustafa Kemal's direction: 'And then someone from goodness knows where has the nerve to come and play the patriot!'

Halit hardly touched his dinner. He refused even the offer of a cigarette. Then he made his excuses and left.

In jail in Bitlis, Yusuf Zia confessed to complicity in the recent mutiny and implicated Halit and various others. Mustafa Kemal had

Mustafa Kemal c. 1923

been reluctant to arrest Halit, perhaps because he feared that this would enrage the Kurds. Now, he felt that he had no choice. On 20 December 1924, Halit of the Cibrans was arrested and sent to Bitlis.

Let us meet the sixty-year-old divine who gave his name to the insurrection, taking control of events in the absence of Halit and Yusuf Ziya: Sheikh Sait. Sheikh Sait was one of the richest men in Kurdistan. He owned large flocks that were driven throughout the region and marketed as far away as Aleppo. Although the sheikh enjoyed most influence among the Zaza-speaking Kurds, he had judiciously connected himself, through marriages that he and other members of his family had contracted, to several Kurmanji-speaking tribes. His third wife was Halit Bey's elder sister.

The sheikh had a refulgent beard, tinged with henna. His eyes were deep and black from antimony. He was met with reverence whenever he toured, receiving funds and obeisance from his followers, and resolving disputes. To hear him preach, as he did often during these arduous tours, or to recite famous devotional verses, was, for many of his followers a deeply spiritual experience. Unlike many other Kurdish divines, whom he regarded as self-serving collaborators, Sheikh Sait was a nationalist. He was in contact with the Kurdish deputies in the Ankara parliament; and he hated Mustafa Kemal.

Even before their arrest, it seems that Halit Bey and the other leaders of *Azadi* had decided that, with a view to rallying as much popular support as possible, the rebellion should be led by senior sheikhs. Shortly after Halit's arrest Sheikh Sait embarked on a tour, starting in Varto and moving south-west among the mainly Zaza-speaking tribes, during which he asked for support for a rebellion and assigned 'fronts' and objectives to supportive tribal chiefs. During the tour, the sheikh issued a decree condemning Mustafa Kemal for rejecting God, the Prophet and the caliph, and stating that it was lawful to rebel against him, but the sheikh planned to wait at least until March before signalling the beginning of the revolt.

In the event, the Sheikh Sait Rebellion broke out prematurely, on 8 February 1925, after an exchange between the sheikh's forces and local gendarmes led the inhabitants of a small town to rise against the Turkish authorities. Powerless to hush up these incidents or prevent an escalation, the sheikh was forced to declare a revolt. Governors were appointed to the 'liberated' districts and unwilling tribes persuaded by force to join the revolt. The sheikh issued another decree in which he declared himself the representative of the caliphate and the leader of the warriors of Islam. The sheikh and his men, who numbered around 7,000, marched south to lay siege to Diyarbakir, the historic capital of Kurdistan, while his fellow commanders opened other fronts in the west and north-east.

A golden chapter in the history of Kurdish nationalism, to warm the heart and move the soul: this is how the troubadours present things in their gusting tenor. It's how they get their tips. Raise your eyes to the sky, summon the epic poem, *Mem-u-Zin*, which tells of love and patriotism under an Ottoman and Persian yoke – even now, your nationalist heart aflutter, you will find in the story of the Sheikh Sait Rebellion reason to wince. A nationalist revolution run by mullahs; a war without generals or strategists; an epic, starting promisingly, that trails off into chaos, backstabbing and division.

In Harput, downstream from Varto along the Murat, the revolutionaries were led by Sheikh Serif, one of the few rebel commanders to boast any military experience, and the people of Harput welcomed him because, in the words of the town's notables, 'these sheikhs are going to reestablish the caliphate and Islamic law and it is your duty to aid them'.

Before the caliphate, however, before Islamic law, there would be looting. The prison was opened, the government buildings sacked, the notables burgled and the régie relieved of its tobacco. The people of Harput reexamined their loyalties, set up a militia and ran the rebels out of town at a cost of fifty lives. Two days later the republican governor, restored to his post, announced the resumption of government services. The government in Ankara sent its congratulations.

Sheikh Sait was forced to lift the siege of Diyarbakir after three weeks, by the approach of a large contingent of the Turkish army. During the siege, the rebels briefly penetrated the town's defences but the Turkish defenders had put up a spirited fight. Of the town's inhabitants, it seems that only the Zaza-speakers, many of whom were related to the rebellious tribes, worked in the sheikh's favour. The Kurmanji-speaking Milan tribe to the south ignored the sheikh's request for help. A ragtag army of religious fanatics, led by a mullah and quaintly armed, in some cases with picks and sabres – such a force, for all its primitive charm, cannot reckon with a standing army, tolerably equipped, defending a fortified citadel.

The lifting of the siege of Diyarbakir and the rebels' retreat north marked the turning point. Several tribes that had hitherto stayed neutral dropped smartly on to the government's side. In Ankara, Mustafa Kemal had taken the opportunity presented by the crisis to oust his moderate prime minister and have him replaced by the hardliner Ismet Inonu. Parliament gave Inonu extraordinary powers to suppress the rebellion and punish those who had supported it. The number of Turkish troops deployed against the rebels rose to at least 35,000, deployed in a ring, vast to start with, tightening as the rebel forces lost their cohesion and purpose. It was a good opportunity for Turkey to experiment with their new air force, bombing Kurds, as the British had done in Iraqi Kurdistan earlier in the decade.

Even after it faltered and died, the Sheikh Sait Rebellion would continue to send out wavelets. Presenting it as a purely religious uprising, neglecting its ethnic character, the Kemalists assiduously prepared the public for more secularising measures: the banning of religious orders and clothing, the promulgation of a secular civil code and the exchange of the Arabic alphabet, the alphabet of God, in favour of the Latin one, that of Mammon. The Kemalists used the crisis as a pretext to increase pressure on 'unpatriotic' or 'reactionary' critics of the government in the press and parliament, a crackdown that intensified after the revelation of a plot to assassinate Mustafa Kemal in 1926.

In foreign affairs, the rebellion undermined the Turks' argument that the mostly Kurdish province of Mosul, in Mesopotamia, and its oil, should be Turkey's because the Turks and the Kurds were indivisibly united by racial affinity. Turkey finally ceded Mosul to Iraq in 1926. And the wavelets produced their own wavelets, in the form of perennial Kurdish unrest. The historians tell us that of the eighteen military engagements or campaigns that the Turkish armed forces took part in from 1924 until 1938, all but one were in Kurdistan.

So much for the wavelets. Down from the crow's nest of history! Here in Varto the Sheikh Sait Rebellion is the story of families we know.

Imagine the fevered mood of Varto town in early March, a few days before the expected assault by Sheikh Abdullah, who was commanding the rebels on the north-eastern front. The rebels' idea was to take Varto and swing south, gobble up Mus and spring Halit Bey and Yusuf Ziya from jail in neighbouring Bitlis. Rabbits anticipating an earthquake, the people of Varto had come out of their warrens and were peering suspiciously at each other.

Varto's Sunnis were guilty by association. Lots of the Cibrans were kinsmen of Halit. Many more were either relations or admirers of Sheikh Sait. There were 120 gendarmes; they served under Turkish colours but were suspected of being secret followers of the sheikh, and potential mutineers. Facing the Sunnis – when had it not been so? – were the Alevi tribes, the Ferons in particular. The Ferons had recently checked a rebel advance at Kasman, their seat. The rebels had regrouped at the old Armenian village of Baskan, a few miles to the south-west. In Varto town, the Alevi tribes were helping the government prepare for the expected assault.

Well over 100 Alevis wandered around central Varto with their rifles and swords. Varto had never witnessed the like. Who would have guessed, to look on the swagger of these men and the insolence in their raw-boned peasant faces, that this was a place where no Alevi lived or had ever lived, and where Sunni mullahs had from time to time declared it religiously permissible to kill Alevis? After the bloody transformation of 1915, Varto's communal balance was changing again.

There was another factor, complicating things: the presence of a turncoat.

Major Kasim of Kulan, cousin, comrade in arms and brother-in-law of the incarcerated Halit Bey, was a tall, gaunt, almost skeletal man. He had a mottled complexion and his hands were covered in blotches. He was well educated and had written on theological and philosophical subjects. For a while, it seems that he subscribed to Kurdish nationalist ideas and for a while, too, he was known for his closeness to Halit Bey. But something, or some things, led him to betray his leader, his tribe and his people.

It was in Erzurum, so the conventional account runs, that he first served notice of his treachery. Kasim had travelled to Erzurum to

join tribal chiefs in a meeting with Mustafa Kemal. Halit Bey did
not attend, but he urged the tribal chiefs to promise Mustafa Kemal
their support only in the event that he granted autonomy to the
Kurds. In the event, runs this account, Kasim offered support without
conditions. After the meeting he is said to have had a private word
with Mustafa Kemal about *Azadi* and its plans.

When the Sheikh Sait rebellion broke out, Kasim and his relation
through marriage, Halit's uncle Ismail, absented themselves conspicuously
from the rebel ranks. As the rebels bore down on Varto, Kasim won
the confidence of the acting district governor, Ali Efendi. Kasim was
showing his loyalty to the government in another way, by dispatching
wire reports to Ankara. He posted his kinsmen on the door of the
telegraph office to prevent anyone from monitoring the ciphers that were
being sent.

Here is a new Kasim, cunningly depleting the defences of Varto town
and, at the same time, using his back channel to urge the attackers
to come at the town from an undefended route. How did he win Ali
Efendi's consent for the redeployment of most of the Alevi forces, so
that a mere twenty remained in Varto town on the eve of the attack?
According to Mehmet Serif Firat, Major Kasim told Ali Efendi that
the rebels would certainly come through the Feron villages in order
to avenge their earlier defeat there. Perhaps so, but who would be
surprised if Kasim, exploiting the district governor's Sunni prejudices,
also told him that the presence of so many Alevis in a Sunni town was
unacceptable to the populace, and should be scaled down?

It is apt that our main source for the battle of Varto, a rich and
diverting domestic fray, should be Mehmet Serif Firat's *History*. His
account is family lore at its most lavish. The prose is turbulent, a little
confused. There is much blood and thunder, Austerlitz transposed to the
steppe, a superb defence, the blackguards Kasim and Ismail running for
cover. The Ferons perform inspiringly, in particular a young man called
Ali Haydar. And we meet another intriguing character, Sergeant Kamer
of the Turkish ordinance corps. He is an Alevi. But he, exceptionally,
has thrown his lot in with the Sunni rebels.

Mehmet Serif Firat begins:

'On the evening of March 11 1925 ... well after dark, a roar raised
by 2,000 rebels and their burning torches, invocations and salutations
filled the air over Alangoz, half an hour from Varto town.'

'In the black of the night,' Firat continues, 'until three o'clock in the morning, the mass of attacking rebels first fell upon Ali Haydar and the auxiliary gendarmes. The gendarmes ... surrendered to the rebels, and then turned their weapons on our national forces and nine Anatolian privates who had stayed in their positions. Performing heroics, the latter stoutly stuck to their positions and battled before those countless rebel forces which flowed relentlessly towards them until the break of dawn, and strew the ground with the corpses of Sheikh Abdullah's uncle Mahmut and five other rebels.'

According to Firat, the rebels realised that they would not be able to uproot these positions, so they outflanked the defenders and in this way entered Varto town, advancing as far as Government House. Ali Haydar and his comrades left their positions and, under the cover of darkness, slipped in amid the rebels and came to Government House.

By now it was dawn. 'The sound of the rebels' invocations and salutations rose into the skies. Along with the [Feron] militiamen at Government House, the district governor and other officials, the two auxiliary captains took their saddle bags and a machine gun and those of the gendarmes that had stayed loyal and went up to Kalcik ... But the game was up. The district had fallen to the rebels.'

The following day Sheikh Abdullah, victorious invader of Varto town, sent a delegation to the Feron chiefs, informing them that if they joined his ranks, they would be given control of Varto and Mus. The Ferons spurned this embassy. Not so Nazim Han's grandfather, Ismail Seyit-Han of the Avdelans.

According to Nazim Han, this is what happened next:

'Four armed men came up here to Kalcik, Zaza-speakers, and they said to my grandfather, "Sheikh Abdullah has summoned you." My grandfather went with them down the road. They didn't know he was a Zaza-speaker and he listened to them arguing among themselves about the positions they'd been promised by the sheikh and my grandfather told them to be a little more circumspect: "You haven't even set yourselves up yet and you're already arguing about who's going to be sub-district administrator!"

'They arrived at Government House. My grandfather saw that everyone of any importance in Varto had been gathered there. The Ferons weren't there, of course. They had taken to the hills. The rebels wanted to say to the people, "We have become the government now, and you must bow to us." My grandfather noticed that everyone was on their feet apart from two people who were sitting down on the only chairs in the room, Sheikh Abdullah and Major Kasim. As soon as he saw my grandfather, Kasim got to his feet and gave him his chair. My grandfather knew what that meant: a death sentence. His legs could barely hold him up. He thought, "Here we are with all these notables and he gives me the very seat that's next to the sheikh! Three or four days from now, when Osman Nuri Pasha reaches Varto and hears that I've been honoured in this way, I'm for the chop!" After he sat down, Kasim turned to my grandfather and said, "Ismail Aga, let's go!" Kasim was a very crafty man but he was the opposite of Halit. He was an old friend of my grandfather.

'When they were sitting in Kasim's house, Kasim turned to my grandfather and asked him why he was looking so worried, and my grandfather replied, "Tomorrow or the next day, this adventure is going to end and our goose is cooked. The army is coming." Kasim rose to his feet and paced around the room in his leather riding boots. "I am Kasim," he said. "I've proved my mettle. If I can save my wife I'll be a hero – otherwise I'm afraid we're all for the chop." '

'So that's when Kasim realised that the rebellion would fail?'

'Kasim was playing both sides.'

Many of the rebels had been against using Kasim. He had promised much support for *Azadi*, especially financial, but he hadn't delivered. He had disobeyed Halit in Erzurum, and he had been thick with the district governor in Varto. He had wired reports for the attention of Mustafa Kemal. But Kasim was an educated man and he was plausible. He went to Sheikh Abdullah and said something to the effect of, 'I didn't used to agree with you, but now I do.' And this is how Sheikh Abdullah came to seat Major Kasim next to himself in Government House.

Sheikh Abdullah entertained grand ambitions of taking Hinis and

Mus and extending his control as far north as Erzurum. But the rebels were constrained by the Alevi militias, and by pro-government forces from Varto's Circassian villages, who harried them in tandem with the gendarmerie. Two rebel offensives, against Hinis and Mus, were repulsed by the government and its allies. Then came appalling news. Halit Bey had been summarily executed in Bitlis, along with Yusuf Ziya. The morale of the rebels plummeted.

Ismail Seyit-Han of the Avdelans turned out to be right, though it took a little longer than he had expected for Osman Nuri Pasha and his force to come down from the north and take Varto back for the government. On 25 March, after a bombardment that destroyed much of the town and left two big holes in Halit Bey's fine stuccoed house, Osman Nuri entered Varto. Some of the most prominent rebels, including Sheikh Abdullah and Major Kasim, took to the Serafettin Mountains to the south, where, a few days later, they joined forces with Sheikh Sait. Two days later, after failing in another attempt to take Hinis, a second group of rebels also scattered.

In Varto, a venerable little turf war, a parish conflict in train for half a century, was approaching its climax. For the third time in a generation, the villages were emptied and pillaged. The women and children, depending on their sect and their instinct for the lethal movements of the gangs and militias, fled to escape the mayhem. The Alevis and Circassians were united now against the Sunni Kurds, and three-day battles sent their plumes and clamour into the sky. What unaccustomed joy, at this feast of reckoning and plenty, to be an Alevi! Oh, to be Halo the chief of the Ferons, giving the sheikhs their comeuppance, on the winning side for a change!

In Varto town, Osman Nuri Pasha set up his headquarters and received the informers, men prepared to tell on other men who had helped the rebels. Ismail Seyit-Han of the Avdelans was among those to be summoned. He went to Government House, from where he was taken to Bitlis. Almost three years would pass before he was freed and returned to his village. Others were less fortunate: the Alevi rebel Sergeant Kamer, for instance. He was disarmed at the steps of Government House and led out of the back door with a score of other men, including some who were quite innocent, and shot in a valley nearby.

There's none of this in the official histories, which put the number of executed rebels at fifty-seven, pursuant to scrupulously fair trials at the Independence Tribunal in Bitlis. You don't read about the Turkish whirlwind tearing through the villages, the village-burning and impromptu firing squads. Justice of this kind was being meted out across the Kurdish region. Thousands – how many thousands, nobody knows – were its victims.

For the climax to this story of ineptitude and betrayal, we must turn to the Turkish journalist Ugur Mumcu. In 1991 Mumcu wrote a book about the Sheikh Sait Rebellion, and this slim volume displays all the contradictory impulses, to even-handed history and leading history, to universalism and nationalism, that beat in the breast of the Turkish Leftist. As well as being a Leftist, Mumcu is a Kemalist, and he does what the Kemalists did back in 1925, which is to privilege the rebellion's religious character. But Mumcu also – and here he differs from many other Kemalists – transmits some of the Kurds' grievances, fleetingly alludes to government atrocities, and deplores the general staff's refusal to declassify important documents pertaining to the rebellion.

Mumcu devotes a chapter to a statement given by Major Kasim, in 1944, in the town in western Turkey to which he had been exiled. Major Kasim made this fresh testimony, which contains many details about his betrayal of Sheikh Sait, in response to a demand from the top Turkish official in the Kurdish region that those individuals that had been exiled be questioned once more. As our only account of events following the fall of Varto, in particular the flight of Major Kasim and Sheikh Sait, the 1944 deposition is a vital document. It tellingly depicts Kasim's ambiguous status among 'the sheikhs' – Kasim's term for Sheikh Sait and his entourage – as something between a prisoner and a guide. It hints, too, at the chaos that had gripped the countryside. But much is left out. At what point did Major Kasim decide to turn in Sheikh Sait? And why did the sheikh, who had been warned several times that Kasim was not to be trusted, continue to consult him on an escape route?

We should assume that now, the rebellion lost, each fugitive was privately calculating how to avoid capture and death. Sheikh Sait's plan was to head east into Iran. Others, it soon became clear, had resolved to go to ground. As for Kasim, a military man who knew the area well, he was aware that between the sheikh and freedom lay not only the Turkish army and its local accomplices, but also the Murat, swollen by spring meltwaters. It is likely that the major, realising that escape was impossible, resolved to save himself from execution by performing a conspicuous act of loyalty to the republic. What more meritorious act than delivering up the sheikh?

Now began an exhausting, circuitous trek, full of rancour. 'After climbing a few hundred metres, we were walking over snow. Sinking and lifting ourselves out, we climbed to the top of the mountain. After two hours we entered Varto and came down to a village in the mountains, Habiban ... I wrote a letter and sent it to the commander [of the Turkish force]. But they were watching me and they told the sheikh, and he summoned me.'

Sheikh Sait did not attempt to punish Kasim for his attempted betrayal. He simply ordered him to recall his messenger. Furthermore, he continued to seek Kasim's advice: 'Sheikh Sait asked my opinion. I indicated some different routes. One of the gentlemen said, "You would stand by and have us killed by the Turks. There are army detachments on the route you have indicated. Why do you feel this enmity for us?" To distract them I shouted, "Did you hope to get the better of a 600-year-old regime with that mouth of yours? If not with these detachments you will meet with other detachments." And then I left them.'

Over the next few hours, tension mounted between members of the sheikh's party. Kasim trotted alongside the others, but his eye was glued to his telescope, looking out for army detachments to which the sheikh might be surrendered. News of the rebellion's defeat had spread, and the inhabitants of nearby villages fired warning shots to prevent them approaching. The party bivouacked in a deserted village overlooking the Murat. Sheikh Sait paid a passing traveller to swim across the Murat and ask some of the villagers on the opposite bank to come to the fording place and help the party across, but Kasim was also busy: 'I took the traveller aside and told him who I was. I told him I was expecting a force of soldiers, and that riders from the opposite village should come and prevent the sheikh crossing at the fording point. And I insisted he say that, if they did not, I would destroy the village and slaughter the villagers' children before nightfall.'

An hour later five or ten horsemen came to the crossing point, and Kasim finally announced his rupture with the sheikh. 'I told [the sheikh] that from here on I would no longer be part of things and that, just as I had not until now descended to showing ingratitude to the Turkish nation, I wouldn't start now, and that they were welcome to cross the fording point if they could.' Sheikh Abdullah threw his lot in with Kasim, too, and Sheikh Sait said bitterly that he had suspected both of them from the start.

Now, according to Kasim, with a column of soldiers visible through the telescope, the sheikhs told him of their intention to surrender. On Kasim's suggestion, they decided to turn back towards Varto town, with the aim of surrendering to Osman Nuri Pasha himself, who had set up his headquarters there. But soon after that the sheikh changed his mind, and decided to cross the Murat and revive his plan to flee to Iran.

Kasim kept the sheikh busy as far as the Abdulrahman Pasha Bridge, which some members of the sheikh's retinue crossed.

'The sheikh dismounted in order to cross. I also dismounted. I told him not to cross, that I wouldn't allow him to. He waved his hand in the air like so, and walked towards the bridge. I turned my gun towards the gentlemen and ... opened fire. They didn't fire back. No sign remained of the horsemen on the opposite bank; they fled. Sheikh Sait crossed the bridge and was intercepted by one or two of my relations and they called me. I crossed the bridge and found the sheikh and three of his men; he was leaning with his back against the rocks and had a Mauser in his hand. Two of my relations were waiting on the road, aiming their guns.

'I was in front of the sheikh. He pointed the Mauser he was holding at my heart and said, "Look!" I pushed the barrel away from my chest. My two relations wanted to disarm both the sheikh and me. Sheikh Sait said, "I'm not handing it over." But my relations seized his weapon.'

Major Kasim wrote a note to the Turkish squadron commander: 'I have arrested Sheikh Sait on the Abdulrahman Pasha Bridge and request the dispatch of a small detachment.'

So far as we know there were few heroes at the Independence Tribunal in Diyarbakir where the captured rebels were tried. In the encounter between a prosecuting team of prim late-Ottoman bureaucrats now employed by the republican government and some broken Kurdish fundamentalists, the former won hands down.

So far as we know – because the official record of proceedings is inaccessible, classified in the parliamentary archive in Ankara, and our chief source of information is the reminiscences of the chief prosecutor, Ahmet Surreya Orgeevren. The best that we can hope for is that Orgeevren, while leaving much out, didn't fabricate what he put in.

The defendants reach us most vividly, as, no doubt, the propagandist in Orgeevren intends them to. They are motley, pathetic, tripping over their beards in their desire to depict themselves as accidental rebels and ingratiate themselves with the court. They are far from the idealised picture of the valiant Kurd that Noel and his ilk drew for us.

According to Orgeevren, the news that Sheikh Sait and thirty-eight others had been captured in Varto had spread 'like a flash of lightning ... there were those that were pleased, and not a few that were afflicted by fright and worry at the thought of the revelations and confessions that would doubtless emerge during the interrogation of Sheikh Sait and his confederates'. In Orgeevren's view, the sheikh harboured a slim hope, 'to convince everyone that the uprising had not been premeditated. Perhaps, he thought, if he was successful in this, he would be able to evade the obvious fate which the law ... reserved for him.'

In the sheikh's interviews with Orgeevren, and in his court testimony, we find him denying that he had ever intended to set up an independent Kurdish state – he first heard that 'absurd' idea, he says, from Halit Bey's co-conspirator Yusuf Ziya. On the contrary, the sheikh explains, his goal had been 'to write a treatise explaining Islamic rulings and requesting that legislation be consonant with Islamic law, and to send it to parliament'. Alas, this had not been 'God's will'. After the unplanned exchange that precipitated the rebellion, 'I couldn't get in the way of events ... I was neither at the front of this affair, nor at the back. Like everyone else, I was inside it.'

So this rebellion, if the sheikh is to be believed, had no leader. According to some of the other rebels, it lacked even commanders.

Take, for instance, the sheikh's son-in-law Abdullah. We have heard that Sheikh Abdullah was a doughty freedom fighter; he took Varto and honoured Nazim Han's grandfather with a seat in Government House. He hoped to take Hinis, Mus and Erzurum. But Abdullah, addressing the court, complains that he has been traduced. Far from occupying Varto, he claimed to have tried to prevent his men from attacking it, even protesting (vainly) at the raising of a Kurdish standard over Government House. What, then, of those reams of orders and directives that have been attributed to him? 'I am illiterate ... everyone wrote under my name so I would be implicated.'

The presiding judge in Diyarbakir is intrigued by the idea of an illiterate divine. 'You don't know how to read or write,' he muses. 'So why are you wearing this enormous turban?'

Sheikh Serif joins the circus of denial. We know him as the man who occupied Harput, whose men pillaged so effectively that the townspeople, rebels by inclination, ended up supporting the government. 'I didn't take Harput,' Serif insists. 'The rebels took it. They all came at once. I went a day later with a servant ... I commanded no one.'

The court has already heard Sheikh Sait allude to his ordering Serif to hold the Gazik front near Harput. 'Sheikh Serif!' the judge cries. 'What do you say to Sheikh Sait's statement? Is Sheikh Sait lying?'

'He's not lying. Only ...'

'Is he telling the truth?'

'He's not lying ...'

At least Major Kasim's courtroom interventions have the merit of clarity. Like the others here, Major Kasim is on trial. But he acts, and is treated, like a witness for the prosecution, and he obligingly demolishes his co-defendants' claims to ignorance or neutrality.

Major Kasim contradicts the argument that Sheikh Sait had never contemplated the idea of a Kurdish state. Religion was a smokescreen, Kasim says, behind which the real goal, independence, could be pursued. He trashes the sheikh's pose of benign ineptitude. Before the revolt, he recalls, Sheikh Sait told his followers that killing a single Turk was more meritorious in the eyes of God than killing seventy infidels.

Kasim undermines Sheikh Abdullah's claims to illiteracy and pacifism when he describes Abdullah's letters threatening him if he failed to join the rebels. He boasts of informing on Halit Bey, whose propaganda efforts had turned 'eighty per cent of public opinion in favour of Kurdish nationalism', to none other than Mustafa Kemal.

Kasim explains his alibi. Far from join the rebellion, as Mehmet Serif Firat and Nazim Han of the Avdelans insist he did, he says he was kidnapped by the rebels after the fall of Varto and forced to flee with them when the government took it back. 'In the morning, when the battle started I heard the sound of cannon and machine guns. The *Kizilbas* had surrounded us. They brought a horse and took me.'

In the stringency of his critique and fidelity to the government's line, Kasim's performance is worthy of any show trial. He assures the court that he was always opposed to the notion of an independent Kurdistan. He casts aspersions on the Kurds' claims to constitute a nation. 'They don't have a language. Even if they're independent, they'll speak English, Persian or Arabic ... it would be not a Kurdish government, but an Arab or an Iranian government.' Then comes the clincher: 'I didn't want to divide from a people we've lived alongside for the past 600 years.'

The verdicts are returned on 28 June. Sheikh Sait, Sheikh Abdullah and Sheikh Serif are among forty-seven 'principal rebels' who are sentenced to death. Major Kasim's purpose has been served. He is among those who are acquitted and released. Shortly after, he will be given land to farm in western Turkey – a soft form of exile.

In this way Major Kasim of Kulan enters the record, already bulging, of Kurdish infamy. His contributions to the court proceedings have certainly been devious and self-interested, but not uniformly short-sighted. During his monologue on Kurdish nationality, for example, he utters two sentences that stand out as sincere and prescient: 'For all of eternity, the Kurds will be incapable of reaching agreement. They unite rhetorically, and then only when testifying to Islam.'

Here one is reminded of another major, the Englishman Noel. For all his commitment to Kurdish nationalism, he had similar doubts, writing in his diary of 1919 that 'the entire lack of any semblance of unity or common purpose between the Kurds must always tend to prevent any real national combination against the government'. Fractiousness and division – they will torment any Kurdish patriot, to Apo and beyond.

The Sheikh Sait Rebellion will never be solved in the south-east of Turkey. The people will never agree on what happened where, who did what, and who, in the shadows, pulled the strings. Kurdish conspiracy theorists argue that the Turks, fearing that *Azadi* would eventually become a force to be reckoned with, precipitated the revolt in the knowledge that their opponents were vulnerable and ill-prepared. On the Turkish side, the belief persists that the British were behind events. There are other, smaller disputes, no less bitter; they concern Sheikh Sait, Major Kasim, the courtroom penitents Abdullah and Serif. The disputants are not objective scholars united in their pursuit of the truth. They are local people coming together to defend Grandpa.

In Varto, among the majority of Cibrans, Halit Bey and Major Kasim are depicted respectively as light and shade. Present-day Cibrans have found that by proclaiming a family link to Halit they can advance a career in public service; one, a politician, has written a respectful account of his life. Despite the mystery surrounding Halit's whereabouts during the massacres that were perpetrated against the Armenians in 1915, it is possible to argue that, had he survived and the rebellion succeeded, he would have made a competent and even inspirational leader for the Kurds, and a potential catalyst for reconciliation between the Sunnis and Alevis.

The descendants of Major Kasim have not entered public service or sought election. They doggedly insist that, while Kasim did not join the revolt, neither did he betray it. They say that Kasim has been slandered by those seeking scapegoats for the revolt's failure, and they point out that Halit Bey's family was later reconciled to Kasim. The Turks executed Major Kasim's father and great-uncle on the road to the Independence Tribunal, they recall, and other family members were executed at Diyarbakir itself. Why has their patriotism and sacrifice not been recognised? But the stain will not wash off. No one in Varto calls his son Kasim.

What was the nature of Kasim's grudge? Some believe he had been jealous of Halit's swift rise through the Ottoman ranks. There is a theory that Kasim was sacked from the Ottoman army for beating a man who had impugned Halit's honour and that Halit did not defend his cousin in turn. Descendants of Sheikh Sait have told me that Kasim harboured ambitions to lead the Cibrans and run Varto. Then there is the question of Major Kasim's relations with Sheikh Sait himself. But we are in the undergrowth of family politics – deeper and darker than I can see.

Sheikh Sait's sole surviving son and many other descendants still live in Hinis, in Kolhisar, the sheikh's home village. Kolhisar was razed by the Turks after the revolt. According to the sheikh's great-nephew, Abdulmelik, around 100 members of the sheikh's family were killed. The survivors were exiled and deliberately impoverished. Land and livestock were confiscated. But the sheikh's name continued to glow, particularly in religiously conservative circles. Abdulmelik is one of several members of the family to have been elected to the parliament in Ankara.

The awkward fact for the descendants of the protagonists is that the 1925 rebellion was a catastrophic failure, which had the unforeseen effect of ending the old dominance of the agas and sheikhs and spurring on Ataturk's campaigns of 'Turkification' and secularisation. Some descendants of Halit Bey argue that he was opposed to the rebellion all along, a dubious claim that finds no place in the impartial accounts of foreign scholars. Others say that the Cibrans are sour that the rebellion should be remembered after Sheikh Sait, not Halit Bey.

With the spread of Marxist-Leninist politics in the 1960s and 1970s, the traditional power sharing between feudal chief and Sunni divine ceased to be romanticised, and Kurdish nationalists, Apo included, started to speak of the rebellion with egalitarian disdain. It is not without significance that the *Vartolu* who rose highest in the Socialist PKK should be Nizamettin Tas, the humble grandson of Halit Bey's ostler – the same ostler whose sharpshooting had saved Halit's life during the Russian advance on Varto in the First World War.

As for Major Kasim, his place in the annals is secure. The republic, from which he may have expected rewards, did little for him, and he was unable to return to live in Varto, even after his exile ended, for fear of popular reaction. The final image we have of Kasim is a sad one – that of a remorseful exile.

The Death of Mehmet Serif Firat

A Kurdish boy called Mehmet Emin, the son of an aga, was on a journey when he was caught in a blizzard. Following his horse through the snow, he arrived, on the verge of death, at a magnificent tent, and collapsed at its door. When he came to, he was being looked after inside the tent, which was held up by twenty-four poles and covered in mirrors, and in which everything had its own place, even the goats and camels. Mehmet Emin's host was clearly a great aga, and he had a beautiful daughter, Adul Khan, with whom Mehmet Emin immediately fell in love. Only after five days, when Mehmet Emin was fully recovered and it was time for him to leave, did his host ask him who he was, and he told him, before asking the same question and going on his way.

When Mehmet Emin got home, he told his father what had happened and asked him to go and seek Adul Khan's hand. Upon learning Adul Khan's identity, the old man replied, 'Son, we have been fighting her family for twenty-two years. How can I go and ask for her?' Mehmet Emin insisted and his father eventually agreed, but cursed him for his obstinacy. 'I will not stand in your way,' he said, 'but let God prevent you from reaching your goal.'

Mehmet Emin's father set off. On the way he came across a shepherd. The shepherd asked him the purpose of his journey and, hearing what it was, told him that he too was an aga's son and that, hopeful of winning Adul Khan, he had spent the past seven years tending her father's flock. He went on, 'Let me tell you that, in all the time I've been working here, I've seen her twice a day come to milk the ewes, but I've yet to receive so much as a kiss! Good luck to you!'

That evening Adul Khan was told by her father to go and make dinner, but she said, 'You tell me to make dinner, but you don't even know who's coming for dinner. I know that better than you do! Mehmet Emin has sent for me. I saw him in a dream.'

Mehmet Emin's father arrived with his retinue. Feeding them, Adul Khan's father brooded, 'For the past twenty-two years this man has been my enemy. Now he comes for my daughter, an act of reconciliation. If I don't give her up my reputation will be ruined.' So he sent Adul Khan off with Mehmet Emin's father. On the road they come across the well-born shepherd. He addressed Mehmet Emin's father: 'So you won the girl after all! Blessings be upon you. You have saved me from a lifetime of drudgery.' He left the service of Adul Khan's father and returned to his own house.

Adul Khan and Mehmet Emin were married. The following morning, kneeling down to say his prayers, Mehmet Emin collapsed suddenly. Adul Khan called her father-in-law, who lifted up the head of his son and saw that he was dead. Looking up to heaven, he gave thanks to God. 'If you had been the one who died,' he told Adul Khan, 'your father would have said, "After all these years of enmity, he took my daughter and look what he did to her!"'

Adul Khan had got pregnant on her wedding night. She gave birth and stayed in her father-in-law's house, and loved him as if she was his own daughter.

ALTHOUGH HE WROTE HIS *History* years after the event, in 1948, Mehmet Serif Firat ended his book with the suppression of the Sheikh Sait Rebellion, and the role that the Alevis, including himself, played in it. Reading the final pages of Firat's account, with its message of thanks to the author from the Turkish general Osman Nuri Pasha and a shorter telegram from Ataturk to the republican loyalists of the east, the temptation is to assume that the story stops here, because from here on it's a dull one of restitution and reward, of the Alevis' being welcomed, belatedly but warmly, into the republican embrace.

But this isn't the way things turned out. Firat wrote his *History* as a pious commission, guided and probably edited by members of the Republican People's Party; he discreetly elided the ingratitude and suspicion that continued to spoil relations between the Alevis and the central government. It is well known that, starting in 1925, Ataturk sent into internal exile tens of thousands of potential troublemakers, including Halit Bey's children and every surviving member of Sheikh Sait's family. What is less well known is that these exiles included several Alevis who had fought on the side of the government, notably Mehmet Serif Firat.

There are three possible explanations for Firat's undeserved two-year exile to western Anatolia. The first is that, for all their heroics, the Alevis of Varto remained indistinguishable in official eyes from the Alevis of Dersim, who had risen in 1921 and 1924 and would rise, in even greater numbers, in 1938. The government may have been swayed by accounts of Alevis collaborating with the Russians during the occupation. But the main reason for the rancour may have been the crudest of all, sectarian spite. For most Sunnis, Turk or Kurd, secular or observant, the word *Kizilbas* carried the same associations, of impiousness and disloyalty, which it always had. It wouldn't do for such people to advance.

There were no Alevi district commissioners in the years following the revolt, and no Alevi mayors. Men from the outside, often from Mus, were appointed to both offices. No Alevi entered the Varto bureaucracy and no Alevi owned a house in Varto town. Until 1929, when he too was pardoned and came down from the mountains, the de facto head of the Ferons, Mehmet Serif's uncle Halo, had devoted himself to warring and brigandage, pursuing Sunni fugitives with his cut-throats and holding up caravans. Mothers across the province of Mus would hush their children with the admonition: 'Be quiet! Halo will come and kill us!'

From 1930, when the hills started to become safer, prowess as a warrior ceased to be the sole criterion for leadership. The Ferons got new chiefs, fighters who were literate. They spoke and wrote Turkish. They were tie-wearers who knew how to address a gendarmerie sergeant and did not flee, out of instinct, upon spotting a tax collector approaching on the high road. They were true republicans, Ataturk men, men like Mehmet Serif Firat. Among the Alevis, the old fear of annihilation, of going the same way as the Armenians, had not quite dimmed, but it was balanced by an appreciation that the interests of the Alevis and the government might sometimes coincide.

The new Alevis entered respectable occupations necessitating constant contact with local administrators. They were country barristers and scribes for the illiterate, and they were supply teachers, instilling Kemalist values and a love of the Turkish language at a time when speaking Kurmanji or Zaza in public was a finable offence. They made sure that their children learned good Turkish. It was the language of government, a shield, and the Sunni Kurds of Varto, traumatised by the rebellion and patriotically attached to Kurmanji, were slower in picking it up.

Suddenly in about 1930 it becomes essential to review, critically and dispassionately, the instincts that come with membership of a reviled sect, an inheritance going back to the persecutions of Sultan Selim I in the sixteenth century. Not everyone is capable of such a review, of moderating the old hatreds and terrors. Halo, for instance. Halo speaks no Turkish and cannot read any language. Down from the hills he drifts wanly, an aimless felon. He cherishes the grudges he grew up with, against rival Alevis, against the Sunnis in general and the Cibrans in particular. He spends a year in a Mus jail for affray and, upon his release, discovers that his nephew Mehmet Serif Firat is on easy terms with the Varto gendarmes and minor bureaucrats. Mehmet Serif is a politician, something Halo will never be.

There is a young Feron, Ali Haydar, whose effect on the Alevis of Varto will rival that of Mehmet Serif Firat. We know Ali Haydar from the Sheikh Sait Rebellion, when he distinguished himself during the defence of Varto town, but it helps to go back to the death of his father to appreciate his impact on the Alevi predicament.

I am sitting in the law office of Ali Haydar's son Ekin in the middle of Ankara, a perturbed sea of grey stone and concrete. This is the place that Ataturk chose for his capital and headquarters during the War of Independence, and the attributes that led him to this decision, Ankara's isolation amid the Anatolian wilderness, far from foreign threats, its being a bare hillock on which to build a new cult, help explain the draining, stupefying effect it has on visitors today. There is nothing here for the neutral, no joy in the drumroll of ministries and directorates-general and central branches, no pause in the official limousines and brass lettering and the gigantic flags that, on a blustery day, whip their gloomy tumult into the sky above the founder's parliament, his university, his ballet and his tomb.

Ekin Dikmen came to Ankara because this is the seat of power. He was once a member of parliament but has now retired from politics, retaining nostalgic membership of the Republican People's Party. He has a law office in the middle of the city. His firm does not get much business, nor does he seem to tout for it. He visits the Ankara Varto

Association, whose president he has been on and off, and lunches with friends in a restaurant under his office. Ekin Dikmen is a tall, friendly man. He wears a tie and a checked jacket and smiles a lot under the white parabola that is his moustache.

It's impossible to sit in Ankara, where Ataturk decided that the Turks must henceforth be secular and European, where he hacked away at picturesque, overgrown Ottoman Turkish, where he decided that men and women should gather at balls to drink champagne and dance – it's impossible to sit in Ataturk's laboratory without resorting to formulations of his devising. So we find Ekin Dikmen, in a conversation about the debt that Alevis owe to the father of the nation, using metallic, republican words such as 'progressive' and 'secular'. He contrasts Ataturk's Turkey with the Ottoman empire in the sixteenth century under Selim I, a 'reactionary' place where each subject must wear a Sunni straitjacket, where there is no 'freedom of speech', where 40,000 Alevis can be murdered for their faith.

There is a black and white photograph on the wall of Ekin's office. It shows a languid young man wearing a well-fitting three-piece suit that was certainly not cut in Varto, and probably not in Mus, and curlicue moustaches of continental inspiration. This is Ali Haydar, in glossy, wistful, rather fragile mood.

Ali Haydar, perhaps even more than his kinsman Mehmet Serif Firat, epitomises the integration of the Alevis into mainstream life. His achievement is there in the upper bazaar, the Alevi quarter that he founded. And it is exemplified by the manner of his death – of natural causes, in hospital in Erzurum, at the age of seventy-two. As Ekin Dikmen says, 'The number of people in our tribe who died of natural causes is low.'

Ali Haydar was the son of Zeynel, the Feron chief who killed his pregnant wife Fatma lest she fall into the hands of his Ottoman pursuers. Fleeing into the mountains after that, Zeynel and his brother Veli entrusted four-year-old Ali Haydar to a shepherd, who concealed the boy under his felt cape. Father and son survived, but the manner in which Zeynel had been betrayed, at the hands of his wife's family, and the circumstances of her death, led inexorably to more violence. Fugitives from the state, Zeynel and his brother Veli seized Fatma's father Ali Aga, the author of their misfortune; Veli 'broke Ali in two', in Ekin Dikmen's phrase, strapped his lifeless body to his horse, and sent it home. In 1912, finally, Zeynel fell victim to the burgeoning feud, when a relation of Ali entered his hut and, according to Ekin, 'killed him by shooting several rounds into his testicles'.

The tribal leaders decided that Ali Haydar was too young to assume clan leadership; Halo would stand in until Ali Haydar's fifteenth birthday. Ali Haydar's brother and sister were taken in by relations but this was a famine year and the boy died of hunger. Ali Haydar himself suffered the indignity of being fostered by Ali Aga's widow.

Ali Haydar grew up independent in spirit. A pupil at the Middle School in Varto, living as the paying guest of a Sunni family, he was insulted for being an Alevi, but he went on to take a Cibran wife – he wanted, he said, to end the enmity between the communities. He resisted pressure from his clansmen to reopen old blood feuds with other Alevi clans.

Rather than perpetuate the disagreement that had cost his father his life, he simply distanced himself from his mother's family. Opportunity arose with Ataturk's surname law. While his mother's family took the name Firat, which is the Turkish name for the Euphrates, Ali Haydar became 'Dikmen', meaning 'summit'.

In the early 1930s, the now Ali Haydar Dikmen took the step, unprecedented for a Varto Alevi, of moving to Mus. Within five months, he had risen to become chief secretary in the Mus governor's office. Imagine it! An Alevi in Government House in Mus, fortress of the orthodox! Later, when Ismet Inonu, who had become president on Ataturk's death in 1938, visited Mus, he received complaints about the upstart Dikmen. The president summoned him and found a highly presentable man who evinced, in accentless Turkish, a sincere appreciation for the republic and the organ that had fathered it, the Republican People's Party. In short, Dikmen was remarkably unlike many of the other bureaucrats Inonu saw in Mus – shifty, speaking ragged Turkish, of dubious loyalty. You would have to be a fool to pass over the value of such a man, and Inonu was no fool.

It was the beginning of a long association between the two men. Dikmen was well received whenever he visited Ankara, and Inonu invited him to become local head of the Republican People's Party. It was 1945. Inonu had successfully kept Turkey out of the Second World War, but now the country was in transition; multi-party politics – democracy of a kind – was the destination. Ataturk's party would soon face an officially recognised opposition. Dikmen did as Inonu suggested.

Back in Varto, practising as a lawyer in the little court there, Ali
Haydar Dikmen tired of living as the tenant of a Sunni landlord. Alevi
ownership of land in Varto town remained prohibited, in the popular
perception, if not by law. Dikmen decided to rectify this anomaly.
He quietly bought a piece of public land behind Government House.
Then, one damp night in 1947, he occupied his land, building a
makeshift hut out of sun-dried bricks. The rain came down. The
structure collapsed. Dikmen rebuilt it. He waited.

The Sunnis of Varto awoke the following morning to learn that
a *Kizilbas* had occupied land in Varto town. They were appalled
by Dikmen's effrontery, but there was division between those who
advocated eviction by force, and those who favoured a negotiated
solution. Eventually some Sunni hotheads came to Dikmen's hut; his
rifle barrel was visible through the window. Alevis arrived from the
surrounding villages to show their support for Dikmen. Then came a
warning from Government House. Ali Haydar Dikmen had broken
no law and the government would tolerate no interference with his
rights as a private citizen. And this is how the Sunni castle of Varto
fell.

In the lopsided history of Varto this is the first instance of redressed
balances, of the authorities ruling in favour of an Alevi over a
Sunni. Gradually other Alevis occupied plots around Dikmen; shyly,
disbelievingly, they brought into being an Alevi neigbourhood. Some
joined the local bureaucracy; determined never to relapse into penury
and exile, they identified education as their safety net. By sending
your child to school, it was true, you lost a farm hand today, but you
gained a bureaucrat or a lawyer tomorrow. So Varto's schools filled
with Alevi children, including dozens of girls. The Sunnis, by contrast,
were distrustful of the republican education system, sentimentally
attached to Kurmanji, and opposed as a matter of course to the
education of girls. Their children lagged behind.

Ali Haydar Dikmen, chief of the Ferons, local Republican
People's Party supremo, received the provincial governor, the district
administrator and the gendarmerie captain at the new home he built
on the site of his famous hut. He accumulated the only library of
consequence in a town whose literary tastes had formerly stretched
to the Qoran and the cogitations of the sixth imam. He flouted the
Muslim fast, drank alcohol purchased at the Varto régie, leafed

through the Kemalist organ *Republic*. Imagine how the Sunnis hated him. This arriviste ... why, he even had the nerve to own a car!

Outside Varto, far away, a reaction was under way: to the perfunctoriness, arrogance and godlessness of the Republican People's Party; to Inonu's planned economy which kept everyone poor; to his abstinent foreign policy. The legal opposition duly came. Its name was the Democrat Party and it was led by Celal Bayar, who had been Ataturk's last prime minister. The Democrat Party started life as an economically liberal version of the Republican People's Party, but it soon discovered the benefits of challenging Kemalism.

In the east, the sheikhs and tribal chiefs were the Democrat Party's natural allies. These men were mostly Kurdish nationalists, which gave the Democrat Party a separatist colouring in this part of the country. Several descendants of Sheikh Sait became prominent Democrats. In Varto the local Democrat Party chief was Halit Bey's son Mahmut Sever, a tall, bespectacled, rather pensive man who was elected mayor in 1946.

Varto in the late 1940s and the 1950s was outwardly calm. It appeared that the people had temporarily exhausted their passions. Brigandage had waned. In the hot summer nights people slept, carefree, on their roofs. When the earth shook in May 1946, killing 2,000 people, the authorities discovered to their consternation that the district contained only twenty gendarmes.

To many Kemalists, however, the pause denoted an ominous drawing of breath. Take Mehmet Serif Firat, for instance, now aged fifty-five or so. In November 1947, he published his *Varto Letter* in a national newspaper, and the result was a sensation.

Mehmet Serif introduced himself as a 'clean-blooded Turk' without political affiliation, a simple villager engaged 'not in politics, but in my own affairs'. But this honest fellow had strong views on a lot of public ills, particularly Turkey's new multi-party system, under which 'seeds of rottenness, sown under the pretext of democracy, have sprouted'. Only a couple of months earlier, the author lamented, Sheikh Sait's son Ali-Riza had been allowed to return from exile to his village in Hinis. Regaled with money, rugs and beasts of burden, feted by the local sheikhs – men who 'poison the republic by teaching Arabic to the children of the homeland, in private cells' – Ali-Riza toured the region, dreaming his 'dreams of deceit and darkness'. Then there was Celal Bayar, the Democrat Party leader, who was greeted on a recent trip to Erzurum with 'one thousand times more love and acclaim' than the great Ismet Inonu had met with. 'Did [Bayar], by any chance, serve this country more than Inonu? No, no … from you, our leaders, and from great God, the real protector of the Turkish people, I solicit a solution.'

Mehmet Serif's *Letter* provoked much comment in the press and was denounced by senior members of the Democrat Party. The talk in Varto was of how, if the Democrats came to power, they would find a pretext to execute him. In his unpublished memoir, extracts of which were subsequently transmitted by his son, Mehmet Serif Firat claimed to detect 'secret activities against me', and 'preparations to assassinate me any day … I ignore these threats and continue along the road that I have chosen.'

Throughout the spring of 1949, convinced that he would soon be the object of an assassination attempt, Mehmet Serif Firat hardly stepped out of his house in Kasman. Then, on the morning of 1 July, in the company of a kinsman called Romi, he set off to visit the gendarmerie captain. Riding through Kasman, Mehmet Serif Firat was approached by a villager who told him of his previous night's dream. The villager had dreamt that Mehmet Serif Firat was confronted by a huge boulder. A man then shattered the boulder and the fragments rolled down the mountain. Mehmet Serif and Romi continued on their way, Mehmet Serif on his handsome Arab stallion.

The two men entered the broad Kasman valley heading east. Suddenly there was gunfire and Mehmet Serif dropped from the saddle, stone dead. Romi turned his horse and saw Halo, Mehmet Serif's uncle, standing among the rocks. Halo shouted, 'Romi! Don't move! If you move I'll shoot you too! Don't go forward and don't go back.'

Halo took Mehmet Serif's horse. He rode to the summer pasture where he knew he would find Mehmet Serif's brother. Stopping outside the brother's tent, he called, 'I've killed Mehmet Serif! Come and take your revenge!' There was no response and Halo continued on his way, having been joined by ten or twelve others, including two of his wives, and the party headed into the Bingol Mountains.

Mehmet Serif Firat might not recognise his home village of Kasman. They moved it from its original site, near the riverbank down in the valley, after the 1966 earthquake levelled the place. They moved it up the hill beyond the cemetery, nearer the main road that takes you to Emeran. Main Street is a muddy track flanked on both sides by whitewashed bungalows with slanting corrugated roofs, and patrolled by big, unfriendly dogs. About halfway up this road, which you climb nervously in your boots, teased by the dogs, you are admitted through a small vegetable garden into a house whose interior reminds you of other houses you have seen in Varto. There is the same stove burning dung patties, the same off-blue walls and threaded chickpea hangings, the same thick carpets and bolsters full of sawdust to lean against – and the same TV, connected to a dish on the roof, sucking in pop videos from Istanbul.

There is something about this house, however, that distinguishes it from the others. There is no masculine fug, no heavy jacket on a hook by the door, no convivial pall of sweat and cigarette smoke. Two women live unobtrusively here, going around the place without slamming doors. They are Ceylan, elderly, moon-faced, and Nadiye – younger, well built, bursting with talk. Respectively, they are the daughter and granddaughter of Mehmet Serif Firat.

Ceylan Bingol and her daughter offer a warm welcome, and this isn't simply down to courtesy (fussing over the visitor, sitting him near the stove, helping him to tea), though of course the hospitable gene is in finer fettle here than in the foreigner's chilly home country. No, there is something else in their attentiveness, an ardour attributable to the pleasure of having one's predictable morning thrown into a different gear by the arrival of an exotic stranger, of being singled out for attention.

There's also an institutional pride to consider, for the Ferons in general, and the relatives of Mehmet Serif Firat in particular, regard themselves as an institution. Perhaps the women experience a mild, belated sense of vindication, all these years after Mehmet Serif was committed to his grave in Kasman, getting the visitors they deserve.

'After his arrest,' declares Ceylan Bingol, 'in Bitlis jail, Halo shared a cell with two other Varto men, and he was very regretful and wept a lot.'

'And in Varto?'

'The Kurds sent out letters saying, "Mehmet Serif has died! Beat your drums! Make merry!" And that is what they did.'

'What about the rumours?'

Ah, the rumours. They abounded, and do so today. Not far from here, in a house owned by a second Feron, I was told that Mehmet Serif Firat was killed because he had impregnated Halo's daughter, Zehra, out of wedlock. Zehra had committed suicide and Mehmet Serif had tried to prevent Zehra's autopsy. Then there were Mehmet Serif's own claims that Halo and his family had syphilis, claims that were apparently slanderous. Behind many a story in Varto, the political one, lies a second, of jealousy and pride, and behind that a third, of dishonour and lust.

At the mention of these rumours, the eyes of Mehmet Serif Firat's daughter and granddaughter fill with wounded dignity. 'He was the sort of man,' Nadiye draws herself up, 'who averted his eyes if a pregnant woman came past.' The suicide Zehra 'turned out to be a virgin. She was clean.' Her mother sniffs hard. 'In matters of propriety, my father was peerless.'

Relations between Mehmet Serif Firat and his uncle Halo had broken down long before Mehmet Serif dropped from his horse in the Kasman valley. Halo had been acting chief of the Ferons, but he had relinquished the position when Ali Haydar Dikmen came of age. Unable to make the transition between brigandage and respectability, he resented those, such as his nephew, who negotiated it with ease. Halo stirred up land disputes between Mehmet Serif and some of the villagers. In response, Mehmet Serif may have been behind several severe beatings that Halo received at the hands of villagers and local gendarmes; he acknowledged in his memoir that 'I was ashamed of being seen with [Halo], and I wanted nothing to do with him.'

When he died, Mehmet Serif Firat was the victim of jealousy and rage; only later would he become a martyr.

The Democrats came to power one year after Mehmet Serif Firat's death. They won the 1950 election by a mile, sweeping up the Kurdish vote. The new president was Celal Bayar and his prime minister the Aegean landowner Adnan Menderes. Theirs was a more dynamic foreign policy. At home, they opened religious schools, ostensibly for teaching mosque imams, encouraged the building of new mosques and reinstated the Arabic call to prayer that Ataturk had abolished. In Varto the old seminaries, those cottage academies run by minor sheikhs, reopened a quarter of a century after Ataturk had silenced them. There were instances of Alevis being beaten up for smoking or eating during Ramadan, and Ali Haydar Dikmen barely escaped with his life when he was lured halfway to Mus one night and ambushed by armed men.

It took a decade, and a second term, for the Democrats to lose their way, indebting the country and veering to authoritarianism. Even now, it was not the electorate that ousted them, but the armed forces – the very 'solution' that Mehmet Serif Firat had solicited, in so many words, even before the Democrats came to power. In May 1961 a group of patriotic officers toppled the government and arrested Bayar, Menderes and others. (Menderes was later executed.) In Varto, the gendarmerie captain took the local administration in hand – and leading Sunnis, including Cibrans such as Halit Bey's son Mahmut Sever, into custody. The Alevis, naturally, were delighted.

By that time the death of Mehmet Serif Firat had become old news in Varto, but the junta were looking for Kemalist heroes to vaunt, and Mehmet Serif fitted the bill. What did it matter to General Gursel, who led the coup of 1960 and went on to become president in 1961, if Mehmet Serif Firat was not, in fact, 'martyred' by 'secret hands' one pregnant week after he published his opus, but gunned down a full year later by his Uncle Halo, a man not equipped to read Mehmet Serif's *History*, let alone object to its contents? Why allow Mehmet Serif to be the victim of some tawdry local score settling? Why not increase his grandeur and standing over his wretched part of the world, and martyr him in the name of truth and progress? This is what General Gursel did in his famous introduction to the 1961 edition of Firat's *History*.

In an age of instant communication, the deception would have been futile, exposed after a few emails sent here and there, but in the 1950s and 1960s the people of Varto were divided into those who were literate and travelled, and the rest. This second group, far more numerous, knew that Mehmet Serif Firat had been killed by Halo, and that Halo spent the rest of his days in jail in Bitlis. But no one asked these people. So, outside Varto, a consensus formed around President Gursel's version.

Today, the majority of Ferons dutifully refrain from challenging this orthodoxy, but not all. In Berlin, Selim Ferat – the great man's nephew, no less – chips away vindictively at the uncle he never knew. Selim is one of the few members of the family to reject overtly Mehmet Serif's assertion that the Ferons are Turks; Selim has Kurdified his surname, learned Kurmanji, and is a strong supporter of the PKK. At this level, the dispute is at its most heated, and within families there is no greater shame than the shame of treachery.

To many Ferons, those who stand behind Mehmet Serif Firat, Selim is a traitor to his uncle, his family and his tribe. Selim retorts that his accusers are traitors to their people and their identity. It was Selim, in a widely publicised article, who denounced his uncle for being a 'denialist', a 'faithful slave' and a 'traitor' – a 'squire who boxes army captains on the ears, a whip-wielding, boot-wearing ... bully'. The Republic of Turkey, he wrote, 'which every day launches a fresh massacre in Kurdistan, calls him a fearless provincial aristocrat, a merry fellow ... the situation is plain to see. In order to win the Alevis, they will make Mehmet Serif Firat a hero and raise him to the skies.'

I have lived with him for so long, he is the pivot on which so much turns. His *History* has been my guide, my deceiver. I have cursed his dishonesty. And yet something in me admires him, for he did not cause his rumpus in the manner of Major Kasim – with weasel words and fancy footwork. He did it with relish, believing himself to be right.

Here is Mehmet Serif Firat's daughter, Ceylan Bingol, out in the wind, framed in the small concrete arch that a later general, another junta leader, raised to her father. Using her left hand, with its man's watch and two rings, one of them inlaid with a small dark stone, she fingers the buttons of her cardigan. She is looking down the valley on to stunted oak trees whose colour is turning.

This isn't the first time that I have been taken by someone's daughter or sister to see his grave. If we broaden our definition of death to include imprisonment, exile or induction into the ranks of the PKK, and our definition of a widow so that it signifies any female left behind, we might say that Varto is a district of widows visiting gravestones, and that its colour, like the rusting leaves below, is mellow and valedictory.

The history here teaches us that to be a woman is to accompany naughty, irascible, rather primal men. Even the sophisticated men here, those engaged in such cerebral pursuits as moving files around the mayoralty, are expected to exhibit the instincts, of carnality, atavism and violence, at which their sex excels. There is no doctrine of passive resistance, no notion of loving one's enemy. There is no opium or *bhang* to conduct one to a stupefied humanism. The women must applaud their men, nurse their men, and defend them after they die their selfish, futile deaths.

We are out on this indiscriminate crag, where the grasses submerge the rough stones, to ponder the traitor/hero Mehmet Serif Firat. A few paces away lie Zeynel and his brother Veli. They buried Zeynel and Veli in unmarked graves, for fear that old enemies would come and dig them up and defile them. No one knows exactly where Zeynel and Veli lie, though they are definitely side by side, 'somewhere over there,' says Ceylan Bingol, indicating an overgrown knoll.

Mehmet Serif got a marked stone. Then in the mid-1980s the junta elevated him, giving him a sarcophagus in cement (now badly flaking), and a stone (maliciously toppled and cracked), inscribed with his own platitudes (fading, mercifully), as well as the arch itself, surmounted by a Turkish star and crescent (no trace). I wonder how long it will be before the whole of this undistinguished structure is pushed over or collapses and a descendant of Mehmet Serif Firat comes up here and waves her hand and says, 'somewhere over there'. And how long after that before they say, 'Mehmet Serif *who*?'

Back in her house I had asked Ceylan Bingol about the PKK and she told me that she had never seen a militant. A safe answer, the answer that everyone gives. But let us suppose that at the height of the PKK's influence here, as the guerrillas roamed around Varto recruiting, propagandising and collecting provisions for the winter, they did indeed knock on her door.

You can be sure that no militant, having extorted his fill of bread and cheese, having procured batteries and socks, needle and thread, would pass over the opportunity to hector the daughter of the traitor Mehmet Serif Firat. He would ask her if she considers herself a Kurd or a Turk, what she thinks of Apo. He would seek expressions of penitence, feed her useful phrases of self-criticism. He might get angry and rant, and she would feel scared.

Gumgum!

Back in Ottoman times there was a man called Kemo, who was inducted into the Ottoman army and took part in an incursion into Iran. Ordered to enter a village and get food, he was surprised to discover that the village was inhabited by Armenians. At that time many Kurds in Varto knew Armenian, so Kemo pretended to be Armenian, and the villagers took him to their headman. When he heard that Kemo was from western Armenia, the headman said that his family had originated from there. He could not say where, exactly, but he began to recite the names of certain rivers and mountains that he had heard of from his father, and Kemo realised that the man was from Varto.

When Kemo left the village the headman confided to him that, before leaving home, his forebears had buried a treasure of precious metals and fabrics; they had buried it with a quantity of red millet grains, a preventive against damp. From the man's description, Kemo understood that the treasure lay somewhere along the Kalcik valley, and, upon his return from military service, he spent several years surreptitiously searching the valley, finding nothing.

Shortly before he died, Kemo, who had no children, revealed to a friend of his, a younger man, what the Armenian had told him all those years before. This younger man was rich and he had decided to build a big house in lower Varto. Digging the foundations, his workmen kept coming across a kind of grain they could not identify. They took them to an old woman, who identified them as red millet, and she told them that in the old days, before wheat was sown in Varto, people had used red millet for making bread.

The rich man heard about the red millet and he remembered what Kemo had told him; it occurred to him that Kemo had never explored around lower Varto, but that this area, also, was part of the Kalcik valley. He changed the plans of his new house, incorporating an enormous central room that, once completed, he would be able to dig up secretly and at his leisure. But his house was destroyed shortly before it was finished, in the great earthquake. When the authorities started clearing up, space was needed for dumping debris, and the lower reaches of the Kalcik valley were chosen. The debris rose high over the site of the rich man's house, and it was many years before it was removed, by which time he was long dead.

ACCORDING TO ROBERT E. Wallace of the US Geological Survey, the earthquake started at 12.22 p.m. GMT on 19 August 1966. It lasted perhaps twenty seconds and had a magnitude of somewhere between 6.7 and 7.25 on the Richter scale. Varto town and many of the surrounding villages were destroyed at a stroke. The neighbouring districts of Hinis and Karliova were also severely damaged. Erzurum, 130 miles to the north, suffered slightly. The shocks were felt as far away as the Black Sea coast.

It was after lunch, and many people were out, swinging a scythe. There was a sound from inside the ground, the sound of rolling stones, a 'gumgumgumgumgum' sound, and the earth began to pitch, first sideways and then up and down, knocking people off their feet. Those inside the anthill houses that Lynch and Brant had seen and Xenophon before them, those snug well-insulated death traps with their metre-thick roofs of rock and mud – these people, mostly women and children and old people, suffocated in the soil of their ancestors. In Karkarut fissures twenty centimetres wide opened up, passing under buildings and tearing them apart. The northern part of Tepe slid down a hill, cutting the Mus Road in two. In Alangoz, not a single house was spared.

In the restaurant in Varto town, a certain Haci Omer threw himself on to his son as the roof fell in. The cinema, where a matinee was under way, buckled, as did the nearby mosque. Government House, the bank, the post office and the new regional boarding school collapsed.

Springs stopped gurgling. Brooks dried up. Human groans rose and mixed with the lowing of livestock dying broken-backed. With each aftershock: another crash, the screams of twisted poplar poles and pulverised boulders, and then the dust would begin to settle again.

Foxes and rabbits pelted down the mountain slopes on to the valley floor. Several people were killed by swarms of bees. In some villages the ground darkened with ants.

Varto had suffered an earthquake the previous month, in which twelve people died. Everyone remembers the big earthquake of 1946. Mehmet Serif Firat writes of a very bad earthquake in 1856, though he doesn't quantify the dead. All in all, when you consider these quakes and the smaller tremors that periodically shake Varto, and the district's location at the eastern tip of the Anatolian fault system; when you consider all this and the unsuitability of the Varto valley, being a saturated alluvial plain, for building activity of any kind, the temptation is to rain curses on the Armenian Vartan Mantagounian who first laid stone upon stone here.

Hours after the event the earth rumbles still. The survivors have no spades or picks for digging at the rubble of their houses, and the groans of their relatives gradually fall silent. The people of Karkarut are terrorised by a buffalo cow which inadvertently crushed her calf and has gone berserk; she kicks and bites and prances furiously. In Varto town, Haci Omer is pulled out from under the restaurant. He is alive but his son has suffocated in his arms.

In Ankara the government stirs. State radio cancels scheduled programming and broadcasts classical music. Suleyman Demirel, the prime minister, tours the affected region. From the newspaper *Milliyet* we learn that the prime minister, addressing people in Varto, has narrowly escaped serious injury, hurling himself out of the way of a collapsing wall. During the same visit, Demirel is castigated by a furious *Vartolu*, who tells him, 'You only come around here when there's a disaster. Not a quarter of what's done in western Turkey gets done here. We are the forgotten people, abandoned to our fate!' The US Air Force flies in a field hospital with seven doctors. The Pope offers condolences. The Greeks send blankets and food. *Milliyet* publishes a shot of Fatma Girik, lissome star of such films as the *Ballad of Kesanli Ali*, giving blood. The governor of Mus pithily observes: 'You could say that there no longer exists a district by the name of Varto.'

Two days after the disaster, *Milliyet* has its correspondent Ozdemir Kalpakcioglu on the ground. He describes black flies feasting on corpses and swarming around the eyes of listless newborns, conscripts sifting forlornly through the earth. 'After staying thirty-three hours under the earth, a six-month-old baby, assumed to be dead, is put on a truck. The tiny babe suddenly begins to cry. A foreign woman immediately cradles the baby and gives it her breast. A babe whose hour has not yet come. No father, no mother. Only God knows what will be the fate of this child.' On the night of 22 August there is a terrifying aftershock, as violent as the original quake, but it does no damage because there is nothing left in Varto to be destroyed. Those who can, leave Varto. Others pitch Red Crescent tents and snaffle loaves dropped by Turkish Army planes. In Varto town a boy is badly injured in a fight over bread. The headman of the village of Leylek is arrested for profiteering. The fortitude of one Nusret Yaman, who lost his wife, three children, mother and two siblings, and yet cares assiduously for his three-year-old niece, is considered admirable. Five days after the event, a three-year-old is found alive.

'And the corpses,' Ozdemir Kalpakcioglu begins his dispatch of 23 August, 'have started to smell in Varto ... until today, I wouldn't have appreciated how important your pickaxe, your shovel, your axe really was. Not for nothing do the villagers cry out for pickaxes and shovels ... they're digging the earth with their fingernails, trying to find and exhume the dead. In waves this smell rises over Varto ... the atmosphere of desperation, discouragement, unease, migration and panic continues. That we might learn to afford people a little dignity.'

The official toll is 2,529 dead, 1,500 injured and more than 19,000 buildings destroyed or heavily damaged. The unofficial toll is higher. Varto district, population 47,000, must begin again.

The earthquake generation will become the heroes and villains of this story. In the 1970s they read their Marx and Gorky. They hoarded grenades and hurled Molotov Cocktails. Fearing for their lives in the aftermath of the 1980 coup, they burned or, in some cases, buried their copies of *The Grapes of Wrath*. They fled. They were hunted down or ended up in exotic foreign refuges. They killed and died. Of those who didn't die, many of them – mellower, older – eventually turned away.

We should know how these people, bumpkin kids gambolling on the scarps, the barefoot offspring of illiterate women who spoke no Turkish and barely ventured from their villages, evolved into sophisticated class warriors conversant with Marxist dialectics and the rotating bolt system of a Kalashnikov. How did they become such promiscuous linguists, speaking, aside from the standard trio of Turkish, Kurmanji and Zaza, the languages of the places they ended up in – German, French, Arabic, the Sorani Kurdish of northern Iraq? Part of the reason for their evolution, the part that is specific to Varto, lies in the earthquake of 1966. But for a broader, more comprehensive answer, it's to the 1960 coup, to General Gursel and the officers who placed him at their head, that we must turn.

The coup had presented an opportunity, some believed, to reform the structure of the east – a structure, bound to tradition and the tribe, that militated naturally in favour of such reactionary phenomena as Kurdish nationalism. In the words of Ragip Gumuspala, a former chief of the general staff, the region contained tribal and religious leaders who opposed the spread of literacy, keeping the villagers under 'every type of pressure'. At least the villagers were 'apprised', in Gumuspala's scented phrase, 'of their Turkishness', but this awareness was vitiated by the Kurdish propaganda of the sheikhs and chiefs. The answer, Gumuspala found, was to resume the policy of exiling leading Kurds that had been pursued after the Sheikh Sait Rebellion, distribute land to the peasants, and revive agriculture.

There was a fresh round of exiles and Sheikh Sait's descendants were deprived, for the third time in the republican era, of their homes and possessions. But comprehensive land reform did not materialise. Turkish bureaucrats and military commanders often found it easier to co-opt the big Kurdish agas than tread on them. In his *Order of Eastern Anatolia*, the left-wing academic Ismail Besikci regretted that almost forty per cent of rural people in eastern Anatolia were landless, and that in some areas relations between lord and peasant remained 'utterly feudal in character'.

The National Unity Committee that General Gursel headed did not run Turkey directly for much more than a year, after which Gursel was elected president by parliament, but the shadow of the armed forces over politics, in the form of consecutive presidents drawn from the upper ranks of the army and navy, remained considerable. (Turkey's head of state is the president, with a head of government, the prime minister, usually representing the largest party in the electoral parliament. The army is the third, if intermittent, actor in Turkish politics.) In some ways, the 1961 constitution drafted by the junta and its allies was a liberal one, providing for religious and press freedom and the inception of labour unions. But it was a racial straitjacket. While the previous constitution had been silent on the ethnic identity of 'the people of Turkey', the new one, at Gursel's behest, included repeated references to the 'Turkish people', and an injunction to promote 'Turkish nationalism'.

The authorities tried to limit contact between the Kurds of Turkey on one hand and those of Iraq, Syria and Iran on the other. In Varto, the bloated bodies of three men, identified as cross-border smugglers, were displayed at the bus station for public edification. There were raids by the gendarmerie and commando units on suspected nationalist villages. Guns were confiscated and the men on occasion stripped in front of their women and abused by a hate-filled young officer: 'Tailed Kurd!'

During the 1960s bureaucrats leaned over maps and plucked, from their imaginations or the dictionary, Turkish substitutes for thousands of Kurdish and Armenian place names. Nazim Han's village, Kalcik, for instance, was renamed Aydinpinar, which means Clearwater in Turkish. (No one uses it.) In the east the conscripts were given a handbook explaining that the word 'Kurd' originated in the sound, a '*kurt-kurt*' sound, that these swarthy people, these 'mountain Turks', emitted while crunching through the snow. When things were calm, the conscripts busied themselves with scraping Ataturk's phrase, 'How happy is he who says he is a Turk,' on to the mountainside.

In Istanbul a Kurd was arrested for devising a 'Kurdish alphabet'. This same Kurd produced a Turkish translation of the seventeenth-century Kurdish epic poem *Mem-u-Zin*, by Ahmet Hani; it was seized before it reached the shops. The following year, a second translation was published and distributed without hindrance, with the differences that this *Mem-u-Zin* was attributed to a Turkish writer, and its contents misrepresented as the story of some Turkish tribes. In Ismail Besikci's words, 'The idea behind a second translation of *Mem-u-Zin* ... is to propagate the idea that there was no such Kurdish poet as Ahmet Hani, and even that there is no such race as the Kurdish race, that *Mem-u-Zin* was originally written in Azeri Turkish and that it has nothing to do with Kurdish.'

The state set up more than forty free boarding schools in eastern and central Anatolia. In Varto, where the earthquake had left few schools standing, there was plenty of demand. Hundreds of Varto children were dispatched to distant boarding schools, to learn literacy and maths, and to imbibe the values of the Republic of Turkey.

'They took us to Mus on the bus,' recalls one evacuee. 'It was the first time we'd been out of the district. They put us in a school to stay the night. None of us had seen electric lights before. We turned the lights on and off. Then we started throwing our shoes at the ceiling, trying to hit the lights, for the fun of it. We did this until we'd broken all the lights, and then we felt a bit silly and sat in the darkness.

'The next day they took us to a boarding school in the Arab region near the Syrian border. We *Vartolu*s were ten or eleven years old, but some of the other boys in the class were twenty. The Varto kids performed much better than the Arabs, which got them angry. They tormented us because we were Kurds. If they had known we were Alevis we'd have got into even more trouble. In public we would keep the Ramadan fast.'

The 1960s was the decade when TRT, the state broadcasting monopoly, opened half a dozen radio stations in Kurdish or partly Kurdish towns – all broadcasting in Turkish, conscientiously observing those injunctions, contained in the TRT charter, to 'serve Turkish nationalism' and the 'indivisible unity of the nation'. These stations lavished airtime on a composition, 'White Flower, Red Flower', which became much loved and was named best Turkish pop song of the year – only it wasn't Turkish, but Kurdish, and had crossed into Turkey with Kurdish refugees from Iraq.

The artists performing songs broadcast across Turkey by the TRT network were often Kurds. One of them, Ibrahim Tatlises, now Turkey's most famous performer, came to prominence with the immensely popular 'Slipper on your Foot'. No one saw fit to inform the public that the song was Kurdish. Tatlises and the other Kurdish singers were in a curious position, arranging and performing Turkish translations of songs they knew to be Kurdish, and getting paid (in some cases) considerable sums to do so.

Into the TRT playlist went not only Turkish tunes, but also Turkish adaptations of Kurdish, Armenian, Arab and Balkan compositions. These artistic debts were rarely acknowledged. TRT presenters, record sleeves, the performers themselves: they gave the Turkish public a specious sense of ownership and, when the real owners belatedly stood up to claim what was theirs, they were resisted. In 2005, thirty years after Tatlises became a star, Nilufer Akbal had the nerve to release a version, in Kurdish, of 'Slipper on your Foot', and was pilloried by the Turkish nationalist press for her presumption.

How to get your cultural bearings at this time, when Tatlises and the others are in lucrative denial and the compass has been obscured? It must be all the harder for a Zaza-speaking Alevi in Varto, at the bottom of the cultural heap, but this is the environment into which Nilufer Akbal, Kurdish pop diva, was born.

Here is tiny Nilufer bawling in her parents' Red Crescent tent in 1968. There is a transistor radio at home, a great prize. Through this medium Nilufer is acquainted with that Turkish-Arab musical form, *Arabesk*, and its hirsute practitioners. A chubby little girl, a bonny dancer, Nilufer Akbal belts out 'Slipper on your Foot' for her father's guests. People gather, for there has been a dearth of joy here since the earthquake. Everyone agrees she has a rare talent.

Nilufer's father is not a Kurdish nationalist. He espouses the political agnosticism that has spread among Alevis since Mehmet Serif Firat's death. But he, too, can tire of the TRT formula. He twiddles the dial of his transistor until … here we are! A minstrel singing in Kurdish, in brilliant bold Kurmanji! The Armenian Karapet Haco!

Karapet Haco is the good that came of the horror. During the massacres of 1915, Karapet Haco observed through child's eyes the annihilation of his village. A destitute saved by his knowledge of Kurmanji and a miraculous talent, he survived and became a celebrated bard. He joined the Sheikh Sait Rebellion, fled the retribution and took refuge in Syria, then a French mandate. When Syria got independence Karapet Haco went to Yerevan, capital of the Socialist Republic of Armenia. The Communist authorities gave him a slot on their Kurdish-language service – provided he avoided nationalist subjects.

One day Nilufer Akbal will ask: Why am I tuning into an Armenian radio station to listen to Kurmanji? And, why is there no Zaza on the airwaves, anywhere?

For now she is a specimen in the republican laboratory. She watches the older boys and girls, including her siblings, come home from boarding school for the summer holidays. The girls have hairstyles they learned from a magazine. They exhibit some meagre acquaintance with instruments called a knife and fork. They brush their teeth. They witheringly appraise their own mothers – barge-like, placidly wearing to bits their whiffy, age-old petticoats.

Daughter thinks: 'I don't want to be like that.' Mother is hurt. 'I've forgotten Zaza,' the ungrateful wretch declares, lying through her (blindingly white) teeth. 'I'm much more comfortable in Turkish.'

Nilufer attends primary school in the village. The teacher is a Varto woman but you wouldn't know it. She has blonde hair of outstanding intensity, lustre and resistance. She has long painted nails that have known neither soil nor teat. Nilufer and the other girls gaze at her. 'What an exquisite thing!' This woman gets Nilufer to stand on the table and sing. She coos and pinches Nilufer's cheeks.

When Nilufer is older she walks to secondary school in Varto town, even in wintertime – four miles through the snow. 'People will die and life will go on,' she thinks. 'We're out here and no one's the wiser. What a painful thing! I don't want to be forgotten.'

But Nilufer Akbal only becomes unforgettable after she has moved to Istanbul, which is both the world's biggest Turkish city and the world's biggest Kurdish city. It is here that she appreciates the difference that remains between her and the Turks around her. She makes some albums in Turkish and they bomb. Then, in 1988, when restrictions on Kurdish recordings lighten, she contributes three Zaza songs to an album that shifts 80,000 copies in three weeks. 'Look what happens,' she says to herself, 'when I sing in my own language!'

Her subsequent albums contain pop songs in Zaza, Kurmanji, Turkish, Armenian, Persian and Arabic. She becomes very famous and tours Europe and America. She is, in her accepting creative spirit, heir to the best of the Ottoman tradition.

The 1970s started in Turkey on 12 March 1971, when the chief of staff, concerned at a sharp rise in political violence and spurred by an

unwelcome bid of a group of radical officers to seize power, forced
Suleyman Demirel to step down as prime minister and to make way
for a technocratic government which would miraculously end the
turmoil. But the turmoil did not stop. In the short term, it increased.
Foreigners were kidnapped and, in the case of an Israeli diplomat,
murdered. Dissidents, the majority of them radical Leftists, were jailed
and tortured and the army imposed martial law on several provinces.
And there was a famous triple hanging, a lesson to all who entertained
dreams of revolution. In the early hours of 6 May 1972, a twenty-
five-year-old armed Utopian, Deniz Gezmis, and two other members
of his Turkish People's Liberation Army, were martyred in the name
of Marxism-Leninism and liberation from imperial America.

'If revolution in Turkey is indeed the longest marathon,' wrote the
poet Can Yucel, 'he ran the most beautiful hundred metres' and was
'the first to breast the rope'. Deniz Gezmis was Turkey's Cohn-Bendit,
but braver and more handsome. He spent the last four years of his
life, from the time that the energising breezes of Paris reached the
Bosporus in the summer of 1968, in and out of different universities,
where he started and ended sit-ins, in and out of jail, where he started
and ended hunger strikes. He went on trips to PLO camps. His
demands: the immediate ejection from Turkish soil of all Americans
and their local agents; Turkey's withdrawal from Nato; land reform;
an amnesty for political prisoners; cultural rights for minorities
such as the Kurds. His Turkish People's Liberation Army set itself
an ambitious goal: 'To liquidate America and all foreign enemies, to
wipe out traitors and set up a Turkey that is completely independent
and cleansed of enemies.' Into his room at Ankara's Middle Eastern
Technical University, the famous room 201, he ushered a considerable
number of tender, attractive young women – captives to his piercing
eye and cleft, proletarian jaw.

In April 1971 Deniz went before a judge in Ankara.

'What is your job?'

'I'm a revolutionary.'

'I don't understand. I mean your profession.'

'I'm a revolutionary.'

What kind of revolutionary? Here, the modern romantic is apt to
be disappointed – not by Deniz's positions, which are as flatly illiberal
as you would expect from a twenty-year-old Marxist-Leninist, but

by their intellectual incoherence. Deniz Gezmis is an advocate of armed revolution. He reveres Ho Chi Min. He models himself on Che Guevara. He sings 'The International' at the top of his voice. And yet he is also a passionate, fanatical defender of Mustafa Kemal – the architect of a state built on ethnic nationalism and anti-Communism. In his interviews and pamphlets, we find Deniz Gezmis trying to smooth over these bumps in the road. He thanks Mustafa Kemal for 'charging us, as students, with the task of participating in the revolutionary struggle'. He invokes Ataturk when characterising Turkey as composed of two sibling races, the Turks and the Kurds. Deniz closes his eyes to the Ataturk who prevented workers from striking, and to Ataturk the racial theorist, who tried to force the Kurds to accept the Turkish identity that he had devised for them.

Deniz is not alone. Rare is the Turkish Leftist at this time who is prepared to accept that Ataturk is no fellow toiler on the boilerplate of Marxist revolution. You find a self-conscious privileging of Ataturk the social reformer, the secularist and emancipator of women, a

Deniz Gezmis, 1971

relegation of Ataturk the perpetrator of state terror. The Left gives unwarranted prominence to Ataturk's brief flirtation with the Soviet Union in the 1920s. The Left buys into the long-discredited Kemalist theory that the Sheikh Sait Rebellion was a British plot to destroy the Republic of Turkey before it could get off the ground.

Deniz is not alone. The far Right claims Ataturk, the armed forces claim Ataturk. The bureaucracy, single-breasted Kemalists to a man, claim Ataturk.

Deniz Gezmis is an internationalist, but a xenophobic one. He thanks his father for telling him about the war of independence; 'ever since, I have hated foreigners'. He is a Communist but he is also a militarist with a soft spot for repressive juntas. He praises the army for launching the 1960 coup. In the wake of the 1971 coup, the Turkish People's Liberation Army makes the following statement: 'The goal has been achieved. The Demirel government has fallen.' It falls – irony of ironies! – to the aged Ismet Inonu, still at the top of the Republican People's Party, to chastise those 'extremists who incited and goaded the army into putting an end to parliamentary life'. This is the Ismet Inonu to whom Ataturk entrusted the republic, Mustafa Kemal's brother-in-arms, the ultimate 'Kemalist'. But Deniz is not so sure. 'Fifty years after Turkey's first War of Liberation,' he says, 'anti-Kemalist politicians have risen to the top of a Kemalist state.'

It's as a man of actions, then, rather than ideas, that Deniz should be remembered, for his actions have a blazing, if rather primitive, integrity to them.

In December 1970, Deniz and his comrades open fire on two policemen standing guard outside the US embassy in Ankara, injuring both. The following month they hold up a branch of a big bank. In February 1971 they kidnap an American sergeant from a base in Ankara and hold him for fifteen hours, in room 201, before releasing him. In March they kidnap four more American soldiers.

The security forces are searching frantically for Deniz and his comrades, house to house, to no avail. Demirel says wryly, 'If I find Deniz Gezmis, I will make him chief of police.' Parliament swirls with rumours. Gezmis is fighting with the cops in Paris Street! He's been arrested! No! He escaped in Kucukesat! The journalist Cuneyt Arcayurek writes, 'I would later learn that on three occasions the interior minister passed in front of the house where Gezmis was hidden ... Deniz's legend grows and grows. The army, parliament, the political parties, the street ... chaos!'

On 15 March, three days after the coup, Deniz and a comrade leave Ankara on a motorbike. (They have already released the Americans unharmed.) They are heading for the hills of eastern Turkey, where they plan to launch their rebellion. The following day they are arrested near Sivas in north-central Turkey. Here's Deniz, splashed over the papers in his famous sheepskin parka, being gripped by white official knuckles as the flashbulbs pop.

From here on everyone knows the order of events. In October 1971 Deniz and seventeen other revolutionaries are sentenced to death. Fifteen of the sentences are subsequently commuted. Deniz and two comrades are to hang. On the night of 5 May 1972, Deniz and his comrades chainsmoke and drink tea. They refuse an offer of absolution from a man of God. Deniz writes a letter to his father in which he states that he has no regrets. The noose is too tight and will not fit over Deniz's head. It has to be loosened. Deniz's final words are: 'Long Live Marxism and Leninism! Death to Imperialism and Fascism!' Deniz hangs for fifty minutes. Then it's the turn of the other two. *Hurriyet*, Turkey's family newspaper, rushes out a 'Lightning Edition'. The front page is dominated by a large, aerial photograph of Ankara's Central Jail, and the headline, 'They were Hanged'.

In Aksehir in western Turkey, where he was at a vocational school learning to be a teacher, a fourteen-year-old Varto boy called Lutfu Balikkaya wept not because he understood much about Marxism or Leninism, but because he believed that Deniz Gezmis had wanted good for the country.

Lutfu Balikkaya told me this in his flat in Kreuzberg, in the centre of Berlin. He told me a great deal more, in between going off in the mornings to run a nearby nursery school, being a father to two children, and repainting his flat. He spoke quickly and quite indistinctly, obliging me to listen hard, and his alert eyes shone behind small round glasses. He was that most valuable of informants: temperate, truthful and much changed.

Lutfu Balikkaya is an Alevi village boy with tight curly hair whose early desire was to smoke Parliament cigarettes like his uncle, a lawyer in a white suit, one of the first members of the family to receive an education. He lost his elder sister in the earthquake of 1966, buried alive as she prepared for her engagement party that evening. A few months later, sad and hungry, Lutfu walked to Varto town after hearing that a bus had arrived to take boys and girls off to school.

In Mardin, a few miles from the Syrian border, Lutfu learned that to be an Alevi is to be beaten and reviled, and he began to feel, not unnaturally, an affinity for the underdog. Back in Varto he fell under the influence of two Leftist teachers. Not quite thirteen, he took part in his first political agitation, marching the length of Varto town, the police in menacing attendance, to protest against a perceived injustice in the education system. When the police geared up to baton charge the protestors, Lutfu and the others struck up the national anthem – to which the police reacted reflexively, by standing to attention. In this way the demonstrators avoided a beating.

Lutfu Balikkaya is one of the men who brought Kurdish nationalism to Varto. He's the passionate young sage from whom the celebrated Haydar, who went on to run the PKK in this part of Turkey, learned about Socialism, independence and justice. He set himself against communal strife. He was arrested, tortured, shoved in a cell, and given time to think. In time the ardour cooled and he came out – out of jail, out of Apo's sphere, out of Turkey and into unlovely exile. But we are getting ahead of ourselves.

Back in the early 1970s, at school in Aksehir, Lutfu became friends with a fellow-student called Hamdi. Lutfu was impressed by the Turkish that Hamdi spoke. It was a plangent sort of Turkish, relieved of the old circumlocutions and energised with European words – *burjuvasi*, for instance, or *oportunizm* or *komprador* – a language of indignation. There were seven other Varto boys at the vocational school. All, like Lutfu, were Alevis, and all considered themselves to be Leftists.

The Varto boys earned a name for themselves early on. Lying on his bunk in the dormitory, Lutfu overheard a Sunni boy boasting about a beating he had administered to an Alevi boy in his hometown. Lutfu called the Sunni boy to order. Insults flew, there was a big fight. Before this incident, most pupils had only heard of Varto in relation to the

1966 earthquake. Now they started associating it with the *Kizilbas* and fisticuffs.

Hamdi was a year older than Lutfu. Upon graduation, he gave Lutfu a collection of fifty books, mainly novels and political screeds, including the translations of some European works. Lutfu did not have time to read all these books, so he took them home with him when the holidays started. A few months after the 1971 coup, when the gendarmes were hauling people off for the crime of reading, Lutfu's father tossed these fifty books into the stove. Lutfu wept hard when he heard the news.

In due course Lutfu graduated and got his first job as a teacher, not far from the Iranian border. It was a febrile time in politics. There was a left-wing prime minister in Ankara, Bulent Ecevit, Inonu's replacement at the top of the Republican People's Party. The Right was led by the corpulent, crafty Demirel and his Justice Party, successor to the Democrat Party, which had been banned after the 1960 coup. Then there was the far Right and the Islamists. These forces contested elections, formed unstable governments and clung to power whenever their partners, as was customary, withdrew and Ankara was plunged into crisis.

Ecevit had declared an amnesty for political prisoners who had been sentenced after the 1971 coup. The jails emptied and old alliances were renewed. Strategies were revisited. Politics got a secret face – the oily presses, the caches and spiky acronyms. The groups that would eventually join battle were in the process of being formed, or evolving; others were in a larval state. The Left was more fractious. By the end of the decade, when Turkey was in a state of anarchy, the Left would fragment into no fewer than forty-nine organisations, the Right into six or seven.

Arriving in the south-east, an eighteen-year-old deputed to instruct the nation's youth, Lutfu was receptive to new ideas. He read voraciously. He was taken with the idea that Turkey was engaged in a second war of independence. He read about the national liberation struggles of Cuba, Mozambique and Palestine. He became an active member of a left-wing teachers' union. He delivered a provocative seminar through whorls of cigarette smoke: 'What is Colonialism?'

'I was a committed Kemalist,' he remembers. 'I was a Leftist, of course, but I was also a Kemalist. On the one hand you're fighting against the system. On the other, you're a Kemalist. Ataturk made you from scratch. You've grown up with the impression that Ataturk created you, he's like God.'

At weekends Lutfu would go to a bigger town, where he stayed in a cheap hotel and hung around with his fellow-teachers. For the first time he was exposed to sympathetic Sunnis. He was friends with a Sunni Kurd who came from near the Iraqi border. This young man had fought on the side of the Iraqi Kurdish nationalists against Iraq's central government. It was a new idea for Lutfu, that Kurdish nationalism might cross existing national boundaries. He was friends with another teacher who supported the Kurdish nationalists without even being a Kurd.

Gradually, Lutfu came to distinguish in his mind between the Turkish and the Kurdish Left. The Turkish Left was the tradition of Deniz Gezmis. The Kurdish Left was this and more. It maintained that the Kurds had suffered specific injustices and that the Turkish Left wasn't paying nearly enough attention.

How is it possible, the Turkish Left demanded, if we accept that the whole of Turkey is being colonised by the Americans and their domestic collaborators, to regard the Kurds as a colony within a colony? That, the Turkish Left argued, doesn't make sense. When Turkey is liberated, the Kurds will be liberated along with everyone else. Let's not indulge in bourgeois splittism here!

In order for Lutfu to decide what he thought about this, he needed to decide what he was. He had known Dersim Kurds who, hearing that he was from Varto, claimed him as their cousin and explained that he was a Kurd. They urged him to consider the language he spoke, Zaza, and its affinities with Sorani Kurdish, a dialect spoken in Iraqi Kurdistan. They reminded him that the Alevis of Dersim and Varto celebrate Nevruz, the Kurdish new year, just like the Sunni Kurds and the Persians – again, unlike the Turks. These Dersim Alevis depicted their rebellions of 1921 and 1938 as Kurdish nationalist events. On they went, painstakingly building evidence, and suddenly the wall, erected by Mehmet Serif Firat and buttressed by Varto's Alevi elders, cracked and fell.

One shouldn't underestimate the pebbly sort of honesty required by anyone prepared to question the foundations of what he has, until now, believed to be his identity. And yet this is what Lutfu Balikkaya, and several other prominent Varto Alevis, did in the 1970s, with profound consequences for their co-religionists. By the time he returned to Varto, in 1975, Lutfu was no longer a Turk, but a Kurd, a smouldering, Zaza-speaking Alevi Kurd.

Lutfu Balikkaya is something of an exception in that he has engaged with his adoptive country to an extent that many other *Vartolus* have not. His German is all but accentless. Although he arrived here relatively late, he has an appreciation of German culture and history – he finds himself seeking in the world around him clues to his own background. His two children are Germans at school, *Vartolus* at home, and they have encouraged his awareness of what is going on outside his window.

In *Snow*, Pamuk's Leftist hero Ka returns to Turkey after twelve years in German exile and plunges back into the life he once led, to the point of starting an affair with a girl he had known as a student. Ka, we learn, did little in Germany. He did not work and he did not learn German. Germany was a ship, advancing with mortal precision, for killing time. It took him around and around and then dropped him off where he had started.

My guess is that Lutfu, if politics and the law allowed him, would go back tomorrow. Compared to Ka, he is a model of integration. He may feel gratitude to Germany, and to Germans, for letting him in and allowing him to stay. But he longs for Varto. He longs to swim in Zaza. And this, aside from his easygoing generosity – a quality, you can be sure, that he learned back home, not here in the busy-bee West – is the reason he gives me his time.

Climbing the stairs to Lutfu's flat, you ask yourself, how many of the names on these doors are Turkish? At least half. Of those Turkish names, how many are held by Kurds? How many people in this building are Alevis? Rich? Poor? It matters little. The German eye, sympathetic, hostile, or indifferent, flattens the differences between these people by heaving on to them the whale of their own foreignness.

Behind the doors, at least, the old identities reassert themselves. Lutfu sits among his once-subversive volumes and the Zaza-German dictionary he has compiled. Lutfu and some other people, including a second *Vartolu* friend in Istanbul, are trying to save Zaza. They start by standardising the language, killing branches to rescue the trunk, and then they go on, inventing or discovering words for ideas and objects that Zaza hasn't been able to express. It's hard not to think of Ataturk playing at language-building after dinner. It's the same idea, and the ideal, of instilling nationhood, is the same.

I have come here, to this pickle jar, expecting to find Varto's history sharper and less inhibited than at source. And so it turns out. The fear that weighs on people in Turkey is absent. There is no Ergun hanging around, no smirking captain. And the people, being refugees in the present, concentrate on the past. Having this past is what distinguishes them from the Ethiopian or the Croat in the street outside. The Ethiopian and the Croat have pasts of their own.

How strange it is to sit talking to Lutfu and the other men he introduces me to in Berlin – men like Yakub Cicek and Mehmet Can Yuce, author of *The Sun that Rises in the East* – about places and people they haven't seen in almost thirty years! In all this time they haven't tasted the sour chalky skimmed cheese or sweet Mus cabbages or strolled along Ataturk Boulevard or headed into the Bingol Mountains. I did all this a few weeks back, but I cannot summon them the way they do. Let's go back to the 1970s; shake a branch and the pears drop down. What was the name of that Fascist mechanic who got shot up and fled to the Black Sea? Necmettin? Mehmet? That's it – Mehmet. Remember him like yesterday.

The earthquake of 1966 opened the eyes and ears of the people of Varto to the outside world. From being, in the early 1960s, a district of illiterates in one of the least literate provinces in the country, Varto leapt up the rankings, and the reason was the large number of Varto children who had received an education – and not a bad one – in the nation's boarding schools. Varto in the 1970s was the scholarship class of the east. At a time when the provincial literacy rate was forty-five per cent, more than four out of five *Vartolu*s knew how to read and write. Almost every young person spoke Turkish.

The town of Varto boasted no less than five professional associations, of which the teachers' union, situated in a British prefab

not far from Government House, was the most influential. Varto had
two bookshops, two printing presses and three restaurants providing
wholesome Turkish dishes at reasonable prices. Varto's cinema
showed the latest Istanbul releases. Accompanied by her brother, who
had taught himself to play the *baglama*, the young Nilufer Akbal won
music competitions and regaled crowds at the teachers' union.

Survivors of the earthquake were cast far and wide. Many of those
who attended boarding school went on to university and entered
a profession in western Turkey. Siblings, nephews and nieces had
followed; communities of *Vartolu*s – well-schooled, hard-working –
had grown in Istanbul, Ankara, Izmir and elsewhere. A second wave
of migrants went further, to Germany and other European countries.
The village of Tatan, for instance, was now populated largely by
women and children. Every summer a caravan of absentee husbands
came clunking across Asia Minor in their second-hand Volkswagens,
and presented their remittances. Spring babies were the norm in Tatan.

Varto had a new entrepreneurial elite. His name was Kadir Aktas
and he was the operator of Varto's bus stop. His family was the first
in Varto to take a holiday on the beaches of western Turkey; his wife
was the first *Vartolu* to wear a bikini. And Kadir Aktas treated himself
to three weeks in Berlin every year, returning with ever more taxing
executive toys, visitor attractions in his office in the lower bazaar.

A showcase for the social engineers in Ankara? A triumph for the
Kemalist model? Not quite, for all the activity had a corollary: ideas
and opinions. Consider those *Vartolu*s, locals and expatriates alike,
talking in the tea houses on a summer evening. The people of Varto,
newcomers to the world at large, were making up for lost time. They
soared on the wings of Allende, Nixon, Pol Pot. They subjected the
colonial paradigms of a) France and b) Portugal to critical scrutiny.
They quoted Sartre and Camus, mostly incorrectly. The Communists
(Chinese faction) accused the Communists (Soviet faction) of social
imperialism, and the Communists (Soviet faction) accused the
Communists (Chinese faction) of social fascism. The Turkish Left
disapproved of the Kurdish Left's 'nationalist tendencies', and the
Kurdish Left deplored the Turkish Left's 'social chauvinism'. Here is
a man sucking at his wilted butt and mounting a brilliant defence of
urban guerrilla warfare as an instrument of social transformation.
'No!' his interlocutor cries. 'We must get the villagers on our side!'

The early 1970s was when dozens of primary schools and three secondary schools reopened across Varto. It was when scores of *Vartolu* teachers, most of them earthquake exiles, qualified from vocational colleges around the country. Fired with improving ideas, many of these young men and women wanted to return to their home district. The majority were Leftists, and the state knew it, but the state could hardly stop the Leftists from becoming teachers; the young would go untaught. So, reluctantly, with misgivings, the Ministry of Education allowed the Leftists to fill the empty posts back home.

Varto in the 1970s was fairly bursting with teachers diligently undermining things. There was a set curriculum, of course, but it was vulnerable to enhancement. You'd find Stalin's speeches being taught in the same class as those of Mustafa Kemal, Fidel crammed into a module with the Ottoman conqueror Mehmet II. The school inspector visits from time to time. At his knock, the blackboard is wiped hastily clean of slogans. 'Welcome, Mr Inspector Sir! Do join our discussion of the Theorem of Pythagoras!'

The Alevis returned from their colleges and universities as Turkish-speaking universalists. They had chanced upon fellow Alevis in Istanbul and Izmir. Sitting there in some association branch, a place – at last! – to enjoy a smoke during the fasting month of Ramadan, a boy strummed his lament for the martyred thirty-nine, those fine Dersim girls, pure of intent, who hurled themselves into a gorge rather than accept to be ravished by the Kemalist enforcers back in 1938. Here it seemed possible to elevate the whole of Alevi history into a paradigm of schism and dissent, and the Alevis into a heroic proto-revolutionary fraternity. If the price of this new security was an enforced universalism, so be it. The Varto Alevis neglected their Zaza without qualm, perfected their Turkish accent and strode forth to the Utopia they had been promised.

Back in Varto these Alevi men and women campaigned for the Turkish Left. In Emeran a young Firat recruited and propagandised in the teeth of the opposition of his father, a Kemalist of the old school, a doomed patrician. You found some elderly Alevi gents, egged on by their children, joining a parade by the Turkish Communist Party, banging skins and singing revolutionary marches. Lutfu Balikkaya taught in the Emeran village school, a lone Kurdish nationalist. A fourteen-year-old student enquired if he planned to appoint a spy in the old manner, to inform on those pupils speaking Zaza out of school. No, Lutfu replied, he did not. Pupils should be able to speak in whatever language they wanted.

To start with, on his return to Varto, Lutfu Balikkaya felt isolated among his fellow Alevis. His father, a member of an important Alevi family, was appalled to find his son identifying himself with Kurdish nationalism. 'That,' Lutfu recalls, 'in his eyes, was big betrayal. He would say that we are Alevis, not Kurds. And besides, we were from a family of agas. We were the last people, in his eyes, who should be Kurdish nationalists.'

Life, as usual, was simpler for the Sunnis. Kurdish nationalists in Alangoz were being galvanised by young Nizamettin Tas, grandson of Halit Bey's ostler. Precocious Nizamettin propagandised on behalf of the Apoists – as they were known after their young leader, a political sciences graduate named Abdullah Ocalan, or Apo. A rival Kurdish nationalist group, *Rizgari*, was promoted by Yakub Cicek, whose village had lost several men to summary executions after the Sheikh Sait Rebellion.

In Berlin, sitting with his old friend and rival Lutfu Balikkaya, Cicek recalls his approach to proselytisation. 'Organising people in Kurdistan isn't that hard, provided you explain things in a way that answers peoples' concerns. You're a Kurd. Has your language been banned? Can you speak your own language in a government office? In primary school in the village the teachers would beat you for not speaking Turkish. Open your hands: three or four smart whacks. When you speak about this, when you link it to a national identity, there's no reason for a villager not to understand.'

In the 1970s no fewer than seventeen Leftist groups were active in Varto. For a while they avoided friction. A shared target, the hegemony of America and its allies over Turkey, overrode nice distinctions of ideology, and, to Alevis like Lutfu Balikkaya and Sunnis like Yakub Cicek, this meant an opportunity. The time was ripe, they believed, for a reconciliation of their respective communities, around the goals of revolution and equality.

In the middle of the 1970s you find a change happening in Varto, that old byword for communitarian poison. You find young Sunnis and Alevis not only chatting together out of doors, but visiting each others' homes. 'He's a nice boy,' concedes a Sunni matron after entertaining an Alevi for the first time in her life. 'They don't eat their children,' an Alevi girl confides to her father upon her return from a Sunni wedding. Then there is the special solidarity that arises between Sunnis and Alevis who do time together. An elderly Sunni rises to his feet when a former cellmate, a much younger Alevi, enters the tea house. This sort of thing has not happened before.

Yakub Cicek remembers intervening to prevent violence when a Sunni boy made off with an Alevi girl. Rather than follow the old course, of bloody revenge followed by a feud, the two communities came together to celebrate the elopers' marriage. Lutfu Balikkaya describes with pleasure the visit that his mother paid to a Sunni village during the fasting month of Ramadan. The Sunni she wished to visit, a friend of Lutfu, not only received her with pleasure, but instructed his wife to kill a chicken for the visitor. 'And this man,' Lutfu goes on, 'for the past forty years, had been an enemy of the Alevis. Imagine it! A generation before, you'd have said to my mother: "Good luck to you! Impossible!" '

But Varto was not, in the end, a sealed republic. Faction leaders enjoyed quite a lot of autonomy but they were answerable to members of a central committee. The currents blowing in from elsewhere got hotter, and the directives more urgent, as Ecevit and Demirel mocked Turkey into chaos and debauched the public finances, and the violence – between Right and Left, and, increasingly, between Left and Left – felled the country eventually, brought it to its knees.

Thirty-four Leftists were cut down during a May Day rally in Istanbul, and neo-Fascist assassins, policemen among them, were implicated in the carnage. Intense fighting took place between Rightist Sunnis and Leftist Alevis: twelve were left dead in north-central Anatolia and well over 100 further south. The jails filled to bursting, Communist academies with their own systems of justice and morality, extensions of the morass outside. The governments of Ecevit, Demirel, and then Ecevit again – they were either complicit in the violence or unequal to the task of stopping it.

In Berlin a former member of the PKK central committee, the *Vartolu* Mehmet Can Yuce, describes the end of peace as he, a young Kurdish nationalist, experienced it:

'You're a colonised nation and you seek your rights. You can bring out magazines and set up associations and enter parliament – in short, you can operate within the parameters that the state has set, but the trouble is that the state outlaws the use of the word "Kurd", they won't let you refer to a place called Kurdistan. Saying these words is a crime, splittism, ample cause to get you arrested, tortured, kept in jail for years on end. So, what is keeping this nation under repression? Force. The army, the police, the gendarmerie, the counter-guerrillas, the far-right Nationalist Action Party. In such a country, where the machinery of repression is so organised and entrenched, you're left with one route, and that's to use force to answer force.'

Scab

There was a man called Mustafa who took to keeping his large flock of goats in the abandoned Armenian church. A survivor of the massacres, a man who had bought his freedom from the caravan, converted to Islam, and returned to Varto, remonstrated with Mustafa: 'Don't keep your sheep in the church! This is a place of worship.' But Mustafa didn't listen. 'Pah!' he replied, 'this place is fit only for infidels and animals.' And he carried on keeping his animals there until, one day, the roof of the old church came down, and his flock was buried alive.

A T THE BLOODY CLOSE to the 1970s, let us consider the predicament of the Turkish police officer unlucky enough to be posted to the Bolshevik stronghold, shared habitat of half-breed Muslims and separatists, of Varto. The groups, cells and parties, and their acronyms, proliferate. The natives jabber illegally in Kurmanji and Zaza. An Anatolian Moscow, they told you on your way here, in Erzurum. Worse than Moscow, you reckon.

After a while, with the help of local informants, you get a handle on the place. The People's Liberation, heirs to Deniz Gezmis, reign over the Turkish Left. The Kurdish nationalists have fractured. Before 1976, the *Rizgari* of Yakub Cicek and his colleagues held undisputed sway. Then, in that year, the Apoists started infiltrating. The Apoists have, by any reckoning, a stellar cast of local activists. They are, furthermore, the only organisation in Varto to boast equal numbers of Alevis and Sunnis at the top level.

Outside Varto town, some groups have a monopoly over entire villages. Other villages contain two or more groups, in competition. Rakasan, for instance, is split between the People's Liberation, the Apoists, and a couple of other groups. In Varto town, the teachers' union is divided. In theory the association exists to agitate for better working conditions and the right to strike – a privilege that the new constitution written after the 1971 coup wisely denied to teachers and other public servants. In reality, the members of this nefarious organisation concern themselves with splittism and stratagems for toppling the regime. Many are armed. You've heard that the loyalist mayor Nazim Han strolled into the association and got into an altercation with a noted Turkish Leftist. The guns were whipped out before anyone could say 'Enemy of the People', though the stand-off was resolved without bloodshed.

There is evidence of stockpiling. The arms enter the district in trucks and on pack animals. They are hidden in feed, among hay bales, underneath floorboards. One day you receive a tip-off. You triumphantly confiscate an Uzi and prepare to lodge a charge against its owner, but your informant promptly offers you a sum of money to get the charges dropped. He wants the Uzi – it's an original, all the way from Haifa. He will sell it on, perhaps back to the original owner, at a profit. You have a wife and three children. Everyone knows the police haven't been paid in months. Who can afford a conscience nowadays?

The task of the state is to disrupt the revolutionary hooligans as they roam about addressing clandestine meetings, distributing pamphlets, scrawling their revolutionary slogans on the mountainsides. But the factions are forever changing form and structure. They learn from each other: how to spread, isolate the cells, avoid detection and at the same time attract prestige and attention. You can't search everyone for guns, can't stop every lorry.

Alas! The state is weak here. To the north lies Erzurum. Mus is to the south. The Nationalist Action Party, lion-hearted friend of the police, is organised in both places. But here in Varto the rightists can be counted on the fingers of one hand. Conservative *Vartolu*s support Demirel if they are Sunnis, and Ecevit if they are Alevis. The main Islamist party is scant and underfed.

The key is to keep the Alevis and Sunnis apart. In his sermons Mullah Zeki, imam at the big mosque, comes down reassuringly hard on the Communists. (By 'Communists', of course, he means Alevis.) Zeki emphasises that Communism means atheism, 'democratic' sexual relations and a host of other abominations. The old duffers nod in agreement, but their children are revolutionaries – what can they do?

When this same Zeki, having learned of a big march of Leftists into Varto, goaded his flock into going out with sticks to defend their religion against the atheists, that reprobate Yakub Cicek calmed them with assurances that the Leftists had no truck with religion, only with justice, and the faithful ended up cursing Zeki for making himself scarce.

The news is not all bad. In Nazim Han the town has a solid loyalist mayor – even if he is a *Kizilbas*. The old Leftist and communal solidarity, much in evidence in middle of the decade, is falling away now that the screws are being tightened and the country placed under martial law. Everyone is on edge. In Rakasan the Leftists have been at each other, with fists if not guns. And what joy, in Varto town, to see the factions prowling, giving each other the stare, asking for confrontation. They consider themselves great thinkers; it is obvious that many of them are perverts and homosexuals.

There is an art to ensuring that Ramadan, traditional month of communal unease, passes off as tensely as possible. Rather than intervene smoothly, in conciliatory style, when a Sunni raises his voice at an Alevi seen chewing in the street, the police officer must do the opposite. He must demand, 'What are you doing eating in the middle of the day? Don't you know this is a Muslim country?' The next thing you know you have a fight on your hands, and the ill will simmers for days.

You have a new man in the team, a good addition. He calls himself Nadir and he's rumoured to have been involved in some rough stuff out east during his last posting. To hear him speak, you'd guess he's no friend of the Alevis. The people hate and fear him already, which seems to give him a strange sort of pleasure.

What's needed now is a mischief-maker of a different order, someone to love the republic and its representatives, invite opprobrium and recklessly generate that paranoia and insecurity without which the state cannot maintain its grip.

Here he is now, resplendent in his flared trousers and Italian leather jacket, stepping forward to kiss you on both cheeks in full view of the lower bazaar: that peacock, Kadir Aktas!

Kadir Aktas is the third of Varto's traitors. He has neither the social graces of Major Kasim, nor the intellectual pretensions of Mehmet Serif Firat, but he shares their respect for power. He is strikingly modern in that he owes his position not to his seniority in the tribe, or to the size of his following, but to discrete, entrepreneurial acts of treachery, to his being an individual in a land of collectives. He is a poseur. His political opinions are hard to pin down.

Kadir Aktas survives in a framed photograph hanging above the desk in a little office, in the lower bazaar, from which his son Ercan runs the empire. Kadir Aktas has been captured in a mellow light; he stares back, dewy-eyed, buoyantly groomed, undeniably handsome, asking only to be judged fairly.

Kadir Aktas was the vainest man in Varto. His wardobe was full of crisp shirts. He wore a different suit every day. He was a rich man. He owned a taxi, a bus, a truck, a jeep and a minibus – besides his famous yellow Renault. His contacts extended north, south, east and west. He was Mr Transport.

Kadir Aktas was a Sunni from the village of Haci Bek, in southern Varto, and it's been suggested to me that old man Aktas had a role in turning in Sheikh Sait back in 1925. The people like such symmetries. Kadir's son Ercan denies this, as well as rumours that Kadir was not a Kurd at all, but a Turk. 'If you go back long enough,' Ercan says, 'you might find some Arab blood in there.'

Speaking to Ercan is the closest I will get to Kadir Aktas. Ercan is half a head shorter than his dad was, and considerably balder, but he possesses what my imaginative voice tells me is Kadir's gravelly throat, his rolling shoulders and his casual menace. Ercan acquiesces; the comparison has been made before. Of course, he adds, the family is better positioned now than it was during Kadir's pomp. Ercan has added to the empire: the taxi stand on the corner of Ataturk Boulevard and the Mus Road; property around the place; the brand new Merc. he drives, with its make-believe licence plate, Barbie-pink: *Ercan*.

A member of the municipal council, an appointed body, Kadir Aktas became acting mayor after the incumbent resigned to contest the parliamentary poll of 1977. Kadir duly presented himself for election at the following municipal election, but lost to Nazim Han by a narrow margin. Ercan is proud of his father's nine months. He built some shops. He built lavatories for the mosque. ' "You know," he used to say, "I love my district, and I love the people. But I've had my fill."

'My father wasn't the state's man, but he was an obstinate man. He was a Kemalist and, although he was a Kurd, he mistrusted the Kurds. He looked around him and saw that they did wrong and then didn't accept that they had done wrong. You swear on your honour and then you go and kill a man. You sell your own daughter for a dowry. Now, I'm against these things, and I'm a Kurd. I'm against them. Do you understand? How do you expect me to accept this society? But I live in this society.

'My father wasn't an educated man, but my father had a passport. In those days, imagine it! My father! Paris! My father! Germany! My father! Holland! My dad spent eight months in Berlin attending a karate course. He was that kind of man, the kind who went to Europe.'

Ercan Aktas does not accept that his father was Varto's most diligent informer since Mehmet Serif Firat, or that, without the protection of the chief of police, the gendarmerie captain and the district commissioner, he would have been nothing. He does not recognise the Kadir Aktas that Lutfu Balikkaya described in Berlin: 'A brave man when his back was warm but, like all those of his ilk, a coward when he was on his own.'

Kadir kept a portrait of Ataturk on the wall behind him, and one of the Imam Ali, the second Shia imam, alongside. 'I asked him,' Ercan recalled, ' "Why do you display the Imam Ali's portrait?" He replied, "Son, I love him because he is God's lion!" My father was very socially advanced. In those days, when there was no whisky in people's homes, my father had whisky at home. You've no idea of the chocolates he had at home ...'

Ercan looks around him for evidence of his father's worth. He seizes what appears to be a glazed meringue, a souvenir from Europe, lying on his desk. 'Look! An ashtray. My father's.' Here is another prize, a cigarette lighter that warbles. Ercan is lost in admiration. 'Think of it; such a man, forty or fifty years ago ... my father's Winchester hunting rifle – you won't see the like even now. He had an inquisitive mind, he liked luxury ...

'But – aha! – you ask me, did he make any mistakes? Of course I would have to hold up my hands and say, yes, he did. You know, to make a crust, you're forced to go at the other man's throat. When he and his brothers started out, there were six other bus stops in this neck of the woods. Exploiting a dispute, causing problems, they made the others their own. They cleared six men out! It was a fight for a crust.'

Kadir Aktas liked money and prestige and gadgets. He liked to walk down the street with the gendarmerie captain, or to sit at the table of the district commissioner. The people who admired him and voted for him were not, in general, those who had not been away for an education. They continued to equate a man's worth with the considerations that he receives from a contemptuous state. Kadir had a braggart's courage and a lean, vole-like *amour propre*. He had cussedness, but not beliefs. He received tips aplenty in his life as a scab, but never a wage.

'I've had my fill,' said Kadir in his son's telling, but he tarried in clearing his desk after losing the municipal elections one Sunday in 1977. It was a historic result; the victor, Nazim Han, had become Varto's first Alevi mayor.

Nazim recalls:

'I won but Kadir didn't leave the mayoralty. I didn't want there to be a fight between the Sunnis and the Alevis, so I gave him all Monday, but he didn't budge. On the Tuesday, even the Sunnis said, "Go and claim what is yours."

'When I arrived, I saw that Kadir was at his desk forcing those municipal employees who had not voted for him to sign affidavits confessing to various irregularities, including theft, so that they could be sacked. His gun was lying there on the desk.

'After sizing up the situation, I said, "Who are you sacking? I've been mayor since Monday and it's now Tuesday. You were only acting mayor. You never had the power to fire employees and you certainly don't have it now."

'He resisted until I showed him my gun under my coat. Then I seized the affidavits, which he'd written himself, and threw them in the stove. As he went down the stairs and out of the door the staff threw everything that belonged to him out of the window, and booed and hissed.'

In Berlin, talking to the Kurdish nationalist Yakub Cicek, I had asked about Kadir Aktas.

'We knew him of course, and we knew he was passing on information. Varto is a small place, and if twenty people gather together, everyone gets wind soon enough. Once, when our group arranged to meet, it was decided that we'd make it look as though we were having a picnic. We all came from different directions. We met at the petrol station.

'We saw Kadir's yellow Renault passing us, going towards Mus, and then it came back again. We moved the meeting to the river, among the trees. A couple of the lads went to the top of the hill there and told us that some army vehicles were on their way. We stripped and some of us went into the water. Others were fishing or preparing a fire.

'Suddenly we were surrounded by soldiers. "Don't move!" We asked what the matter was and they said they'd received information about us. They came down and searched our clothes and found nothing.

'Later that day I went to buy some shampoo and the man in the chemist's wrapped it and gave it to me, and as I was walking home I passed Kadir's front door. I was going into the upper bazaar when suddenly the police surrounded me. My hand was in my pocket. I made as if to bring my hand out of my pocket.

' "Don't move your hand! Don't move! We'll shoot!"

'I asked, "What's up?" and they replied, "We have information about you. Raise your empty hand!" They opened my bag and saw it was only shampoo. At that moment, Kadir passed by, pretending to be minding his business. Yes, the deceased did have such propensities.'

Things got worse over the course of 1979 and the first eight months of 1980. The third Ecevit government fell and Demirel formed his fourth administration. The shops were empty and electricity blackouts were commonplace. Inflation cleared 100 per cent.

The death toll from violence around the country rose to 600 per month. Even Dersim, overwhelmingly Alevi, was being torn apart by rival left-wing groups. Parallel administrations had been set up by Leftist and Rightist groups in various parts of the country.

The people of Varto could read the auguries. The Apoists were resigning from their jobs in the public sector, severing their links and preparing for a settling of accounts. Some of them were already fugitives. The Apoists and the People's Liberation were at each other's throats. The fist fights were giving way to armed clashes and people were being injured. Before, the factions had cooperated. Now you found them seeking excuses to fight, giving petty rivalries and enmities a political colour. Everyone was on edge.

One night two *Vartolu*s were shot dead at a petrol station in Mus. They had just delivered two injured students from the Varto boarding school, which had been damaged by fire, to the hospital there. That same night, back in Varto, hundreds of Leftists received and buried the bodies. The anxiety was acute, the speculation rife. Had the school been deliberately set on fire? Who had informed the Fascists in Mus that these Varto men were on their way, easy targets in the darkness?

The reviled cop Nadir chased a group of pamphleteers down the street and into the garden of a tea house, from which they were able to escape through the trees. Having lost his quarry, Nadir turned on Yakub Cicek, who was sitting in the same tea house, and there was a noisy altercation. The same Nadir was involved in a firefight with armed Apoists outside Varto town. One night the police lodgings were sprayed with bullets. The following day the town was full of soldiers. The people suspected the police of shooting up their own houses in order to have a pretext for more arrests.

Nadir was nailed, eventually, one evening as he played dominoes. A man entered the tea house – a stranger, eyewitnesses said – and tapped him on the shoulder. 'Are you the man,' the newcomer asked, 'who wants to turn Varto into a lake of blood?' Nadir reached for his gun but it was too late. He fell off his chair with five or six slugs from an Uzi in his head and chest, and the assassin fled.

The authorities pinned the deed on Yakub Cicek and his comrades. They said that Yakub's nephew, a trainee teacher in Bingol, had pulled the trigger. They arrested dozens in Varto and Bingol and sent a team from Mus, including an old colleague and friend of Nadir, to carry out raids and conduct the interrogations. Nadir's friend oversaw Yakub Cicek's questioning in Varto police station. They tied his feet to a *falaka*, or wooden rack, and beat his soles with their truncheons. Then they made him walk barefoot over rock salt. Yakub resisted for eleven days. He admitted nothing and then a judge freed him. His nephew was sentenced and jailed.

Kadir Aktas continued to stir things up. He flaunted his relations with senior officials and it was widely believed that he continued to pass on information about Leftist subversives. But he was vulnerable, despite his bulletproof vest and licensed gun, and his karate skills. It was drawn to Kadir's attention that a certain Alevi, Hizir, had vowed to kill him. Stay clear of Hizir! One lunchtime, walking into a restaurant in the lower bazaar, Kadir saw Hizir entering through the back door. Kadir shot first and missed. Hizir shot back and hit a bystander. Hizir fled.

The senior people up at Alangoz, a progressive Sunni village that admitted no sectarianism, were alarmed. They contacted some of Varto's most influential Alevis and proposed a meeting of members of both communities, with Kadir in attendance. It would be the most important meeting since the Sunnis appealed to the Alevis to join the Kurdish nationalist movement in 1920.

Ercan Aktas takes up the story:

'They said to my dad, "Kadir Bey, you've done a lot of work for the state in this part of the world, and we'd like to get together with you and talk about this." And they said, "You'll come on your own." And my dad said, "I'll come on my own. I've no outstanding account with anyone, because my conscience is clear." So he gets in his jeep and he says to the driver, "Take me to Alangoz." One of our relations also got in, saying, "I'm coming too." But my dad said, "If I go with a handful of people they'll think I'm scared and that won't help me at all. I'll go on my own."

'So my dad is taken to a house in the village. At the door they try to search him, but my father doesn't let them. And they lead him in and he's questioned. They criticise him for hours and the majority are against my father. And then it's time for the sentence, and when the sentence is delivered, it's delivered as they would in the courts of the

Republic of Turkey: the judge snaps his pencil in two. That means: execution! And when that happens my father gets the picture and ... well, at the end of the day, life is sweet! So he whips out his two guns and fires some rounds into the ceiling. Everyone in the room hits the deck and my dad bolts out the door and into his jeep. "Step on it!" '

Not everyone agrees with Ercan's account of the Alangoz meeting. A second account, related by others who were present, depicts it not as a trial but as a large public meeting, in which Kadir was tactfully dissuaded him from stirring up communal tensions, before being permitted to leave. Kadir, these people add, turned in a truly abject performance, full of protestations that he had been 'misunderstood'.

Everyone agrees that Kadir Aktas kept a low profile after Alangoz. He became, in the words of one man who had been there, 'As quiet as a mouse ... the tip of his nose would touch the ground whenever he saw me: "My dear sir, how is your health today?" '

It was the summer of 1980.

Military coups in Turkey are named for their dates. They vary, like siblings, in character and complexion. The 1960 coup is called 'May 27'. It is the coup of General Gursel and Mehmet Serif Firat. The 1971 coup is called 'March 12'; it is the coup of Deniz Gezmis. These were important corrections, but corrections only. The 1980 coup, 'September 12', dwarfs the others in scope, power and ambition. The violence that preceded it, and the punishment dispensed in its name, have no parallel in the history of republican Turkey. A rescue operation carried out by rational men, it succeeded in its urgent objects, keeping Turkey alive, and keeping it alive for the West, at a time, after Iran and Afghanistan had been lost, when America and its allies felt acutely vulnerable. But what a price! A generation, brutalised; ethnic conflict, entrenched; a culture, already impoverished, clapped in irons.

Among those Turkish citizens who fervently hoped for strong measures to end the chaos of the late 1970s, who cursed their politicians for incompetent swine and longed for a martinet to take the hooligans in hand, was Nazim Han. Uncle Nazim, it will be recalled, had been elected mayor of Varto, but he was not enjoying his first term.

In Varto, like everywhere else, the state had been emasculated. The factions were rampant. 'Every day,' he recalls, 'fighting and disputes!' The factions put him under pressure to support them. He found no opportunity to formulate policies, let alone implement them. Varto was like a goalmouth scramble after hours of rain: a bath of mud and flailing figures.

The Turkish people had grown used to coups, and looked out for the signs: unexpected troop movements in the wee hours; martial music on the radio. The army had made known its displeasure with the politicians. The patience of the chief of the general staff, Kenan Evren, was running out. In the days leading up to September 12, Nazim got into the habit of turning on the radio early in the morning. 'If God wills it,' he told his wife, 'there will be a coup.' Then at dawn on September 12 Nazim's dogs made a din. Nazim went to the window with his gun and saw soldiers in the road. He turned on the radio; sure enough, the military march, 'Forward, O Turk, ever Forward!' was playing. He opened the door to the officer who had come for him. Dressed nattily, he was taken off to Government House, where he found Varto's other senior civilians, also detained.

'Everyone was there. They asked me how I was and I said, "Capital!" One of them said, "Every military coup retards our democratic development by fifty years." To which I replied, "There is no such thing as Turkish democracy. The state has disappeared. We can't even go to Mus in safety!" '

At five on the same morning, Turkey's top politicians, including the prime minister, Demirel, had each been awoken by an officer and handed a letter from General Evren. 'In the face of all warnings,' the general wrote, 'the confrontational stance adopted by the political parties, and their sympathetic or actively supportive attitude towards extremists, have boosted anarchy, terrorism and separatism and brought our country to the point of disintegration.' The letter informed the leaders that the armed forces had taken control and that the government and parliament were suspended.

In this way Kenan Evren became the martinet that Nazim Han and others had longed for. Over the next three years, before he restored to the country an army-supervised version of civilian government, he conducted a massive purge of extremists from the bureaucracy, muzzled the press, implemented a stabilisation programme that brought down inflation and wrote a new constitution that was overwhelmingly endorsed in a referendum. In the words of Hugh and Nicole Pope, authors of an authoritative history of modern Turkey, 'the perceived need to control, to avoid the disorder of the 1970s, shines through almost every article of the 1982 constitution', which exhaustively lists the rights enjoyed by the citizenry, and, with equal thoroughness, the circumstances under which they may be abrogated.

After the coup *Time* put General Evren on its cover, with a collage of the Istanbul skyline in his hands. The legend read, 'Holding Turkey Together'. This is what Kenan Evren did, and many were grateful. Across the country, and in loyalist areas of Varto, the months following 12 September witnessed the birth of many babes called Kenan. It was too bad that, as an antidote to the anarchic pluralism of the 1970s, the generals found no more imaginative solution than a fresh campaign of cultural homogenisation, expressed in the dictum, 'Everyone bound to the Turkish state through the bond of citizenship is a Turk.' At least the violence had stopped.

Rather, it had not stopped, but it had stopped in the streets and universities. In the months after the coup the locus of Turkey's violence moved to the villages and the mountainsides where the fugitives had fled and the security forces sought them relentlessly, and to the police stations, garrisons and jails where they were held, tortured and, not infrequently, killed.

According to official figures, over the four years that followed the coup, 180,000 people were detained, the great majority of them Leftists, 65,000 charged and 42,000 convicted. Some 640,000 handguns and 48,000 rifles were confiscated. The majority of Leftist organisations in Turkey, whether Turkish or Kurdish, were either wiped out or enfeebled. In the past, the People's Liberation had spoken of the need to provoke the regime to 'take off its mask and reveal its true face to the people', as a final galvanising step towards revolution. But the coup did not galvanise the extreme Left. It all but annihilated it.

The number of executions was small, twenty-five. No political leader was tried for his life. It was in torture, that instrument of confession and revenge, that the junta found its genius. No official figure exists but, from the ubiquity of torture in the reminiscences of former Leftist prisoners, and the casualness with which they discuss it, we can only assume that it was commonplace to the point of banality.

In Varto, the Leftists had gone to ground. They moved from village to village, or slept rough. The weather was still fine. Then one day the fugitives awoke and discovered they had been snowed on.

The fury arrived after 9 December, when Haydar Firat was shot while tramping through the snow. He had been a voluble Kemalist, and so the military authorities were displeased at his death. Political murders were supposed to have stopped. That was the point of coups. The army poured men into the area and two suspects were shot dead.

In this way the junta joined the battle for hearts and minds. The squaddies barged into the villages, yanked hair, hurled ornaments to the floor. In the words of one Varto man: 'Breaking down doors, stripping the men and yanking their sexual organs with rope in full view of the women; these became normal occurrences.'

'If the intention was to arrest you,' Lutfu Balikkaya told me in Berlin, 'they simply found you an organisation. I was arrested for membership of three different organisations. First arrest: one organisation. Second arrest: another organisation. Third arrest: a third organisation.

'Before September 12 someone had ripped up the Turkish flag at the Varto boarding school and they wanted a scapegoat. They tortured two pupils and got them to say it was me.

'When I was in jail in Mus there was a teacher who was arrested sixteen times. Even the police got tired: "Look, sonny! Don't come here again!" "But you keep arresting me!" "What can we do? You keep getting denounced."

'He was arrested sixteen times, each time for membership of a different organisation.

'They arrested a fellow called Cemalettin. They had mistaken him for another man, of the same name, who had killed a prosecutor. Cemalettin the assassin was a university graduate. Our Cemalettin, on the other hand, could barely speak Turkish. They'd only arrested him because he had the same name. His mother had died. His father had married again. When it came to dividing up the property and goods, he said, he had got the ewes and his stepmother the rams. His Turkish was so bad that he said this in a way that implied that his stepmother had had sexual relations with the rams. The police would sit and laugh at him. It was inconceivable that this was the man who had killed the prosecutor. They knew it as well as we did. But they kept him for sixty days all the same. Every day the policemen would come and laugh at him.

'I remember another kid. His father had a shop in Malazgirt. He gave the police lots of names. One day one of the policemen came in and said, "You little shit! We went all the way to Siirt and we arrested a teacher and it turned out he was one of ours. Why did you do this, little shit?" The kid replied, "Isn't it obvious? You burn my hand with a lighter and you only stop when I give you names. So I give you names. I've given you the names of all my father's customers." '

'I'd been in Ankara on the eve of the coup,' recalled Yakub Cicek. 'That night I came back to Mus. I got there late so I stayed in a hotel. The next morning I came downstairs and they said, "There's been a coup." General Evren was on television. I stayed that day in Mus and saw a few comrades and then, changing my vehicle twice, came to Varto.

'The martial law commander had brought out a poster with the names and photographs of those who were wanted, and my face was on it. I would have meetings in the mountains with other comrades. People who weren't suspected by the state would pass on messages. If we were in a village, we didn't show our faces for fear that someone would inform on us. A few times raids were launched on villages I had just left. They raided my own house several times. We buried everything we had in the way of books or papers or photos; everything not buried or destroyed was taken off during the raids.

'We had a bit of land, and all our houses – mine and those of my brothers – were on this one piece of land. One day I came down from the mountains. Some workmen were on our land, building a stable for the animals. I climbed up on to the half-built roof and saw that soldiers had all but surrounded us. There was nowhere to flee. I jumped down off the roof and climbed under a big sheet of polystyrene that was lying in a jumble there. It had been laid over the roof to protect the animals from rain. Now they had put it on the ground. My older sister was standing by. I whispered to her that she should tell the workers to carry on working, not to panic, and to pile more things on the polystyrene. The soldiers arrived and searched everywhere, including the house. My sister, out of fear, was standing near me. The Turkish officer asked, "Do you speak Turkish?" And she replied, "No." He said, "Look! You do speak Turkish!" and she, guessing what he had said, replied in Kurdish, "That's all I know."

'The captain walked off with the headman of the village, my relation. I learned later that the captain told him that he knew I was under the polystyrene but that he also knew I was armed and didn't want bloodshed. So he walked on. He wasn't doing me a favour. He wanted to avoid a fight.

'Some of the *Rizgari* leaders had been arrested before September 12. They were in Diyarbakir jail. But the rest of us were still active ... Kurdistan is a rural area, where everyone knows each other, and if you're a stranger and you arrive somewhere, two days later you're under the microscope. The intelligence agencies want to know who you are and where you've come from. It's a lot easier to hide in Istanbul. You just have to create a legal identity for yourself, have a home address and a professional address. But you should be aware that all the concierges in Istanbul are informers!

'After staying in Istanbul for a while I came back to Varto. I came to Diyarbakir, no trouble. I had my teacher's identity card. I spent a couple of days in Bitlis talking to comrades and then I went to Mus. I had wanted to go all the way to Varto but when we got to Mus the driver of the coal truck I was in announced that he wouldn't go any further. I couldn't roam around Mus for fear of being recognised. I hailed a taxi and said I wanted to go to Sekawi, at the northern end of the Mus plain. I told the taxi driver that I had a sick uncle in Sekawi and that I was going to visit him. I gave the name of the father of a man I knew from Sekawi. I thought to myself, "He's old. He must have some ailment or other."

'We got to the bridge over the Karasu and there was a long queue of vehicles at the checkpoint. I told the soldiers, "I have a sick uncle in Sekawi, Haci Mahmut, and I want to go and see him. That's why I came. I don't want to stay in this queue." The soldier said, "Haci Mahmut? He just got out of hospital," and he waved us past the queue. As we were about to move off, he asked, "Will the taxi driver be coming back this way tonight?" and I said, "Yes," and he said, "Will you send us some bread with him?" And I said, "Not only bread, but cheese too." And he let us pass.

'We came to Sekawi and the driver asked, "Which way?" and I said, "Straight." On we drove and he noticed that we were now leaving Sekawi and I said, "Just drive straight!" I knew there was one more checkpoint before Varto town, at the Abdulrahman Pasha Bridge. Before we reached it, I said, "Stop!" I put my hand in my pocket to get out his fare and he said, "Please don't hurt me, I won't say a thing to anyone." I said, "I don't want to hurt you. I just want to pay you." He said, "Honestly, I don't want any money." I said, "The price you asked was too high. I'm going to give you the correct fare. Don't over-charge in future, got that? And when you go back, tell that soldier you dropped me by the road because the car wouldn't go up the hill to Haci Mahmut's house." He replied, "Don't worry about me. After you, dealing with the soldiers will be a breeze."

'I walked over the hills to Varto. If I crossed the Abdulrahman Pasha Bridge I'd fall foul of the soldiers. I took off my clothes. I'd forgotten how slippery the rocks were; I slipped as soon as I entered the river and everything I was holding got soaking wet. I wrung out my clothes at the other side and put them on. I got to Varto town just as they were calling the morning prayer. I went to my father-in-law's house. No one had known I was coming. I got in touch with one of our people and told him I wanted to come to the village that night.

'The comrade walked in front and I came behind. I wanted some water and I told him I'd go down to where I knew there was a spring. There was a bend in the road and the spring was below the bend. But the soldiers were waiting behind the bend with the lights of their vehicles turned off. Suddenly the place was full of light and I heard the sound of rifles being cocked and a voice shouted, "Hands up!" I made as if to raise my hands but then I hurled myself down the hill and they opened fire. I was down and they were above me. Their fire went over me. I scrambled between the rocks and up the hill and from the top of the hill I saw that they were stopping all the cars that were coming along the road, and lining up the cars so their lights went into the valley, and firing away. But I wasn't there any more.'

Pity the scabs. Major Kasim lived out his days in exile, reluctant to return home for fear of retribution. Mehmet Serif Firat was loathed and reviled by the majory of *Vartolu*s. Now, in the 1980s, it was Kadir Aktas's turn.

For a while, after the coup, with the Leftists scattered and democracy prorogued, Kadir walked tall again, sporting his Ataturk rosette. Then over-confidence led to a mistake. He filed a complaint against six alleged conveners of the Alangoz meeting, claiming that they had set up an illegal 'people's tribunal' there.

The trial was a significant one, much discussed. Unitary states attach much importance to infringements of their jurisdiction; it's the symbolism that counts, the whiff of parallel government.

It would be Kadir's final performance. In court he fulminated and cursed. On the pavement outside he offered smiles and a handshake to the men he had accused. Asked to describe Kadir, one of the defendants answered, 'Like JR in Dallas,' which amused the judge. One night the defendants were hauled off, blindfolded, and paraded for national TV in front of a cache of arms they had never seen before. The following morning, without explanation, they were released.

After months of hearings, the prosecution case collapsed. A witness called by Kadir abruptly changed his statement. He had, he said, been pressured to make it. The prosecution failed to prove the 'Apoist' character of events. Acquitted, the defendants went their separate ways.

Some returned to Varto, where they saw Kadir Aktas every day. And so began his final isolation. He offered to make peace with the men he had dragged to court, but his offer was contemptuously rejected. Now all of Varto was united against him. His ostracism was irreversible. He got ill, died sunken, embittered and remorseful: sad, shabby old peacock.

The Siege of Varto

I would like my identity to be a tree, but probably it is a river. It would be nice, in times of loneliness, to lean against it, warm and striated.

For me, identity was always a matriarchal legacy. Growing up in London, my father's roots in France and Belgium seemed distant. My mother, in a way, was herself a reverse immigrant, the daughter of a father and mother, themselves English, who had emigrated to Canada after the First World War, and she never, even after (re)settling in England, quite knew where she belonged. After her death, by her own hand, when I was thirteen, as I memorialised, even martyred her, I resented her origins. I felt obscurely that they had contributed to her death.

From this flowed the spirit of flight, which took me abroad after university and kept me there for thirteen years. To some degree that life, spent observing things through a journalist's eye, fostered in me a superior sort of neutrality. There was no need to define myself except in relation to my close environment, from which, clearly, I was different. Equally, I saw no reason to get angry about events back in England, for that no longer was my home and the events in question did not affect me directly. So gradually, my passion for my native place, already weak, degenerated further. Less than a citizen – I was not called on to pay taxes, found it mostly inconvenient to vote – I slowly, almost without realising it, detached myself from any sense of collective destiny. If I roused myself to outrage, such as when America and Britain invaded Iraq, I did so self-importantly, as a citizen of the world. When it was convenient, I played the Brit abroad, but only when it was convenient.

Until! Fatherhood twice over and the primal instincts released like pollen. To protect and teach, to allow, to curtail, to let live, to make live. I found that the need to inculcate and instil, above all to instil a sense of belonging, was as strong in me as in the exotic people I had observed for so long. And that instinct was there, *albeit in a subtler, more elegant form, in my Iranian wife. Suddenly we were no longer two worldly members of the community of nations, teaming up for a secular appreciation of life, but products of wildly differing cultures captive in a room with two gleaming tablets awaiting the chisel of culture and upbringing.*

Now, in the tall stalks of identity, I am drawn to movement and exile. Why do they seem tragic to me, when displacement – the histories of migrant communities concur on this – has so often furnished opportunity? Is it because I, a world roamer, hanker for a place where I belong, from which never to stir? Certainly I am a conservative, enamoured of the illusion of continuity. And yet ... is it an illusion that we are witnessing a rotting of the bonds, and the death of the local imagination?

I mourn the passing Armenian-ness of Salahettin and Sukran Cakar. They seem happy in their new place, in Wuppertal in western Germany, and they are certainly more accessible to me. But I mourn nonetheless. I wish they were still Armenian, living Armenian lives in Armenia.

Or Lutfu Balikkaya, that other new German; he thinks he belongs somewhere else, in Varto, and he is engaged in a struggle, for reasons that he might be hard pushed to define, and with no hope of material reward, to save the Zaza language. I should like nothing more than to meet Lutfu Balikkaya for tea in Varto's upper bazaar, and yet I fear that he would find his Varto gone, and be disappointed.

He would realise then that Varto is no longer the district of Varto in the province of Mus, but the sum total of the various diasporas: a Gundemir Armenian speaking from upstate New York; the PKK fundraisers in Berlin; scattered cousins in Yerevan and the Kandil Mountains of northern Iraq. In time, with the indifference of the generations, even this Varto will cease to exist, for its component parts will have drifted further downriver and been washed into the featureless ocean that someone once, with sublime optimism, named the global village.

THE WIDE INDIFFERENT STREETS of Kreuzberg are lined with call centres. They cater to homesick minorities. The people in your adopted country consider you to be a member of the biggest of these minorities, the 2.6 million-strong Turkish minority, because you arrived here from Turkey and the passport you carry remains, after all these years, a Turkish one. How odd it is, how it cracks you up – you, who went to such lengths to become an orphan, embraced once more, against your will, by the parent you rejected!

There is a smaller, rebellious minority within that vast, 2.6 million-strong Turkish community of Kurmanji-speaking Sunni Kurds. You are a Kurmanji-speaking Sunni Kurd and thus distinguished from the other subaltern groups, the Zaza-speaking Kurds, Alevi Turks and Turkish-Armenians. There is a certain amount of solidarity between these different groups, and now, increasingly, some intermarriage. In your eyes, however, there are tall barriers between them, matters of culture and faith, which cannot be leaped over.

Then there is your geographical identity. You come from Varto in the province of Mus. Your grandfather was a participant in the rebellion of 1925.

One Saturday night you and a couple of friends go to a big, barn-like nightclub. This place is owned by a fellow *Vartolu* and is packed with young Kurds with small fistfuls of Euros to burn. Towards the end of the evening a human chain is formed, linked by little fingers and culminating in a bright strip of cloth describing arabesques. The dancers inch, crab-like, around the room. The English writer joins in. Everyone is having fun.

Hold on! The dance is Kurdish, but the music, performed by a *baglama* player from Hinis, is Alevi music from Dersim, and mostly in Turkish. You're drinking your *raki* and working with methodical enjoyment through side dishes of yoghurt and purslane, beans, and aubergine, but there is nothing Kurdish in these dishes; they evoke soft evenings in the eastern Mediterranean. The young people at the tables around you are chatting in Turkish. The parents of these kids, people your age, were Kurds when they left Anatolia two or three decades ago. How is it that their children, despite spending all their lives in Berlin, seem to have become Turks? Your own son, for instance; he speaks Turkish better than you, and Kurmanji with curmudgeonly forbearance.

You told yourself you'd go back: the classic immigrant self-deception. You own an internet café and a travel agency running tours to Cappadocia. Such is the depth and breadth of this community, such is the ability of its members to duplicate the services provided by the host nation, that it's possible to spend the day in productive and profitable activity and not be required to utter a word of German. Even now, thirty years after you got here, you're uncomfortable speaking the language of your hosts.

The following evening, in the train, riding a packed car through the suburbs, you are accosted by two loud drunks, looming unsteady scum. They are shouting into bottles of beer. The scum fling out some horrid song. Then they lose the thread and see you – short, diffident, foreign.

They address you. They would like to know – nothing personal, no harm meant – if you are by any chance from Israel. 'That's right, sir. Israel!'

You reply quietly, evenly, as the conditions require. You have been here before. 'No, I am a Kurd.'

'Not even a Turk?'

'No, a Kurd.'

They are fiery-faced from mirth now, gasping, burping. One of them composes a few words. He'd like you to remind him of the name of that Kurd, you know, the one with the moustache …

'Abdullah Ocalan.'

'What?' More howls.

'Abdullah Ocalan.'

'Is he your president?'

'We don't have a president.'

How nice it would be to have these two freckled donkey-fuckers out in Varto, and to gather some of the boys with a gelding knife and show them some real Kurdish hospitality.

At the next station the scum dismount. The car is relieved by their departure, the atmosphere brightens, but still no one looks at you. A few minutes later the train stops again and everyone is invited to dismount and wait on the platform for the next train. It's an unscheduled stop. You decide to check that this is indeed the right platform for the airport – which is where your companion, the English writer, is going. Walking up the platform, you see a likely candidate, a swarthy dark-haired fellow.

You ask, '*Bu trenin son duragi havalimani mi?*'

The man stares blankly.

'Must be an Arab,' you mutter. 'Where's a Turk when you need one?'

I set out from Varto one autumn morning in 2006. The rainwater ran in torrents down the Mus Road. I read in *Gundem*, the unofficial PKK newspaper, that flooding had taken dozens of lives across the south-east. 'The State is an Observer' ran the headline. The newspaper criticised the government for not declaring the region a disaster zone. In the stricken town of Batman, the paper reported, the mayor's request to borrow the governor's helicopter, in order to tour affected areas, had gone unacknowledged. The coverage was designed to underscore the Kurds' self-image as a people neglected and undervalued by a chauvinistic state.

I took a minibus to Mus, then another across the Taurus Mountains, gashed by the rain, towards Diyarbakir. A roadside sign ironically summarised the PKK's tactics: 'Fire; Kill; Gloat.' On the contrary, I read in *Gundem*; the state's relentless attacks on guerrilla units were

© Getty images

Kurdish protest in Diyarbakir, September 2006

destroying hopes of peace – they were a dishonourable response to
the PKK's unilateral ceasefire. At least the ceasefire seemed to have
relaxed the conscripts on the road to Diyarbakir. Our minibus was
waved down just once. My press card elicited no comment from the
sergeant who inspected it. We pulled away and the driver put his
Kurmanji cassette back in the player.

I stayed three days in Diyarbakir, capital of a putative Kurdistan.
I went from meeting to meeting, visiting Apo stooges and the state's
men, crossing and re-crossing the big desolate square to hear about
solutions and empowerment. Since my last visit, in the late 1990s,
Diyarbakir had become a habitat for stray boys, the children of
Kurds expelled from their villages during the big clearances. In thin,
threatening packs, they begged, played football and smoked or sniffed
whatever came to hand. Earlier in the year, on a signal from the PKK,
they had run amok, trashing banks, police stations and shops. Then,
on a signal from the PKK, they had stopped.

One of the people I spoke to in Diyarbakir put me in touch with 'the
TV station' – this is a reference to the PKK's unofficial TV station, *Roj*,
in Copenhagen, just as 'the organisation' refers to the PKK. The man
at *Roj* gave me the name and telephone number of someone in Erbil,
across the border in northern Iraq. I should call him when I got there.

The following morning the TV in the breakfast room of my hotel
was full of Ecevit's death. Ecevit, loathed by the Kurds because it
was he, as prime minister, who had triumphantly announced Apo's
capture in 1999; Ecevit, the archetypal, conflicted Turkish Leftist.

That evening I drove south with two men. We crossed the Iraqi
border. 'Welcome to Southern Kurdistan!' The next morning I was in
Erbil, capital of the autonomous Kurdish region in Iraq. This is what
Diyarbakir would like to be: a capital with a president, parliament
and flag. There was foreign investment and talk of direct flights to
Europe. The people were proud.

I visited the ministry of extra-regional affairs, which is responsible
for the autonomous region's relations with the outside world. There I
found a Dersim Alevi employed as the minister's adviser, well dressed
and underemployed. She had felt a midwifely urge to help out at the
birth of an independent Kurdish nation. Wandering around the old
citadel I came across a Frenchman presiding, in some style, over the
Arthur Rimbaud Arts Centre; he deplored the philistinism of the Quai

d'Orsay. The lobby of the Sheraton Hotel clattered with the two-wave radios of ex-servicemen guarding dozens of British businessmen as they piled into the buffet lunch.

The following morning my contact came. He was a Kurd from Turkey. He drove this route often. I was not to worry. We went from Erbil towards that corner where Iraq, Iran and Turkey rub hard against each other. After climbing for three hours we went through a checkpoint, a sign that we were entering a part of the Kandil Mountains that the PKK has made its own. The rains had been here too, exposing tree roots and gouging the soft, flint-strewn mountainsides. The villages, providers of amenities and services to the PKK, smugglers of medicines and alcohol into Iran, looked prosperous; each had a fat haystack and gaudy beds of mountain flowers.

We rounded a bend and there, on the mountain opposite, was Apo: his portrait dug into the mountainside, angry and blue.

My hosts brought me tea, enquired politely about my journey. As the sun went down, Murat Karayilan, the PKK's acting leader, arrived. He wore the regulation PKK rig of baggy Kurdish trousers, zip-up tunic and cummerbund. He was podgy and cheerful. The other militants treated him with respect, but not awe.

Karayilan was accompanied by a slight, strikingly attractive young woman whose hand was softer than you would expect in a guerrilla fighter. She had only recently come to Kandil, she told me, after growing up in exile in Scandinavia – the recent Turkish bombardment, in which several militants had been killed, had been her baptism of fire. She had been assigned to look after me because she spoke several languages. It had not been anticipated that I would be a Turkish speaker.

She and Karayilan and I sat cross-legged and watched the Turkish TV news while eating sunflower seeds. It was the first anniversary of the firebombing by Turkish military agents of a Kurdish nationalist bookshop in Semdinli, just over the border. A judicial enquiry had been opened but had gone nowhere; the man leading it had been sacked under pressure from the generals and their allies in the mainstream press. The TV news covered the anniversary perfunctorily.

After the news I interviewed Karayilan. We spoke of the ceasefire that the PKK had announced a few weeks before, relations with the Iraqi Kurds whose territory they had occupied, and America's plans for the region. Given Apo's incarceration, I suggested, and his vulnerability to Turkish government pressure, wasn't it time for the PKK to choose a new leader? The young woman shot me a glance. Karayilan replied smoothly. 'It was Abdullah Ocalan who gave the Kurds their spirit and their voice. To abandon Abdullah Ocalan is to abandon Kurdishness.'

The following day, waking to the partridge's stabbing cry, tramping up and down the hillsides with the Scandinavian and two male guerrillas, driving over the tracks to visit camps and emplacements, watching the kestrels on the headwinds, I found it hard to reconcile the extremes, of beauty and selfishness, idealism and cynicism, which coexisted here.

The camps, particularly the women's camps, were pastoral idylls, the trees hung with blankets drying in the sun, spotless huts fronted with herb gardens and beds of pansies. The larger camps had timber schoolrooms. A black volcanic sea, snow-crested, rolled out beneath us.

These young people had laid out a modest lunch under a willow tree, pasta and home-grown tomatoes and parsley and cold spring water. Behind that mountain, remarked one of the women, revellers at a wedding were once turned to stone by the curse of a jilted lover – their petrified forms are visible today, dancing still. That way, she pointed, fell the legendary Kurdish hunter Abdul Kovi. And here, just before you, is where the ark came to rest.

After lunch I watched the Scandinavian smoking with élan, her dull trousers set off by a florid cummerbund, watched her knot a scrap to a wishing tree.

She had sat in the timber schoolrooms and rote-learned, in the deadening manner of novices everywhere, the incandescent wisdom of her leader. 'As the Leader has said ...' she would begin her responses to my questions.

She had been pitted like fruit, her self-ness gouged out and stuffed with Apo's rage. If ever she dared to become an individual again, she would cease to be an asset to the PKK. She would flee or be killed.

According to the Varto Alevi Mehmet Can Yuce, a member of the PKK's central committee before September 12, in his book *The Sun Also Rises in the East*, the coup was a response to the emergence of the PKK. This is self-aggrandising exaggeration. Of the tens of thousands of suspects who were tried for political or security crimes during the three-year period of military rule, only a small fraction were charged with 'separatist activities', and not all of these, by any means, were associated with the PKK. Nor was there an appreciation within the junta that, of the dozens of organisations that had been targeted and, to varying degrees, neutralised, the PKK was the most dangerous. General Evren told the people that terrorism had ended. The country could look forward to an era of stability.

The PKK survived because Apo saw the coup coming and got himself and other senior figures out of the country in good time. The organisation was able to grow after 1980 because, alone of the illegal groups in Turkey, it attracted an impressive range of foreign sponsors: the Kurds of northern Iraq; the PLO, then in exile in Lebanon's Bekaa Valley; and the governments of Syria and Libya, which saw in the PKK a means of prosecuting their own disputes with Turkey. From his base in Damascus, Apo was able to stage congresses, train militants and build links with Kurdish nationalists who had fled to Europe.

Abdullah Ocalan is a dumpy fellow whose modest background and intellectual grandiosity set him apart from such other, more familiar Kurdish leaders – aristocrats and sheikhs. It is striking that even in Yuce's account of the PKK's rise, an unabashed hagiography, Apo is depicted as cold, remote and angry. His addresses are 'effective' and his thought processes, when Yuce roams unbidden into his brain, steely and unbending. Apo's belief in his historic mission is 'total', though he regrets the amateurishness of his comrades. They, according to Yuce, invariably concur with the chairman's criticisms, and even volunteer ones of their own. Yuce capitalises the object of his admiration – 'Chairman APO' – which has the effect of turning him from a person into an acronym. He fails to mention that Apo stole another militant's fiancée; he denounces those 'traitors' who were, from early on, purged or killed. 'The participants in the meeting,' Yuce writes with unwitting candour, 'unanimously accepted the Chairman's proposal.' There is much else in this vein.

Certainly, Apo was – already, in 1980 – a megalomaniac, a dangerously isolated autodidact whose sounding board was a row of nervously clapping comrades. But he was other things besides. He had saved himself and the PKK at a time when plenty of other groups were either blind to the impending coup or willing it with millenarian logic. His goal, the creation of an independent, Marxist-Leninist Kurdistan, was, for many, an attractive one. He would go on, starting with the attacks that shocked Turkey on 15 August 1984, to turn the PKK into one of the outstanding, and seemingly immovable, features of the Middle East. Apo's is a remarkable achievement.

The attacks of August 1984 left two soldiers dead. Some Kurds were dismayed by the readiness of the newcomers to kill conscripts, whom many Leftists regarded as allies in a putative proletarian revolution. But many others experienced a kind of euphoria. It took pluck and skill to deal a blow to the Turkish army, strong arm of the Kemalist state and author of much Kurdish woe. Here in the Kurdish east, the scene of dozens of failed insurrections, it is the aura of daring and success, as much as the goals being pursued, that wins hearts.

For the next two years, there were doubts as to the PKK's staying power, the ability of a small, inexperienced organisation to ride out the determined military response of the Turkish government. Recruits had to be found, trained and deployed. A stream of high-profile attacks needed to be maintained. The people needed to be educated about the PKK's aims and methods, and the organisation's sphere of influence expanded from the border area. It soon became clear that the PKK's ambitious early goals, which included the setting up of 'liberated' zones in 1986, could not be realised. But the people were impressed, both by the PKK's growth under unpropitious circumstances, but also by the prestige and attention it quickly won.

In the Turkish state, Apo found his best ally. Civilian government had been restored in 1983, when the liberal economist Turgut Ozal became prime minister and General Evren president. But Turgut Ozal responded to the PKK's emergence with militarist logic. The government described the PKK's attacks as 'isolated incidents' and the work of 'bandits'. Troop numbers were increased and, in 1986, northern Iraq was bombarded for the first time. Turkey's political and military establishment defiantly refused to address the PKK's central complaint, which was that the Kurds had been subject to a systematic campaign to strip them of their identity. Ozal's chief adviser reportedly suggested that official recognition of the Kurds would lead to an increase in racism.

The late 1980s have a late Ottoman feel to them. There are no Armenians to fear, but the old Hamidiye Regiments have been revived in the form of the 'village guard' system, under which thousands of loyalist Kurdish peasants have been armed and paid to fight the PKK. The unruly south-east has been placed under the authority of a regional governor based in Diyarbakir. The Republic of Turkey, which has for much of its existence deplored the hegemony of 'reactionary' tribal chiefs over the Kurdish regions, is now cutting deals with loyalist leaders, pitting them against a rebel army that pursues such 'traitors' – and, on occasion, their hapless families – without mercy. The foreigners raise a predictable stink about human rights abuses: the burning of pro-PKK villages, the indiscriminate arrests, the widespread use of torture. In a way, the Turkish establishment is right; the European Union has become to the Kurds what the Powers were to the Armenians.

In Varto things were quiet. There was a pause, partly due to the absence of the Leftists, who had fled or been imprisoned; older rhythms had resumed. But everyone followed events in the south, and everyone knew that the violence was getting closer. Varto had more televisions, and more people who understood the evening news. In general, the Sunnis were excited and the Alevis apprehensive. Many elderly Alevis argued that Apo was a common murderer.

PKK defectors had accused him of executing some sixty militants who opposed his policies. Many women were heartened by the PKK's strongly feminist ideology and their recruitment of female guerrillas. Obvious to all was the gap that seemed to exist between the aspirations of the PKK, to set up an independent Kurdistan, and the reality here in Varto – of the Turkish republic, strong and determined, going about its business. The authorities had just built a new army post, suitable for 200 men, at Ustkuran. They were improving roads in the district. Were these the actions of a state preparing to relinquish control?

Several *Vartolu*s had joined the PKK. Nizamettin Tas was in the Bekaa somewhere. Mehmet Can Yuce was a prisoner in the military jail in Diyarbakir. The aim of those administering this jail was not to extract information, but rather to destroy the inmates, physically and mentally. Aside from the usual techniques of food and sleep deprivation, electric shocks, the *falaka* and severe beatings, inmates were sodomised with truncheons and forced to eat faeces and rats. Well over fifty are thought to have died as a consequence of torture in this jail, and many committed suicide or died prematurely after their release, but the campaign of disobedience conducted by many of the inmates – their refusal to buckle under unimaginable torments, popularly known as the 'Diyarbakir Resistance' – was an inspiration to Kurdish nationalists everywhere.

As the 1980s wore on, and the PKK became operative in Mus and other nearby places, the question on everyone's lips became this: when will the first group enter Varto? Some shepherds spotted armed men in the Bingol Mountains; were they PKK scouts? In the summer of 1989, in the pastures above Ustkuran, a body was discovered. No one knew whose it was. The body of a militant, killed by the state and left there as a warning? The people were scared, and they left the body to rot.

The first PKK group to arrive in Varto was headed by a Varto Alevi, codename Haydar – Demir Celik's brother-in-law. A second group entered soon after, also headed by a Varto Alevi, codename Ismail. By deputing Alevis to begin the campaign in Varto, the PKK showed its acumen. The Sunnis of Varto were already in their camp. It was the Alevis they needed to win.

Haydar is well remembered, for it was he who introduced Varto and the PKK to each other. Touring the villages clandestinely, recruiting logisticians, fundraisers and guerrillas, Haydar and his men impressed on the Alevis that they were Kurds, that the republic had robbed them of their identity, and that Apo would help them win it back. The people knew Haydar and reckoned he was a decent, brave fellow. Slowly, particularly among the young Alevis, Haydar made progress. He had less to do in the Sunni villages. It was as if the Sunnis had been waiting for the PKK since the final shot of the Sheikh Sait Rebellion.

The PKK's goal was not simply to attack police stations and kill village guards. It was to humiliate the state and demonstrate its powerlessness. The PKK first did this in Varto by convening a meeting of some thirty men, mostly poor Alevis, who had been induced, by the promise of a government wage, to take up arms as 'forest rangers'. The result of this meeting was that the forest rangers resigned and returned their weapons. And that, Kurdish nationalists in Varto recall proudly, was the closest the district came to having a village guard system.

Schoolboy and schoolgirl committees were formed. At the Varto Lycée an angry adolescent, who later joined the PKK and fell in combat, explained to his peers what Kurdishness meant, and recommended texts – available in the form of grubby photocopies – by Apo and other luminaries. The teachers, futilely drumming into their pupils their Turkishness, stood little chance. In the villages, young boys ventured out at night to take pot shots at the garrison building. The conscripts inside – terrified kids, for the most part – longed for Mother and home.

Haydar took care not to expose the people to reprisals by the state. He restrained militants who urged the assassination of a prominent member of the Cibran tribe for being openly critical of the PKK. And when his wife Zinet – Celik's sister – was killed by the security forces further east, and her body brought back to Varto for burial, he is reputed to have contacted the local garrison commander and threatened a major attack if he did not have the road to Zinet's village cleared of snow so her cortège might pass. The garrison commander did as he was told. What chutzpah!

Young Kurdish PKK recruits, 1991

On one occasion, Haydar and his men had set up a checkpoint on the Mus Road, and were stopping buses and cars. One of the buses contained a policeman and his family. According to PKK rules of combat, the policeman should have been shot out of hand as an enemy combatant, but Haydar was moved by the entreaties of the man's wife, and spared his life on condition that he leave the force and never show his face again. The terrified policeman agreed, but he did not keep his side of the bargain. He returned to Varto and became known for his cruelty and use of torture.

'After the guerrillas came,' recalls one *Vartolu*, a young man at the time, 'there was a change in the attitude of the people. Whereas before, some of the older people had described them as murderers, now we young people realised that these "murderers" were in fact like our elder brothers.' The people referred to the militants as 'our children' or 'our children in the mountains'. On the morning minibus into Varto town a man might remark, 'The village got a visit from our children last night,' and everyone would be happy. A PKK fundraiser, a poor boy, was roundly scolded for buying his mother a chicken with the party's money. 'There was a strong feeling,' recalls the same *Vartolu*, 'that by next spring, by next autumn, we would be living in an independent Kurdistan.'

Where did that feeling come from? It came from the sudden leap, in recruitment and prestige, that the organisation made at the beginning of the 1990s. According to Ismet Imset, a highly experienced journalist who wrote extensively about the PKK, by 1992 the PKK had 6,000 men and women under arms and its network of recruiters and logistical operatives, misnomered *milis*, a bastardisation of the French *milice* or militia, numbered 45,000 people. The PKK was able to mobilise huge demonstrations in major towns across the south-east, and lockouts and strikes in protest at growing human rights abuses. The PKK had transformed the Kurdish New Year festival of Nevruz from a low-key cultural event to a massive annual protest. Militants roamed freely across large areas of eastern Turkey, entered into local truces with Turkish commanders and imposed 'visa' requirements on foreign journalists wanting to visit. The People's Labour Party, a PKK front, returned twenty-two deputies in the 1991 general elections, including a Varto Cibran. And still the Turkish establishment, unrepentant believers in a military solution, called on the militants to surrender.

By targeting 'traitors' with greater precision and economy, and by offering the village guards an amnesty, the PKK was able to contrast its restraint with the state's increasingly brutal behaviour. 'Special Teams', made up of PKK defectors, hoodlums and right-wing ideologues, had been deployed to take the fight to the PKK and its supporters. It was the beginning of a fracturing of the security forces that would dirty Turkey's patriotic war – hand it over to criminals, Turkish supremacists and sadists. There was a new feature, the extrajudicial execution of members of the *milis* and other supporters. Cracks appeared in relations between the armed forces and civilian administrators, some of whom refrained, out of fear, from criticising the PKK publicly. One district governor told Ismet Imset that he received constant abuse over the telephone from Turkish army commanders in his area. According to a 1992 report issued by the Turkish Human Rights Foundation, the security forces were implementing a 'terror' campaign; more than 1,000 non-combatants, including children caught in army crossfire, had lost their lives in the first six months of the year.

Varto would never experience total war. The Varto valley was too flat and treeless to accommodate large groups of militants, who gravitated to the Bingol and Serafettin Mountains. Fighting – an assault on the Ustukran garrison building in 1990, a running battle in Varto town during the 1991 election campaign – was exceptional. Rather, the state was being overwhelmed, gradually and insidiously. Outside Varto town the checkpoints proliferated – PKK checkpoints, where polite guerrillas in baggy trousers and cummerbund checked identity cards and collected 'donations'. The number of people bringing civil court actions dropped sharply as the PKK's tribunals, headed by militants, assumed responsibility for public order and private ethics. It only took a word from the *milis* for both bazaars in Varto town to shut in protest at some government atrocity, or in mourning for a fallen guerrilla. And, one 15 August, the anniversary of the PKK's first ever attack, hundreds of *Vartolu*s from dozens of villages converged on Varto town, chanting, 'Long Live Kurdistan! Long Live Chairman Apo! Long Live the PKK!' It was the biggest day of action in Varto's history, even if the entrances to Varto town were blocked by tanks and there were dozens of arrests.

Being highly disciplined, the PKK insisted on a disciplined society. Blood feuds became less common, and those that did break out were generally resolved peacefully. 'False friends', in Apo's words, those 'middle-way revolutionaries' pursuing impure goals, were punished with exemplary severity. There was the Varto petrol station operator, for instance, who failed to pass on money he had collected for the party and was found dead in his slippers, his mouth stuffed full of notes. His name was Kerem Geldi and years later, when I arrived in Varto, the gendarmerie captain would tell me that he had been killed simply for opposing the PKK.

Everyone had a son or a daughter, a father or uncle, 'in the mountains'. You got recruits coming from as far afield as Izmir, arriving on the bus, being greeted by the *milis* and transferred to the Bingol plateau. On one remarkable morning some twenty-five pupils at the Varto Lycée failed to turn up for school. They completed their education in the open air.

'My cousin was one of the first *Vartolu* guerrillas to fall. When I was five years old he came to our house. Everyone was sitting around the stove, talking and laughing, and he turned to me and said, "Are you a Turk or a Kurd?" I didn't know what he meant, but I remembered what they had told me at school, and I said, "I'm a Turk." He slapped me. Then he looked at me and said, "You're a Kurd!" From then on I was a Kurd.

'After he was martyred they brought his body back and a huge crowd went to meet it. He'd fallen in Elazigi. He'd gone to a village and the village headman had informed on him. His body was one of the first to come back to Varto. I shouted his name. And I thought, "I'll join and I'll avenge you."

'The guerrillas came to the villages but my family kept me away from them. Ours was a nationalist family – my ancestors had fought alongside Sheikh Sait – but they didn't want me joining. I asked my mother, "If I go, what will you do?" She said, "I'll kill myself." She told me to help the guerrillas, to give food and provisions, but not to go. I said, "If the soldiers come and take you I won't be able to stand it, and I'll attack them and they'll kill me." She said, "Why would they come and take me away?" I said, "They're taking away all sorts of people these days."

'I knew the guerrillas were going to the house of a friend in another village. I said, "When they next come, let me know, so I can make contact." A little later his elder brother came and spoke to me and I said, "I want to join." And he said, "Well, there's a group that's going."

'I thought it over for a couple of days. I didn't sleep. I said to myself: "There's winter up there, and hunger and thirst, and death, but it's better than this." To die with honour. I went to my school friend Erkan and told him, "I'm joining." He began by saying, "Don't go this year. We'll join together next year." Eventually he said, "All right; we'll join together." I had a girlfriend at that time. I phoned her. I wanted to say, "Sorry. It didn't work out." But she didn't answer. I told the *milis*, "My mind is made up."

'We went to the appointed spot in Alangoz. The *milis* were there. We stayed the day under the trees, but no one came for us. Then we went home. Word had got around that some people were trying to join. I bumped into my father in the street and he said, "What are you doing?" I said, "Nothing. I went somewhere, that's all." My father said, "I'm sending you to Mus to stay with your uncles."

'We had a new departure time: Sunday at five p.m. I had to go to Mus first, to my cousin's wedding. If I didn't go, my family would know something was up. I told Erkan I would be back that evening and that we would go together. I went to the wedding. I danced and sang and had my photo taken with the bride and groom. I said to my cousins, "Let's go to the market and wander around." We shot some pool and then I said, "I'll just pop out to see an old school friend and then come back." My cousin said, "If you're not back in an hour, I'll turn Mus upside down."

'I went to the bus station and boarded the first minibus. It was about four p.m. The minibus seemed to be going slowly. "Go faster! Go faster!" The driver said, "It's Sunday. The banks and post office are closed. What are you in such a hurry for?" We came to a checkpoint. The soldier told me to get out. He looked at my identity card and reeled off the names of my dead cousin and two other members of my family who had become guerrillas. He said, "Where are they?" I replied, "My cousin was killed. I don't know where the other two are." I thought to myself, "Tomorrow you'll be able to add me to your list."

'I rushed to Alangoz. I saw Erkan among the willows, smiling. Two of the others hadn't come. There were two *milis*. Night fell and we moved off, on our bellies, going up the hill. Armoured cars were on the roads, using their searchlights. The authorities had got wind of something.

'We decided to split up and wait for the signal – three whistles. The signal came and we carried on climbing. When we reached the top we hugged – now we were guerrillas!

'We walked across Varto in the direction of Karliova. At Inali we stopped at a house but the woman inside wouldn't open the door. She told us there were soldiers around but to help ourselves to what food we could find. We found some bread in the stable. There was some yoghurt in a trough in front of the well.

'We kept walking. There was no water. Not a drop. We stopped to smoke, shielding the burning end with our hands. They took us along a route that we didn't know; if someone decided to flee, he wouldn't know where he was. We started to tire. Our feet hurt. Erkan dropped from thirst and I said, "Come on!" One of the comrades advised against eating the yoghurt we had picked up at Inali, saying it would make us thirstier, but I decided to have some anyway. The yoghurt seemed to have solidified. I realised it was plaster, not yoghurt! I offered some to the others, and we had a laugh. One of the comrades told us to wait and he would bring water. He came back an hour later with water. We walked on.

'We slept the following day, under the trees, and that's when we lost our deserter. One of the comrades fell asleep on duty and the deserter slipped away.

'We chose our codenames that day. I chose the name of my nephew. We met up with another group at Emeran. We set out for the HQ in Bingol. It took us three days to get there. We went through a couple of villages and they gave us food. Everyone behaved warmly towards us. They were good families. Our morale was sky-high.

'We reached HQ and we saw lots of people we knew. Twenty or twenty-five of them were from Varto. Everyone took care of us. Before drinking themselves they insisted we drink. Before eating they insisted we eat. It was a beautiful place. Then it was 15 August – the anniversary of the PKK's first attack. The comrades brought twenty villagers to the camp. There was dancing and we held races and competitions. We gave the villagers our expensive watches; we had no use for them now. Then we took them back to their villages.

'That day we left HQ. We were about seventy in number. We went to another open place. Three days later there was an engagement. The army was on one side, we were on the other. They injured two of ours, and we counter-attacked to evacuate the injured. Then it was fighting at close quarters. I saw a female guerrilla cut to pieces. There was nothing we new recruits could do, unarmed, wearing civilian clothes. They had taught us how to take a gun apart, but we still didn't have our own. We simply protected ourselves.

'The soldiers were shouting. They were swearing. They had heard the voices of our female guerrillas. Our people were swearing. In the end three of ours were martyred, one of them a *Vartolu*. The soldiers withdrew to one of the peaks. When we recovered the bodies, we saw that they had cut off their fingers and their ears. They'd cut off their penises. They'd cut them to bits. I took a gun that had belonged to one of the martyrs.'

'That winter was really bad. Our camps had fallen into enemy hands. We were always outside. Sometimes we didn't see anything for a week. We were in tents. We would sleep on the warm ashes of the fires we had made during the day. We ate soup: water, flour and salt. I barely remember seeing bread that winter.

'In theory every squad had its own radio, but then there were battery shortages. Or you'd have the batteries but no radio. You had tea but no sugar, tobacco but no cigarette papers. A bear or a boar might find your provisions and ruin them; the enemy might do the same. We received some rudimentary training. What is Socialism? What is communal living? Then we were thrown into the practicalities.

'During a long engagement I remember hearing one of the Turkish officers shouting into his radio, "We're stuck here dying of hunger and you don't send us food. You're not being fair!" And the other officer said, "Aren't you ashamed? On the other side are people who haven't eaten for fifteen days." Even the enemy sees your power of resilience. On eight or nine occasions, in order not to fall into the hands of the enemy, I was prepared to pull the pin and blow myself up. You think, "I'll die, but I won't surrender."

'Summer was our season. We would cut the electricity line to the army post; that would force them to come and carry out repairs, and then we'd attack. Or we'd lay a trap when they were on their way back from an operation. They might have been out for two days, looking for us in vain, trying to kill us. And then, dog-tired, resigned, they'd come back. We'd take out the first two or the last two vehicles in the convoy. Two minutes flat. Then you had to flee, lose yourself. If you did that, they would have a hard time finding you. Our message was this: "Don't come into my territory. If you come into my territory, this is what happens."

'The enemy's approach was to surround us. We might find ourselves encircled by three rings. The answer was to break out at the earliest opportunity and get away. If you couldn't, you kept them at bay until nightfall and then slipped through. If you were on a peak, in a good position, you stayed put.

'Our objective was to wake the Kurdish people. We said to the enemy: you may have the power to take our wives and to kill us and torture us, but we have our power too, our guerrillas. The object wasn't to kill. The key objective was to bring into being a people who say, "We are Kurds."

'The state burned most of the villages where we were in Bingol. They left three or four people in each village. We would go to these houses for supplies. After we'd gone the villager might go and tell the authorities, but only after giving us a head start. Sometimes we'd go and get supplies from a neighbouring district. It would take us a week to bring them back on mules. Or we'd give some villagers a list of things. The villagers knew that by going to buy batteries and sugar they ran the risk of being arrested, but they went nonetheless. The authorities kept tabs on the amount of batteries and sugar being sold. The villagers would slowly hoard things for us ... who else were they going to help, if not us?

'I didn't speak to my family for two years. I said to myself, "I won't remind them of me. I won't upset them." I was in Karakocan, where my cousin had been martyred. I'd fallen and a sharp stone had gone right into my leg. I bound it and went to a village and the villager looked at me and said, "Aren't you going to call your mother?" The other comrades said, "Call!" I was feeling emotional because of my cousin. I took the phone and dialled. My mother picked up the phone.

I was in two minds as to whether or not to talk. She said, "Hello," twice, and then she said, "Son? Is that you?" I said, "Yes," and she fainted. My father came and spoke. He cried a bit. He complained: "Why don't you call?"

'Here's a photograph. It was developed years after it was taken. That's me. I didn't have a beard back then. Here's a comrade from Diyarbakir. He blew himself up after running out of bullets. This comrade was martyred. This one's in jail. That one's in Europe. Here's one from Varto. Martyred. This one: also martyred. And this one. Note that everyone is smiling.'

Briefly it seemed that the PKK might force the state to moderate its policies. After Turgut Ozal stood down from the premiership and succeeded General Evren as president, he softened his former militaristic position somewhat, allowing the use of the Kurdish languages in music and books, developing relations with the Kurds of northern Iraq and even (so the rumour went), considering the possibility of turning Turkey into a federal state. Hopes rose further when a new prime minister, that survivor Suleyman Demirel, assured delighted crowds in the Kurdish region that he recognised Turkey's 'Kurdish reality'.

Ozal's sudden death in 1993 came during a unilateral PKK ceasefire that had prompted the government to consider a limited amnesty for PKK militants. The ceasefire ended soon after, with the slaughter by the PKK of more than thirty unarmed conscripts in the Bingol Mountains, which in turn was met with a military response of great severity. Demirel had ascended to the presidency in place of Ozal, and Turkey soon got its first female prime minister, in the form of the inexperienced and little known Tansu Ciller. Ciller came to power full of ideas about the Kurdish question. She proposed Kurdish-language broadcasts on state TV and devolved government for the Kurdish region along the lines of that provided for the Basque region of Spain. But her proposals were opposed by the establishment and she, concerned not to lose the support of her party, quickly became an advocate of a military solution, accelerating the process of village clearances and initiating moves to have several pro-Apo parliamentary deputies jailed. It was in Ciller's time, a later judicial inquiry was to find, that 'an execution squad was set up within the state', a squad responsible for the deaths of many of the estimated 5,000 Kurds who were mysteriously killed between 1990 and 1996.

And so, seventy years after Sheikh Sait, the state continued to apply military logic to a problem of culture and identity. Its budget swollen, its arsenal improved, the army got better at fighting the PKK. Troops flooded into a much expanded war zone: 300,000 ranged over a much larger area against a few thousand militants. The army learned to infiltrate the enemy, recruit informers and penetrate the illegal drugs trade from which the PKK derived much revenue. Above all, the state got more brutal. A twilight counter-insurgency, at one remove from the ordeal of the gendarmerie conscript seeing out his eighteen months, came into being. Its stock in trade was torture, targeted killings and the burning of villages, and its practitioners were those sickos and opportunists, peddlers of arms, narcotics and murderous xenophobia, who never wanted it to end. The war had long been in the bloodstream of the east. Now it came to dominate policy-making in Ankara on issues as diverse as foreign relations and democratisation. Inflation; corruption; the sluggish pace of economic and political reform; Turkey's every ailment seemed hostage to the next big military push in the east.

According to the Turkish journalist Nadire Mater, some 2.5 million young Turks served in the war zone between 1984 and 1999 in carrying out their compulsory military service. Taking into account their families, the number of Turks involved in the war was around fifteen million, a little less than a quarter of Turkey's population. Mater's *Mehmet's Book*, made up of the reminiscences of forty-two conscripts, is a portrait of young people who go off to kill and die – in some cases, without knowing why. For every tub-thumping chauvinist she spoke to – those who, upon returning to civilian life, found themselves longing for the consoling certainties of rage and patriotism – Mater came across many others who evinced bewilderment, sadness and cynicism. The sons of rich men were rarely to be found in the war zone; exploiting their personal connections, they would arrange cushy postings to the Black Sea. Amid the fear and boredom and the beatings that were a feature of garrison life, the manipulation of casualty figures and the vast operations which cost millions and yielded a dozen PKK bodies, there was a sense that the burden of conflict was the poor's to carry.

'Two teams enter,' recalled one infantryman, a participant in a village clearance. 'Searches; clearance; destruction and burning. The petrol catches, the sides of the houses are burning. We're watching the village burn ... I found the answer to all my questions here. I saw that the state wants this to go on. For, if the state attended to the cultural, linguistic and racial rights of these people, and improved their living conditions, there would be no war.'

Implicit in these accounts is the conviction that the war, against a guerrilla enemy, can never be won. 'You can't put a soldier everywhere,' observed one interviewee. 'There are twenty-five or thirty of you. You can't compete with ten terrorists. Because the terrorist is changing his position all the time, day and night. We tire more quickly ... the soldier is the seeker, and the seeker is easily hunted ...'

Mater's soldiers spoke with awe and fear of the Special Teams, those well-paid neo-Fascists who had turned the region into a charnel. 'They all wore bandanas,' ran one description, 'all ex-policemen, completely sold on a warrior image of themselves, guys dressed like Rambo.' Wilder still were those freelance assassins whom the state would not publicly acknowledge: men like Green. Green was allegedly responsible for the deaths of dozens of PKK militants and supporters, until his own disappearance in 1994. He appeared thus in the reminiscence of a conscript serving in Mus:

'A tall well-built bearded fellow arrived. He was accompanied by a beautiful woman. We knew this was Green, we just didn't know how famous he was. They sat for an hour; I waited on them. In the garrison they told me how many people he had killed. They speak of him with admiration ... five people who killed soldiers are brought to the Mus garrison for interrogation. After interrogation, it's said that Green took them outside the town, stuffed their mouths with grenades, shot them from a distance and then brought back their bodies ... a dynamic man, like a legend ...'

You can't give latitude to people like Green and expect to retain sight of the values, of justice and accountability, on which the republic is supposed to rest. You don't offer, as the state is rumoured to have done, twenty million lira per terrorist scalp without getting a lot of non-terrorist scalps.

The murder of a counter-terrorism commander reportedly involved in narcotics smuggling; the suspicious death of the head of the commandos; the scandalous association of a senior policeman, a Kurdish tribal chief and Turkey's most wanted hitman, which lasted for years before coming to light in 1996 – these attest to a blurring of the battle lines.

The cost, for the general health of the Turkish state, was high. But the meeting of terror with terror bore fruit. The mid-1990s, when the state gave itself over to violence, was also the time when civilian Kurds finally appreciated the distance that continued to separate them from their cherished goal of an independent or autonomous Kurdistan, and recalibrated their relations with the PKK accordingly. The number of *Vartolu*s joining the PKK levelled off, then started to fall. The walls in Varto town, formerly daubed with nationalist slogans – 'Long Live Kurdistan!' – received a new message: 'Surrender to the state's magnanimous embrace.' The Kurdish eye had been clouded and its heart corrupted, and that was the state's great achievement.

Qarapungar, in the foothills of the Serafettin Mountains in south-eastern Varto, exemplified the change. This was supposedly a nationalist village, inhabited in part by descendants of Sheikh Sait and Halit Bey of the Cibrans, a village that had provided several recruits for the PKK. Cracks appeared when several of the villagers were induced to take up arms as village guards. In 1992 one of these men was killed by the PKK. A second man, with a Kurdish nationalist past and a pro-government present, was also killed. Then, in 1994, four guerrillas fell in an engagement with the security forces near Qarapungar, followed by three local shepherds, the latter slaughtered, allegedly, at the behest of a village guard.

What followed was typical of thousands of villages across Turkey's Kurdish region, now that the countryside was being depopulated and laid bare. The security forces stripped naked and tortured two Kurdish nationalists in view of the other villagers. They destroyed several houses and drove their owners out of the district. Over the course of the next few months the bodies of more PKK militants were found in the vicinity of Qarapungar. Who had killed them? Green? Local men who were once in good standing with the PKK? The effect of these incidents was to deplete the population and to turn the villagers against each other. It was no longer possible to tell who was an informant, and who was not.

The state's tactics, to terrify people and humiliate them and divide them, were being replicated across Varto. Several villages that received a lot of PKK visits were partly or completely emptied. The inhabitants ended up in Diyarbakir and further afield. Severe beatings and sundry humiliations were administered.

> SOLDIER: My son, are you afraid of me?
> SUSPECT: Yes, I'm scared.
> SOLDIER: What? Am I God that you should be afraid of me? (Beats him viciously.)
> SOLDIER: Now tell me, son, are you scared of me?
> SUSPECT: No, I'm not scared of you.
> SOLDIER: Why aren't you afraid of me? (Beats with greater vigour.)

Bans were placed on the summer migration to the upper pastures; hundreds of sheep and goats, sweltering on the valley floor, fell ill and died. A group of village headmen were pressed into building latrines for an army post. The entire population of Badan, a village that had produced some fifteen guerrillas, was held for a day in the blazing heat in the garrison compound. The gendarmes put it about that the people of Badan were in fact Armenian – a lie. (The same lie that the captain fed me when I arrived in Varto in 2005.) The network of informants had spread to almost every village. The arrival of a militant, or even of a stranger, was immediately reported to the gendarmerie.

Some informants played a double game, acting as advocates for arrested nationalists, arranging the payment of a sum to secure release. They denounced their own enemies and rivals, regardless of guilt, and scooped up the perks. Green cards, issuing from the district governorate and affording the bearer free health care and other advantages, were distributed as sweeteners. The PKK *milis* may have been infiltrated. Strikes were now being called with counterproductive frequency; the people grew weary.

It was hard nowadays to be sure of anything. The district governor was accused of being a Sunni extremist. The state suspected the mayor of having PKK sympathies, but the PKK started threatening him. The headman of a village in eastern Varto was murdered, allegedly for informing on some guerrillas; others thought money was the issue.

A second village headman, a friend of the PKK, was also murdered. Every week or two, at night, Varto town would be disturbed by gunfire, which started in the evening and went on until dawn. The PKK raided the town, said the state, but no one saw any militants, there were no dead bodies or spent PKK shells, and the houses of prominent Kurdish nationalists got shot up. These 'engagements' were in fact pieces of theatre, staged by the state, to introduce fear and uncertainty into the lives of the people.

No more was this a romantic war of liberation. There would be no liberation. The population of Varto started to fall dramatically as people went away, and the rural economy to die. For many the alternative to migration was destitution, repeated beatings, and the possibility of a violent death at the hands of the state's assassins.

Sitting one evening with Naci, the owner of the Karinca stationery shop, I asked him to tell me about the time that the Karinca was burned to the ground.

'There had been gunfire the whole night. Lots of people got caught in their workplaces or in the tea houses by the shooting and had to stay there until dawn.

'They came to our house at about 10.30 p.m. There were six of them, masked. They asked for my brother Kazim. Another of my brothers, Cemalettin, said, "Kazim's not here. How can I help?" They said, "It's Kazim we want." One of them spoke into his walkie-talkie, saying, "Kazim isn't here, but Cemalettin is." And the voice replied, "Take Cemalettin."

'The only other people at home were my mother and father. They didn't know how to use the telephone. The sound of gunfire was coming from outside. Cemalettin said to them in Kurdish, "Give the word that they've arrested me."

'Off they went, walking down the street. The garrison was a mere fifty metres away. "Maybe," Cemalettin thought, "they're taking me there." But they passed the garrison building.

'Until now, it had seemed possible that the six men were guerrillas, even if their use of Turkish military terms suggested not. But by walking brazenly past the garrison building, they showed they were not guerrillas. They made as if to take the village road, up the hill. Cemalettin said, "No, I'm going no further. If you want to kill me, kill me here."

'They dragged him up the hill until they got to an open piece of land. He was handcuffed and blindfolded. The sound of gunfire was still coming from around the town. They were saying, "Where's Kazim? It's Kazim we need." Cemalettin was saying, "I don't know where he is." Time passed. At about five in the morning the voice came over the walkie-talkie: "Did you find out where Kazim is?" They replied, "No."

"In that case," came the response, "kill Cemalettin."

"They got Cemalettin down on his knees. He heard the sound of the bullet being loaded and the gun being cocked. And then another order came through the walkie-talkie.

' "Leave Cemalettin. Torch the stationery shop."

'Cemalettin didn't understand much of this. The words he heard were, "You can go home." He didn't believe his ears. Overjoyed, he walked back down the hill and went to our uncle's house. He banged on the door. "Open up, Uncle; I'm frozen." Uncle woke up his children, got them up and told Cemalettin to lie down in their warm bed. Lying there, Cemalettin remembered what the voice had said over the walkie-talkie: "Leave Cemalettin. Torch the stationery shop." He phoned home. No answer. He phoned our sister. She said, "We got news that they've burned the shop. Everyone's down there now."

'Someone had phoned my mother and told her, "Run! Your shop is being burned to the ground! Run and stop them!" But when she got there she found armoured cars parked in front, and the Special Team prevented her from intervening. Then Kazim turned up. The window was broken and the counter was burning. The shelves were beginning to burn. Kazim tried to intervene but the Special Team wouldn't let him. "Let me in!" he begged them. Then he ran at the window and smashed it with his elbow but that only let more oxygen in; there was a roar and the flames spread everywhere. Someone ran off to get the fire brigade but the Special Team attacked him on the way and his head was injured. Somehow the fire brigade was informed but the Special Team prevented them from getting to the fire. Still Kazim was shouting, "Let me in! That's fifteen years' work in there!" They beat him. He started swearing. They started swearing. My sister leaped on Kazim to prevent him being hurt but the Special Team beat her with their rifle butts and broke her arm. And they beat Kazim so badly he was left in a coma and had to be taken to hospital in Erzurum.

'Cemalettin arrived, still wearing his suit. Everyone else was covered in mud and dust. He said, "Let's go home. Leave it. It's better that property burns than lives are lost."'

We have seen this before. Something similar happened on a larger scale at Sirnak, to the south, in 1992, when the state half-destroyed the town after a force of PKK militants tried to liberate it. Then, when the dust settled, and guerrilla numbers were revised steadily downwards, and the locals started to talk, it became clear that there had been no PKK force, not even a small one. The Battle of Sirnak had not been a battle but a drawn-out punitive spasm, a two-day spree by vandals wearing the colours of the Turkish state and trashing anything they saw.

Varto town's version of the Battle of Sirnak is called the Siege of Varto, and here, too, the headline is misleading. We cannot be sure, of course, for we are dealing with recent history, whose purveyors are unreliable, incorrigibly biased eyewitnesses. The Siege of Varto started at around nine p.m. on 17 September 1996. More than that, it is hard to say.

Taking its cue from the governor of Mus, the national newspaper *Milliyet* announces in its 19 September edition that the town of Varto was 'blockaded' by terrorists on the night of 17 September and that a Special Team policeman was killed and two further Special Team policemen, two civilians and seven soldiers injured. The terrorists, *Milliyet* goes on, fired their rocket launchers and rifles indiscriminately on houses and public buildings. A curfew was imposed, skirmishes continued at various points, and 'piles of hay that were on the roofs of outlying houses, along with those houses that had been hit by rockets, started to burn'.

On 20 September the newspaper reports that the PKK force numbered sixty people. Varto has now returned to 'normal' and the curfew has been lifted. According to the governor, thirty people have been questioned and five arrested in connection with the incident; he denies allegations that the security forces, succumbing to sectarian spite, have singled out Alevis for particular harassment: 'we have tried very hard not to vex the people during the searches'. Peace reigns over the town, though the façades of houses are riddled with bullet holes. Tansu Ciller's successor as prime minister, the Islamist Necmettin Erbakan, has expressed his chagrin, ordering that all 'necessary help' be afforded to the people of Varto.

What, after this heartening news, is the *Milliyet* reader to make of a report, published the following day, that there has been a fresh round of fighting in Varto, in spite of the presence of hundreds of security personnel? These new developments have raised 'questions', the newspaper observes, without identifying the questions, let alone answering them. The district governor in Mus has refrained from commenting on this latest fighting; the questioning of thirty suspects from the original incident 'continues'. And that, for now, is the sum of *Milliyet*'s coverage of the Siege of Varto.

An awful lot is missing. What of that unlucky bystander, a visitor to the district, who was shot dead at his window in the Berlin Hotel? Why is there no mention of the streets, teeming with armoured cars, tanks and soldiers, of the ruined shopfronts and cars? The hundreds of male *Vartolus* who were dragged on bleeding knees to detention points in the centre of Varto, and there humiliated and reviled – they, too, have been forgotten. Finally, what about the arrest of a number of Kurdish nationalists, including one whose interrogation, directed at extracting a 'confession', featured the passing of an electric current through his penis and testicles? What is the meaning of these events, and why are they not in the nation's newspaper?

A clue comes some days later. A parliamentary deputy called Fuat Firat (no relation of Mehmet Serif Firat), a Kurdish nationalist with connections in Varto, makes a sensational declaration to journalists in Ankara. According to Fuat Firat, Varto was not the object of a PKK attack on 17 September, but the scene of a dispute between a regular policeman and some members of the Special Team, over a 'prostitute' living opposite the police station.

When the policeman was in the woman's house, says Firat, the Special Team raided it. The policeman was killed at the door to the house. 'It was announced that the PKK had carried out an attack and that fighting had lasted for hours between the PKK and the security forces.' On the contrary, Firat says; the security forces, embarrassed by an egregious disciplinary lapse, shot up the town to make it look as though the PKK had attacked. And it was the Special Team, he adds, not the PKK, that set fire to the hay.

From now on the truth will be shrouded behind speculation and innuendo. The 'prostitute' in question turns out not to be a prostitute, but a civil servant. She happens to have a family connection to a prominent Varto Alevi, a famous supporter of the Turkish state, who, in his youth, took the republic's side against Sheikh Sait. Her detractor, Fuat Firat, the man who destroyed her reputation, is a prominent descendant of the sheikh. Might this be a new instalment of an old story?

The lady in question will be forced, from unsolicited celebrity, to leave Varto for distant Izmir. From there she will open and win a legal case for defamation against Firat. Firat, after paying damages, will maintain that the witnesses he called were intimidated into silence by the Special Team. The majority of *Vartolus*, pruriently fascinated, remain convinced that there was no PKK attack that night. How, they ask, might the PKK gain from shooting up the houses and setting alight the hay of their supporters?

We know, or think we know, the following:

The Special Team issued a call for help, after the first shots. It went something like this: 'All of Varto is in insurrection! For God's sake, come and save us!' Reinforcements arrived and, that night, in the words of the mayor at the time, Varto became 'Texas'.

The following day, after the shooting ended, after the whole town had been searched for guerrillas and the detention centres filled, there was a standoff between the regular police and the Special Team outside the police station. According to one eyewitness, the regular police fired over the heads of the Special Team to dissuade them from turning their fury on the populace prone before them; there were fears of a general massacre.

That night, twenty-four hours after the event, Special Team policemen set out from Mus, intent on avenging their colleague. The head of the Mus army garrison, concerned to avoid a bloodbath, ordered them turned back at the Abdulrahman Pasha Bridge. ('If they had got to Varto,' recalls the mayor of the time, 'they would have laid it waste.') Then there is the curious decision suddenly to release the hundreds of detainees without charging any of them, and, after that, a statement issued by the Varto gendarmerie disclaiming any involvement in the incident.

Some good did, in the end, come of the Siege of Varto. Less than a week later, the general staff put out a public relations manual, aimed particularly at the Special Team, urging representatives of the state serving in the south-east to avoid establishing their authority 'on a basis of pressure and fear'. A few weeks later – on the urging, apparently, of the regular army and the governor of Mus – the Special Team was abruptly withdrawn from Varto, and the people breathed a little easier.

The Siege of Varto was not a siege, but a misunderstanding.

'It was the first time I had entered Varto in all those years. We were a group of eight. We stayed with the family of another *Vartolu* guerrilla. I was full of emotion, back on home territory.

'We were to recover our stores, meet up with another group coming from the north-west, and send them off east into the Serhat region, and from there into Iran. We were to do some scouting, learn the routes, bring up the Erzurum force and link them up with the Serhat force. That was the plan. And we were to collect provisions and bury them so the next groups wouldn't need to enter the villages. We set off in two or three groups. We dug our emplacements and went off to get provisions. We collected some equipment that had come from Europe the previous year.

'We were in a village right on the border between Hinis and Varto. On our tenth or fifteenth day one of the villagers informed on us. The army was ready. It was early morning. The enemy came along the road from Hinis, into the valley. Not a big valley but a good valley, lots of trees, suitable for fighting. They filled the head of the valley with men and blocked off the bottom of the valley and started firing. We were now only four, but they thought we were seventy. They wanted to wipe out seventy guerrillas. They had put men across in the Bingol Mountains, too. Everywhere that lay within a day's march.

'We listened to their radio contact. The soldiers were saying, "Sir, we've killed and wounded a great many of them. They're evacuating their wounded." They'd thrown three rings around us: one narrow ring, one wider ring, and one ring at a day's march.

'We stayed there among them for five days, moving around. They couldn't see us for the trees. We didn't fire at them. We said, "Until they see us, let's not start anything." Eventually we were forced to return fire and it became obvious that we were only four.

'Still, they didn't dare come closer. A conscript does eighteen months. He's got a child at home. People are waiting for him. He's got a life before him. We don't have that. I'm staring death in the face. But he's waiting for his eighteen months to end. He's scared even to shoot, for fear that we'll know his position and fire back. We throw stones. Everyone fixes their eyes on the spot where the stone lands.

'They withdrew a bit. The Cobras came and shot up the place. They brought up the mortars, but still they didn't know where we were. That night we slept twenty metres from the nearest soldier.

'This went on for four days and then our batteries ran out and we were unable to listen to the enemy. On the fifth night they used night-vision equipment and saw us. They were about one mile away. We moved at five the next morning. Three enemy squads were approaching from behind us. We could hear them moving through the trees. They thought we were still asleep. Then they were upon us. We fired. The four of us escaped unscathed. We were wearing Turkish army hats. I mistook one of my comrades for a soldier and took aim and almost shot him. I was in a cold sweat.

'That night we covered our faces in mud and waded through the water so their thermal detection equipment wouldn't pick us up, and we got through the first circle.

'Think of it; that was the welcome we got when we returned to Varto: 5,000 soldiers turning out to greet us!

'We got some information from a shepherd. We got some batteries from him. We headed towards the forest at Kunaf. The road was full of armoured cars. We had to prolong our route. We stayed a couple of days near Kayalidere; the operation was still going on. They burned part of the forest. They thought we were still in there. They tossed some chemical bombs down from the planes. That was on the fifth day. We couldn't enter the village to get food. The soldiers had surrounded it.

'We were heading towards Varto town. Fifteen days had elapsed; no one had heard word from us. The TV announced that four terrorists had been killed. Still we didn't break radio silence. Our comrades thought we'd been martyred. The comrades in Iraq announced our names, and that we'd been martyred.

'We went to my uncle's house. My hair was very long. I'd just started growing a beard, and I had sideburns and a thin moustache. My hair was filthy. I'd got much thinner. My clothes were in a state. That's how I arrived.

'My aunt brought tea. She forgot to bring a spoon. She went to get the spoon and forgot to bring the sugar. She was very excited, crying. I said, "Don't tell anyone I'm here." Then my mother came. "I want to kiss your feet," she said. The first night the others slept and I didn't sleep. The following morning my sister-in-law came in holding a tray and saw me. Her knees bent and she dropped the tray. She wrapped her arms around my legs and I bent down and got her to her feet. She wept.

'My brother came and he couldn't speak. He went bright red. Everyone made a point of showing equal affection and concern to my comrades. My family said, "You've got us around you but their families aren't here. If we hug you they will be unhappy." So they hugged the others more than me. My mother said, "I'm going to wash your hair now." I said, "Come off it; I've grown out of that!" I think she wanted to look over my head and check I hadn't been injured. She used one and a half packets of shampoo.

'We spent three or four days there. Everyone thought we were dead. The enemy didn't know that we'd got out of their circle. It was a question of waiting until the atmosphere calmed. They wouldn't guess that we'd go to our own village. I looked out of the window and saw old school friends pass. For a moment I wanted to live like a normal person.

'When we left I didn't cry. I thought, "If I cry, they'll cry all the more." We set up the radio near to Kulan and established contact with our comrades. Everyone was astonished to hear our voices. They shouted. They'd written poems in our memory. We reported what had happened. We went to Karliova, joined another group, and then headed towards Bingol.

'Later I learned that they had been to my father's house and said, "Your son's dead; come and collect his body." They'd done that several times before. It's one of their tactics. A few days later they came and asked him, "Where's your son?" He replied, "You just came and told me he was dead!" '

Deep State

At the first thaw, a shepherd saw them. They were sitting at the base of a rock: three men. The shepherd was alarmed and didn't come close. The following day he saw them again. They were in the same position. He approached warily and saw that they were dead.

They had been denounced and forced to flee the village they were wintering in. They had been making for a hiding place and got caught in a blizzard, losing their way. They froze to death there, wrapped in socks and plastic bags, and they had stayed, embracing against the cold, until spring.

IN FEBRUARY 1999, FIVE months after Syria expelled him under pressure from Turkey, sojourning unhappily in Kenya, Apo was delivered up – by the Americans, it is thought – to Turkish special forces. The prime minister was Ecevit once more, an old man now. He trembled as he announced the news at a press conference. The president, the elderly Demirel, called it 'The most important event in the history of the republic.' Millions of Turks were delighted. The Kurds were shocked and angry. Dozens set themselves on fire in protest.

That November, after his trial on the prison island of Imrali, off Istanbul, Apo was convicted of treason and sentenced to death. Soon after, the parliament in Ankara outlawed capital punishment, and Apo's sentence was duly commuted to life imprisonment. The action of the parliament upset many Turkish nationalists, but it had the advantages of keeping alive Turkey's application to join the European Union, averting the possibility of civil strife between Kurds and Turks in the cities of western Turkey and, perversely, preserving an expedient ally of the Turkish state.

For this is what Apo had become. Since his capture, in statements and during his trial, Apo had disavowed the principles in whose name he had dispatched thousands of young men and women to their deaths. The Kurds, he declared, 'lie within the Turkish national entity'. The PKK's original objective, an independent Marxist Kurdistan, was a 'demonstrably unattainable and unnecessary ... fantasy'. Apo's respect for the Turkish flag was complete, his desire to 'serve' the republic unimpeachable. His regard for Ataturk shone brightly. From Imrali he ordered his guerrillas to withdraw from Turkey into northern Iraq and observe a ceasefire.

By allowing him to communicate through his lawyers with the PKK's leadership council, the Turkish authorities enabled Apo to preserve his dominance over an organisation that had looked, immediately after his capture, as though it might fracture. The leadership council had declared all directives from a captive Apo to be non-binding; it now reversed this decision. Apo's order to withdraw from Turkey was implemented without demur, his 'sacred cause of peace' adopted *in toto*.

Apo's arrest, and his craven performance in court, did indeed spur a small number of PKK commanders to break away and form splinter groups, based in northern Iraq, which subsequently came into conflict with the PKK. In Istanbul a few publishing houses run by disaffected Kurdish nationalists began to print books critical of the Chairman and his way of doing things.

In one of the best-known of these critiques, whose title, *Apo's Verses*, ironically underscores the leader's claims to Prophet-like authority, the Bingol Kurd Selim Curukkaya described Apo's hostility towards those former prison inmates, veterans of the 'Diyarbakir Resistance' of the early 1980s, who were freed under an amnesty and rejoined the guerrilla ranks. Apo seems to have felt insecure among these heroes, and he bridled at their unwillingness to submit to the culture of self-criticism that he had promoted during their incarceration. Over time, using his favoured methods of denunciation, public humiliation and violence, Apo was able to destroy the legend of the Diyarbakir Resistance and the prestige of its survivors.

A second critic was none other than the Varto Alevi Mehmet Can Yuce, author of the hagiographic *Sun that Rises in the East*. Now, in a new book, *Upshot of a Misapprehension*, he wrote an account of Apo's capture and capitulation. 'He dropped to his knees before the enemy ... He surrendered in the full sense of the word, he committed his betrayal and gradually established the paramountcy of surrender, betrayal and the practice of elimination in the party; in this way he brought about a defeat unparalleled in our history.' Yuce blamed the 'personality cult' that Apo had enshrined at the heart of the PKK, and the 'arbitrary leadership' he exercised.

I wonder why it took Yuce, one of the original and longest-serving adherents to the cult, a former champion of arbitrary leadership, so long to walk away. The same goes for Selim Curukkaya – and for Nizamettin Tas, the boy from Alangoz who defected from the PKK in 2003. It must have been obvious early on that Apo was turning his movement into a personal dictatorship, and yet these men remained enthralled. Power is part of the explanation, for these village boys

Abdullah Ocalan handcuffed, 1999

retained, as long as they basked in Apo's favour, a gratifying influence over comrades in the field and compatriots around Kurdistan. Fear, too, must have been a factor: the fear of being branded a traitor, and perhaps a more philosophical fear, lurking in the mind of every fanatic, that the cause for which he has killed and suffered, spilt blood and ink, will turn out to be a fraud.

During my time as a journalist in Turkey, writing from my Kemalist perspective, the aspirations of the Kurds for independence or autonomy had seemed presumptuous and unwise. I doubted whether this, in fact, was what many of them wanted. Now, after spending time in the rebel land, I have revised my opinion; it is a solecism on the landscape that the Kurds of Turkey, living contiguously and without large minorities, fired with a strong national consciousness, should not enjoy – at the least – considerable autonomy.

But what if the autonomous region of Turkish Kurdistan were run by Apo and his myrmidons? It is hard to envisage a happy future for such a place. One imagines it with its own apparatus of repression, its secret policemen and torturers – and a brimming Diyarbakir military jail.

The PKK did not, in the end, become a vehicle for the Kurds' uplift. It incorporated some of the worst aspects of life in Kurdistan – the culture of denunciation and the personal despotisms – and put them at the service of a monstrous cult. 'No philosophical definition or theoretical judgement is sufficiently commodious to accommodate Abdullah Ocalan.' Thus a line from the preface to *The Language and Operation of Reality* (author: A. Ocalan). To confound is also to dazzle, and the majority of Kurds in Turkey have preferred to be dazzled than confront the cruelty, hypocrisy and cowardice of their leader. Blinded by the iconography, unwilling to disavow their past beliefs, they have found reassurance in the chimera of Apo's genius and omniscience, the impossibility of knowing him and the necessity of trusting absolutely to his mysterious ways. In the Kandil Mountains the young dupes justify his U-turns with such platitudes as, 'It is easier to make war than to make peace.'

Not for Apo, it wasn't.

Of all those who have taken up their pen to criticise the PKK, it's perhaps the female militants who have the most compelling things to say. For them, wrote the author Nejdet Buldan, prefacing a compilation of interviews with female former guerrillas, *Being a Woman in the PKK*, the very act of joining was 'a bomb that upset all the values of the Middle East … they went to fight at a time when most women feared even to go to market'.

Reading this, I was reminded of Gulseren Erdogan of the village of Emeran, who was kidnapped by a spurned suitor and his family – and only with the greatest of difficulty, and no help from the state, recovered from her captors. Gulseren was one of the lucky ones. The majority of kidnapped women are regarded as lost, their honour irreversibly compromised, and the thoughts of their families turn not to recovery but revenge. This, of course, involves inflicting suffering on another young woman.

When I was in the Kandil Mountains in 2006, I was shown around a gun emplacement that was manned by female guerrillas. These women politely answered my questions, and most said that they had initially been attracted to the PKK because it offered an escape from patriarchal Kurdish society. One told me that she had arrived at Kandil from south-eastern Turkey as an illiterate, and that the PKK had taught her to read. But it did not seem that these women's feminist aspirations had been served by their membership of the PKK. They had privilege and responsibility in the field, and Apo spoke in his seminars of the warrior woman as 'beautified'. But their enslavement as militants was complete: not to a father or a husband, but to the Chairman.

Every new recruit, recalled one of Buldan's interviewees, a Varto Cibran called Aryen, 'had first to undergo her rebirth in the image of the party … In Damascus, we drew a line underneath our past; taking on a new form in the party, we struggled against our emotions and our beliefs. In class it was repeatedly impressed on us that the family was a feudal, duplicitous institution … so now we saw our own families as being duplicitous and feudal. For this reason a few comrades and I got together and ripped up the photographs we carried of our families.'

The PKK is justly notorious for its ban on romantic relations between male and female guerrillas, and for the harshness with which it punishes transgressors. This ban may have been designed to aid military efficiency, but it became an essay in social experimentation and control.

'By flirting with one man,' said Apo in Aryen's recollection, 'you belittle yourselves, finish yourselves. By forming an attachment to one man, you are serving yourselves up – there are plenty of examples of this. There are plenty of women who have loved one man, or been with one man, and have eventually had to leave the struggle [he didn't mention those women who had been killed or exiled, or those comrades who remained in detention]. Do not flirt with one man. Let there be ten men, 100 men. Make all of them dependent on you. Only do not belong to one man alone.'

Apo's recommendation was not meant to be acted on; monogamous or polygamous, sexually active militants were punished with torture and re-education at best, a death sentence at worst. Scores of PKK militants were executed for having relationships, many as a result of denunciations by comrades.

The Turkish government and its allies have tended to portray Apo as a libidinous old tyrant who flaunted the very prohibitions he brutally enforced. The PKK has dismissed this as malicious propaganda, but the frequency and variety of such reports appear to confirm the accuracy of this depiction.

'Every month,' recounted one of Buldan's interviewees, 'four women would be selected to go and live in Apo's house. The women would generally have attended university. Most of them were physically attractive, girls who grew up in the cities, or in Europe. Each month there would be a rotation. "The Leader will nurture them," it was said. "They will flourish at the Leader's side." I don't know how much they flourished. In the Bekaa, after classes, Apo would come and give his class. After lunch women would be selected to play ball with him. Doesn't that say it all? Every girl who was arrested or left the organisation had things to say about this; it's impossible that all this was a fiction. As they say, where there's smoke there's fire. Lots of the women who stayed in his house became mentally unstable … lots tried to commit suicide. Is it possible that this happened for no reason? Some of the women refused to stay in his house. They were immediately … taken in for re-education. There was never an explanation. Why not, do you think?'

It is striking that, of Buldan's ten interviewees, all went to live in Europe, and eight married former guerrillas. Membership of the PKK cannot easily be undone. Even those militants who have benefited from government amnesties, or served jail terms, find it hard to reintegrate into Kurdish society. They gravitate to spouses who understand their predicament.

It was my last day in Iraqi Kurdistan. I was due to fly out that evening. I had arranged to meet Nizamettin Tas in my hotel – Nizamettin, the Alangoz boy whose father was a prime mover behind the 'trial' of Kadir Aktas, and whose ostler grandfather had saved the life of Halit of the Cibrans during the Russian advance of 1916. He had become a senior PKK commander but had quit in 2003 along with more than a dozen others, and the organisation now regarded him as a traitor.

When Apo was captured they asked him to describe his top-level cadres. Nizamettin was number seven. He was a good and resilient soldier, Apo said, if lackadaisical and not overly worried about loss of life. But Nizamettin had not always been number seven. He had benefited from the purges. He had been contrite, reverential and self-critical when the occasion demanded. In Munich, a *Vartolu* guerrilla told me that Nizamettin had been too much the yeoman soldier to appreciate Apo's subtlety in re-orientating the party after his capture, and that this explained his treachery.

Here, in the first floor coffee shop of a dingy hotel, smoking heavily, speaking over Lionel Ritchie, sat a slack-bottomed politician. His face was amiable and plump, his eye untrained. It may be that urban habits – the oily food and the endless tea and cigarettes; perhaps a peg or two at sundown – had sapped him. Up there, at Kandil, in the border regions where he had made his name as a commander, he had lived on clean air and adrenalin.

He recounted the decision of the dissidents to take over the PKK following Apo's capture – to transform a Marxist guerrilla army into a legal, pro-western political party without abandoning its guiding principle, Kurdish nationalism, and its minimum demand, federalism. They had organised a Congress and changed the PKK's name. They had been working on a strategy to turn the Iraq-based fighters into Turkey-based political propagandists. There had been talk of relegating Apo to the status of a 'spiritual leader' – the Americans, with whom Nizamettin said he had held secret talks, were apparently keen on this.

But Apo himself, in Nizamettin's telling, scuppered the plan, ordering the arrest of the reformers and precipitating their flight. Apo's lawyers had come to Kandil to reimpose his writ. They had returned to Turkey with recordings of the recent Congress proceedings – recordings that they had handed over to the Turkish general staff. The PKK had assassinated, Nizamettin added, no fewer than seven of his fellow dissidents.

Here was the thread running through Nizamettin's account: Apo's alliance with those army officers, neo-Fascists and criminals, whom citizens of the republic call the 'Deep State'.

The theory runs as follows:

The Deep State wants to perpetuate the war to avoid losing the prestige, political influence and, in the case of the armed forces, enormous budgets that the fighting has generated. It fears the prospect of the PKK disarming and turning legitimate – tidying itself up in the manner of Arafat's PLO – and winning more support inside the European Union and the United States. A third fear is that, if the PKK disintegrates, its successors will turn out to be more indiscriminate in their use of violence, particularly against civilians.

Apo can help. His fear is that he will lose control of the PKK. The Deep State, by permitting Apo extensive contact with his lawyers, and thus with the militants, allows him to keep his grip. So, the war continues, albeit less intensely, punctuated by ceasefires, and Apo stays in charge, hobbled, fatally compromised, but too strong to be toppled.

It's an attractive theory, neat and symmetrical. Yes, they deserve each other, Apo and the Deep State.

A couple of days earlier, up in the Kandil Mountains, I had talked with a Varto guerrilla called Jihan about lambing in the foothills of the Bingol Mountains and the unsettling effect that Mehmet Serif Firat's *History* had on a young Alevi. Now, with Nizamettin, the conversation turned to the earthquake of 1966 and the Sheikh Sait Rebellion.

'I was in your village a few days ago!' I told him, as I had told Jihan, and his reaction, of slightly wary indifference, was the same as Jihan's. Jihan had severed relations with his father, an Alevi of the Mehmet Serif Firat school, because the old man had opposed his joining the PKK. As for Nizamettin, he hadn't seen Alangoz since the 1980 coup. His two brothers no longer lived in Varto.

Nizamettin vaguely remembered someone called Kadir Aktas, but he had not heard of the 'people's tribunal'. He did not know that his own father had been tried for his involvement in it. 'For thirty years I didn't even ask a question about my village,' he said. 'If you asked, it was considered a sign of weakness. "Aha!" they would say, "He misses his family." '

I smiled. I had come all this way to talk about Varto, and no one wanted to know.

That evening, on the plane to Istanbul, I thought of the fighters I had spoken to – in Germany, Iraq and Armenia – and those whose books I had read. I had found myself identifying with some and abhorring others. But what had decided my reaction?

The difference, it dawned on me, was often the difference between those militants who had spent years in the camps of northern Iraq, mired in 'education' and the politics of self-hate, and those for whom the struggle was real – fighters in the field. There was little to admire in the modified products of Kandil and the Bekaa. There, 'family' life was a match to capture and bask in the favourable attention of Apo, and to destroy rivals for that attention, to accuse them of reformism, feudalism and defeatism. Here, fidelity to the Kurdish cause was measurable in contempt for the Kurdish people, a contempt so odious, it bore comparison with the worst of Turkish chauvinism.

For those in the field, on the other hand, up in the mountains of Bingol or Dersim, I found I had different feelings: pity, even sympathy. For the men and women there – outnumbered and outgunned, reliant on the people in whose name they fight and resist – there was the simple chemistry of insurrection.

I wish I had been there to see the meeting, two weeks after I left Iraqi Kurdistan, between those two Varto revolutionaries, Lutfu Balikkaya and Nizamettin Tas. Lutfu had been invited to Erbil by the ministry of culture, and he and Nizamettin met. Nizamettin was speaking about his new political movement when Lutfu cut in and asked, 'This is all very well, but don't you think, first of all, that you owe an apology to the Kurdish people?'

The Kurdish people will only get their apology when they dare to demand one. Until then they will be stuck with Apo.

Down in the valley it was election time.

For the past four years the Kemalist establishment had tolerated the government of Recep Tayyip Erdogan and his Justice and Development Party. The Justice and Development Party was an Islamist party; the Kemalist president, Ahmet Necdet Sezer, had constrained its transformative instincts, vetoing legislation and appointments that had, to his mind, a reactionary blush. But 2007 was the year when Sezer was to step down, and Erdogan and his party had intended to replace him with one of their own, Abdullah Gul. Secularists in parliament, the bureaucracy and the army were aghast and, using methods of doubtful legality, they had ganged up to stop parliament electing Gul. This, in turn, had provoked Erdogan to seek a fresh mandate. If the people re-elected him resoundingly, he would interpret this as a vote for his party's presidential choice, and challenge the Kemalists to defy the clearly expressed wishes of the people.

Such was the view from Ankara and other places in western and central Turkey, but national elections have their own colour in the Kurdish-majority east. For the Kurdish nationalists of the Democratic Society Party (which has close but informal links to the PKK), the election presented an opportunity and a threat. An opportunity because this year, by running as individual independents without party affiliation, the Apoists would circumvent a law which barred parliamentary representation to parties that won less than ten per cent of the vote. And a threat because now, for the first time since the 1950s, Turkey's ruling party was attracting mass support among the Kurds. It was getting hard for the Apoists to portray Erdogan as an enemy. His government had sharply reduced the use of torture by the police, alleviated poverty in some eastern regions, and lifted some residual restrictions on the use of Kurdish. More than once Erdogan had dissuaded the armed forces from pursuing the PKK in Iraq. He promoted the unity of Turks and Kurds, not as Turks all together, but as Muslims under God. If only the Deep State let him, it was optimistically rumoured, he would seek a comprehensive settlement with the PKK.

The inhabitants of the province of Mus were currently represented in parliament by three members of the Justice and Development Party and one member of the Republican People's Party. Now, with the Apoists standing as independents, the Kurdish nationalists were tipped to capture at least two of the four seats available. The independent candidates had divided up the province's districts so as not to split their share of the vote, and Varto had been allotted to a controversial *Muslu*, Sirri Sakik. Sakik was the brother of Semdin Sakik, a top PKK commander who, after falling out with Apo, had been captured and had obligingly trashed his old boss in a book written in Diyarbakir military jail. Sirri had been deputy for Mus while Semdin was busy blowing up army posts in the same province. The state assassin Green had frequented a Sakik-owned bar in the provincial capital. A curious and oddly poetic triangle.

I had seen photos of Sirri in the press following the PKK's slaughter of thirty-three unarmed conscripts in Bingol in 1993. The national newspaper *Cumhuriyet* had printed Sirri's photo next to that of his brother Semdin – the man who had allegedly planned and overseen the atrocity. *Cumhuriyet* had wanted to point out the anomaly of letting one Sakik sit in parliament while a second Sakik murdered unarmed squaddies. By choosing a file photo of Sirri grinning frivolously, the paper had given the impression that he approved of what his brother had done.

In Varto the election is about all of the above, and it is also about the rivalry between two men who are not even standing: Demir Celik of the Democratic Society Party and Abdulbari Han, his predecessor as mayor, now the local representative of the Justice and Development Party.

Abdulbari Han was once a proud nationalist; the Sunni clan he leads provided dozens of recruits for the PKK. Now, however, he is an advocate for Erdogan's conciliatory, development-based regionalism – bridges, not bombs; handouts, not Apo. He accuses the independents of 'playing politics with the blood and tears of the Kurdish people'. He makes fun of Demir Celik for travelling long distances to attend the funerals of PKK guerrillas who had no Varto connection. His opponents counter that Abdulbari Han is trying to revive the old Alevi–Sunni conflict, stirring up Sunni resentment against the Alevi mayor. They recall that he was a bruising, profligate mayor, surrounding himself with burly clansmen and ruining the local finances. Communal relations are increasingly strained. A local Alevi boy recently murdered his Sunni business partner. The Alevi's brother, living innocently in Ankara, was shot dead as a reciprocal measure. It's a time for conciliation, Abdulbari Han's critics say, not opportunism.

Yes, even now, in 2007, when the country faces pressing dilemmas in foreign, home and economic affairs, the election here will be decided, or heavily influenced, by the old curses of clan and sect.

There is a wild card, the irrepressible Ercan Aktas, Varto's Berlusconi. Yes, Ercan is up for election, on the ticket of a small pro-establishment party which stands little chance nationally and no chance in the east. Ercan is the best dressed of the candidates, tossing *bon mots* from the Mercedes's open window – campaigning most vigorously, it has been unkindly noted, behind closed doors. Ercan's aim, everyone agrees, is not to be elected, but to prepare himself and the people of Varto for the next municipal poll, when he will go head to head with Demir Celik. Kadir Aktas never won an election; Ercan wants to go one better than his old man.

Finally, we gentlemen of the press: Murat, editor and reporter for the pro-Celik *Gimgim News*, dean of the corps, as wary as he is courteous and handsome; the recent arrival Serkan, *Muslu* editor of a new pro-Abdulbari Han rival, the *Varto News*; and myself, sole representative of the foreign media, a journalist once more, dutifully interviewing the candidates, attending the rallies. It is the first time that the *New York Review of Books* has covered the elections in Varto with such exclusive and flattering attention.

Visiting Varto for the third time, after Germany, I had been pleased to discover that my stock had risen. Word got around that I had seen Lutfu Balikkaya and Mehmet Can Yuce and Yakub Cicek. I brought introductions from *Vartolu*s with whom I had stayed. It became known that I had conversed freely with these people, over many hours. I had become more knowledgeable about Varto. This made me a more penetrating questioner, less easily fobbed off. One's ability to pull the wool over the eyes of another is surely predicated on his ignorance; I had got less ignorant.

On this visit, my fourth, it became known that I had been the guest of the PKK in the Kandil Mountains. My stock rose further still. It was not widely appreciated that my visit to Kandil didn't necessarily denote support for the PKK. It was assumed that I was a sympathiser, and I didn't disabuse people of this misapprehension. Several people asked me to recount what I had seen. One man could not restrain himself: 'The Turkish army is no match for our fighters! The morale up there in Kandil is good!'

The candour now being shown me by some *Vartolu*s did not prevent others from developing a novel theory about who I was and why I was here. Having been alternately a spy for my home country, Britain, and a spy for my adopted country, Iran, it was now suggested that I was the descendant of Armenians who had been deported in 1915, and that I was here in Varto to retrieve a cache of ancestral gold.

The context of this rumour is as follows. The Armenians were the Jews of these parts, working hard, earning well, storing like squirrels. They had a thing for silver and gold. Their women liked to glitter. During the deportations, the more trusting of the Armenians, those who believed the government's assurances that they would soon be allowed to return home, decided to bury their riches rather than cart them along. They did this under their houses, under a tree, under a church crossing.

Armenian gold has become a curse in all the lands where the Armenians once lived. I have seen avarice enter a young Varto Alevi so he gives up his job, pours his money into a costly metal detector, and spends his time doltishly scrutinising the landscape. I have even seen it invoked as a pretext for murder.

I have never heard of Armenian treasure being retrieved in Varto. If you found such a treasure, I was asked, particularly if it was on someone else's land, would you advertise the fact? And yes, as it happens, over the years, there have been instances of precipitate departures – people upping sticks without prior warning, poor men or debtors embarking on a new life they could never, under normal circumstances, have afforded.

I had decided to stay at Varto's newest hotel, the Azak. The boys on the desk were young and friendly, and seemed not to regard me as someone they should automatically dislike. I appreciated this. Otherwise, in terms of amenities and comfort, the Azak was not very different from the Teachers' Hostel.

I had fallen out with Demir Celik. I had led him to believe, he told me angrily one evening at the mayoralty, that I wished to write about Varto's flora and fauna, its cosmopolitan character and culture; now I was asking questions about the PKK. I asked him to recall our first interview, our discussion of his growing up an Alevi and a Kurd, and of the Turkish republic's attitude towards minorities. I had not concealed my interest in politics and history. Celik said that our acquaintance had been problematic for him and that he wished henceforth to disassociate himself from me.

Of all the people I had met in Varto, it was to Demir Celik that I had hoped to speak without reservation about Varto and its place in the world. It was to the well-read pharmacist that I hoped to divulge my feelings about the PKK and the facts that I had accumulated concerning the annihilation of the Armenians. By doing this, by appealing to the democrat and pluralist in him, I had hoped to coax Celik to speak about his own poignant position: as mayor under the Turkish star and crescent, brother to a Kurdish martyr, and proxy to a cause, the Apoist cause, that was tawdry and debased. We would have ranged all over Turkey, he and I, before returning to the strange, enchanting, bloodstained district of Varto. It was to have been one of the highlights of my professional life, this magnificent conversation, and now it would never happen.

But Celik was a decent man and even now he did not try and obstruct my research. He was cordial, if distant, when we bumped into each other. A few days before the election, we went campaigning.

The Democratic Society Party minibus had already visited some ninety villages and hamlets across Varto; a handful remained. Twenty party workers, most of whom I recognised, were on board. We came off the Ustukran road and careened through Tatan, blasting Kurmanji election jingles through the tannoy. Beyond Tatan, high above the wide Murat, we passed three neat stone piles. They marked, I was told, the spot where the security forces slaughtered three captured PKK militants in the early 1990s. (The official version is that the militants were killed in combat.) I marvelled, yet again, at the precarious balance of power here, which had induced the authorities to overlook such symbols of defiance.

The men working in the fields laid down their scythes and gave us the victory sign as we passed. Stopping for a few minutes in each village, encircled by women and girls dancing, smothered by kisses from the men, Celik mustered his grimace-smile. The aim of the tour was not to convince voters or change minds. It was to generate a sense of anticipation prior to Sirri Sakik's arrival the following day.

The Sirri Sakik roadshow duly rolled into town. Varto was filled with honking horns and blaring music and election banners fluttering in the wind. Sakik and I spoke for a few minutes in a shoe shop owned by a party worker. Sakik was suave and handsome and rather patrician; he was, in his expensive striped shirt and cufflinks, an improbable advocate for a movement that continued, even now, to proclaim its Socialist character. He was at pains to stress how much had changed since the Kurdish nationalists were last represented in parliament. 'The Turkish establishment has accepted the Kurdish reality.'

The Kurds, for their part, had modified their demands. 'Back then we were demanding an independent Kurdistan. Now our eyes are fixed on Ankara. We are going to parliament to make peace.'

Sirri Sakik appeared on a platform that had been positioned at the intersection of Ataturk Street and the Mus Road. The people applauded rapturously – not out of any great love for him, but from respect for the PKK and rancour for the state. The turnout, well over 3,000, was testimony to the organisational skills of the nationalists. I bumped into people from all over the district, and a few who had come down from the summer pasture. Behind me, the steps of Varto's main shopping centre heaved with Sunni village women in their headscarves, chortling among themselves or with their babies. Expatriate *Vartolu*s, back from Europe for their summer holidays, conversed loudly in German.

The speakers stepped up, one by one. They shouted a great deal and that turned their voices hoarse. A lot of good lines were drowned in the distortion. Those who had come from outside the district did not fail to praise Varto's cosmopolitan character; the word 'mosaic' was uttered a great deal. No true Kurd, ran the Apoists' cautionary message, should pay attention to the blandishments of the Justice and Development Party; this election was about something more important. 'They are trying to steal our votes by promising water and electricity,' thundered Demir Celik. 'Our votes are our honour.'

This – bashful, encoded – was a reference to Apo. The value that the Kurds place on Apo is the honour of a nation that has no seat of government, no currency. To forget or forsake him in his incarceration, to vote for any party other than his party, would be the heinous act of a denialist and an opportunist. For fear of prosecution – propagandising on behalf of an illegal organisation is the crime –

the speakers in Varto couldn't make this point explicitly. But everyone knew what they meant.

I imagined the Chairman on Imrali, putting the finishing touches to his Democratic Ecological Paradigm, the latest in a series of incontinent treatises on the right way to order the world. Apo should by now have become a perfect irrelevance, the living dead, a Kurdish Ariel Sharon. And yet he had not. His every delusional sally, every spasm of self-pity and promotion, was greeted by his supporters as evidence for an ability to outsmart his jailers. In a curious way, by elevating him yet further, by putting him up there with Mandela on Robben Island, they were turning his lies into truths. He had become what he always insisted he was: a genius.

Sakik was the last of the speakers, sweating through his stripes. He declared himself 'the slave of this people'. The people roared, in Kurdish: 'Long Live Apo! Long Live Apo!'

When Sirri Sakik last addressed the people in Varto, in 1995, the intersection we now occupy was encircled by those Fascists from the Special Team, mouthing their obscenities, fingering their rifles. Now, observed by the occupants of a single armoured car, and a few dozen impassive cops, thousands of people have gathered to chant illegal separatist slogans. After the speeches there will be a concert, with songs sung in Zaza and Kurmanji. And after that, everyone will go home. No arrests; no torture; no killings.

Eastern Anatolia has changed for the better, but the Apoists cannot claim sole, or even some credit. It's the government of their electoral rivals, the Justice and Development Party, which checked the brutality and excess, pensioned off the torturers and reined in the Special Teams. It's the Erdogan government, ostensibly to demonstrate Turkey's European vocation, which gave the Apoists the democratic oxygen they now enjoy. So it's understandable that some Kurds – how many, we will discover on polling day – have decided that it is not, after all, a dereliction of their patriotic duty to vote for the people who brought about these modest but appreciable improvements.

On the last day of campaigning I attended a rally organised by the Justice and Development Party. It was smaller and less impressive than the Apoists' rally, attended by Abdulbari Han's supporters and some party members from outside the district. Afterwards I sat with Abdulbari Han and his latest, rather implausible ally, my old friend

Nazim Han. How was it that Uncle Nazim, having been, at the beginning of our acquaintance, such a staunch supporter of Demir Celik, had now gone over to a party that was known for its hostility to Alevis? I never learned the answer, though the Apoists had plenty of theories, few of them flattering.

That evening I was strolling along the upper bazaar when I came across an angel at the intersection of the Mus Road and Ataturk Road. He was wheeling about the deserted intersection, and his wings were some election posters.

He saw me and stopped flying. He bounded up. He was about eight years old. 'Who will you vote for?' he demanded. 'Vote for my dad!'

'Who's your dad?'

'Ercan Aktas.' He showed me the posters. Ercan looked out: resolute, compassionate and rich.

'I certainly shall. And what is your name?'

'Kadir.' And off he soared.

Polling day dawned. Turkey, the foreign media informed their subscribers, was a strategically important country, the world's sole functioning Muslim democracy, a bridge between East and West. Everyone should pay attention to what was happening in Turkey.

At the Azak Hotel all was quiet. The night receptionist was snoring. Walking up the hill, towards the lower bazaar, I met a police car. Erkan the cop was driving. The baby-faced chief of police sat next to him. Both wore civvies. The chief had recently become a father. His tour would shortly come to an end. He was in good humour. 'Christopher Bey!' he greeted me. 'Climb in, and we will go and see Turkish democracy in action!' I sat in the back.

We started our tour at a polling station in a school in Varto town. There were lots of voters, all in good spirits. Then we went off to tour the surrounding villages. Erkan asked me casually whether, after my last visit to Varto, I had gone anywhere else. I had gone to Diyarbakir, I replied. And from there? Into Iraq. Where specifically? To Erbil and Kandil. Ah, Kandil. Erkan and the chief exchanged sideways glances. It so happened, Erkan went on, that he had come across a commentary in a newspaper on an article that I had written about Kandil. The columnist who had written the commentary was a very clever and influential man. 'It was actually a favourable commentary,' he added, a little surprised.

I asked the chief about the recent Alevi-Sunni murders. He was proud of the police's role in bringing the Alevi suspect to book. 'We arrested him on the night of the murder and he confessed soon after.' The chief began to lament the tendency of people here to fight each other for tribe and sect, as in medieval times. 'What I should like you to do,' he said, 'as an outsider, is to conduct an investigation into why they behave like this. The municipal authorities think only of politics; why don't they concentrate on bringing these people into the modern world?'

We entered a Sunni village and the chief remarked on the absence of vegetable gardens outside the houses. 'Where I come from,' he said, 'near the Black Sea, you hardly find a house that doesn't have a garden full of root crops and vines and all sorts. Why don't they have that here?'

There are answers, of course, to the casually superior ruminations of the state's administrative class, to that familiar blend of revulsion and pity, refined by three years among the inferior dross of eastern Anatolia, that forms the attitude of Turk towards Kurd.

It is worth reminding ourselves that tribal and sectarian violence was once, briefly, virtually extinguished here. When? In the early and mid-1990s, when the PKK was at its most influential. What are we to infer from the state's reaction of princely indifference to the abduction of Gulseren Erdogan, carpet weaver of Emeran? Was that the reaction of a state working diligently to solder the rifts of sect and tribe? We know that the state, when its interests demand, is capable of exacerbating those rifts. It's called divide and rule.

On the question of vegetable gardens, it is true that the Kurds, being pastoralists by tradition, have come to vegetable gardens late, if at all. Equally, it is true that the mountainsides and meadows are their gardens: home to hundreds of herbs and fruits, remedies and tonics, that you and I may not recognise.

On we went, from polling station to polling station, and there was, between the cops on one side and the voters on the other, a curious mixture of bonhomie and distrust. In one of the villages Erkan expressed shock at the dilapidated condition of the local school, and promised to send up some conscripts to paint and rewire it. Then he ruined the goodwill he had generated by remarking to a local man that many Kurds had achieved high office in the republic. Everyone smiled wanly. No one volunteered the obvious answer: 'Only by forgetting that they are Kurds.'

We reached Abdulbari Han's village, Inaq. I had visited the graves on the hillside above, scratched with Arabic script and attesting to the execution here, by firing squad, of several participants in the Sheikh Sait Rebellion. Abdulbari Han stood outside the village school. He was charming and solicitous. But I remembered the first time I had arranged to meet him, when his goons had come out of nowhere and bundled me into his car like mafiosi.

I got a call on my mobile from Serkan of the *Varto News*. There had been reports of voter intimidation in the village of Karkarut. Serkan was tied up; could I go? I left the cops and went by taxi to Karkarut. The open space in front of the village school teemed with troops. Upon learning that I was a foreign reporter, the soldiers drove off in their Land Rovers.

Escorted by a Karkarut man, I entered the polling station. A sullen, nervous-looking election officer sat behind the desk. He was an outsider, my companion told me, no friend of the Kurdish cause, and he had been seen guiding illiterate voters so that they voted, against their will, for non-Kurdish parties. There had been an altercation; the election officer had found himself on the floor. The Varto prosecutor and dozens of soldiers had arrived, and the election officer's alleged assailants had been arrested. My guide insisted that no punches had been thrown. 'The election officer threw himself on the ground,' he said, rather endearingly.

It was late afternoon when I got back to Varto. I went to the headquarters of the Democratic Society Party. It occupies a whole floor of the newer of Varto's two commercial centres. It was crammed with hundreds of people talking and smoking and looking up, every now and then, at a long table occupied by Demir Celik and other party officers. I recognised most of the people there, and I realised that now, at last, I knew Varto quite well.

An old man who had, two years before, accompanied me to the Urartian citadel at Kayalidere, looked at me vaguely and said, 'I know your face, but I can't remember where from. Which school do you teach in?'

I saw an old Armenian who had spent the previous morning telling me his family's story. He gripped my arm, his eyes gleaming, and whispered in my ear, 'I have information, dear boy, definite information, that you are one of us. But remember, if anyone tells you there is gold in Baskan, it's a lie. A lie!'

The results began coming in from the villages. The district party chief was on his mobile phone, taking down results. He held up a hand to shush people. There was a thrill of anticipation. For the first time in more than a decade, the Kurdish nationalists would be represented in parliament.

The district party chief turned on his microphone and began announcing results. 'The results from Dadina! Sirri Sakik: 260! Justice and Development Party: ten!' There was a resounding cheer. 'The results from Kaynarca! Sirri Sakik: 387! Justice and Development Party: seventeen!' An even louder cheer. He also passed on results that he was receiving from other districts in the province. It became clear that the province would return two Kurdish nationalist deputies. Sirri Sakik would be one of them. Some women sitting near the front wept for joy. There was a call for the bard Selahattin to take the microphone. Selahattin got grinning to his feet and sang in gusts his Kurmanji panegyric to Apo. The room resounded with the refrain, 'Long Live our Leader Apo!'

As the evening wore on, I realised that the district party chief had announced the results from the nationalist villages first. The Alevi vote had been split between the Republican People's Party, some centre right parties, and the independents. Some of the Sunni villages, notably those allied to Abdulbari Han, had voted for the Justice and Development Party. The Kurdish nationalist share of the vote in Varto had dipped from sixty-three per cent at the previous election, in 2002, to fifty-four per cent. And the number of Justice and Development Party votes had risen substantially, from a mere 336 in 2002, to 1,967. Ercan Aktas had picked up 338 votes. I visited him, watching the results with his campaign manager. His party had failed to secure the ten per cent it needed to get into parliament. He failed even to raise a smile.

Later that evening the bookshop owner Naci, Kamer and a few other nationalists gathered in a small booze shop in the upper bazaar. I joined them and we sat on stools and talked, all the while following the national results as they came in. The Justice and Development

Party had won by a landslide, scoring stunningly well in several Kurdish provinces. The nationalists around me suspected that results had been rigged against them in one or two marginal seats, but they shrank from drawing the obvious lesson, which was that Apo's claim to be the sole representative of Turkey's Kurds no longer held true.

It may be the case, as Sirri Sakik had told me, that the ground for the government's reforms – the state's acceptance, as he put it, of the 'Kurdish reality' – had been laid by the PKK and its armed struggle. But the victory – if that, indeed, is what it can be called – had come at a huge cost: 40,000 lives lost, the vast majority of them Kurdish; thousands of villages destroyed or evacuated; millions displaced.

Back at the Azak, I went over some notes I had made in Mus while talking to an articulate Kurdish nationalist – a *Vartolu*, a Cibran, but a man whose relations with the PKK were uneasy.

'One of the consequences of this war,' he told me, 'is that now there are Kurds all across Turkey. There are now Kurds in every single small Turkish town. If you propose an independent state or a federation, sixty or seventy per cent of Kurds will oppose it. They'll say, "We're mixed up now; we can't be separated. We've married. We have children. Mum's a Kurd. Dad's a Turk. Mum's a Turk. Dad's a Kurd. The children are neither Kurd nor Turk. How, then, to split up? How to split up the country? How to split up the state?"

'Let's suppose the state throws up its hands and says, "All right! I accept a federation. This will be the Kurds' autonomous region: right here." So what happens to the Kurds of Istanbul and Izmir and all the other towns in western Turkey? Won't that lead to ethnic cleansing?

'Alternatively, you can say, "We're going to democratise the republic, we're going to build a state that's founded on human rights and applies no discrimination on grounds of race or sect." Fine, but if that's really the case, is it necessary to fight and kill for such goals?'

The Kurdish movement in Turkey no longer has an objective, a method or a leader. It is a mirage.

The Captain's Victory

In the spring the Alevi girls came out to pick cardoon stalks and one of the Armenian girls in the village, a blind girl, asked to go with them. So they took her along. They reached a nice shaded place and the Armenian girl said, 'You leave me here. I'll sit here a while.' She sat and started to sing a song and then she heard the sound of running water. She put out her hand and discovered that a stream was running close by. She brought the water up to wash her face and when the water touched her eyes she was cured of her blindness. She shouted to the other girls, 'I can see! I can see!' They came running but they saw no sign of water, just an old dried-up spring. And the spot is a pilgrimage place to this day.

I WENT NORTH FOR the last time. On a previous occasion I had shared a taxi with some men from Varto. But the taxi had been stopped so frequently on my account, and my papers scrutinised with such spiteful attention, that my companions had regretted our association and requested, at Hinis, that I complete my journey by minibus.

It was now more than two years since my first visit. I had met the people I had hoped to meet. I had filled my nostrils with what Rebecca West, archivist of Balkan atrocities, called the smell of skunk. I had admired feats of loyalty and self-sacrifice, poppies amid the refuse, and the pleasing, symmetrical propensity of those who hate with passion, to love, disinterestedly, with passion also.

I had been drawn here to the east by a longing to taste vicariously these passions. And I was leaving secure in the knowledge that I would live the rest of my life without experiencing the agonies that prick one to kill and wreak vengeance – that pounding of opposite emotions until they merge, the interstices narrow, and the senses become purely, brilliantly animal.

I sat on my plane. My eyes were wet. I grieved because I was unable to stop Varto where it was now, to prevent it from continuing to change and go around in ways that I would not be there to record.

Above all, I was nervous. I would be back in England soon, with my little crowd, and we would see if I belonged – and what, if anything, there was to belong to. I had been away thirteen years. Not as long as Lutfu Balikkaya, but long enough to feel like a stranger.

My neighbour engaged me in conversation. He was a soldier going home at the end of his military service. He chatted about the studies he would now embark upon, his mother who had fretted, the tedium of garrison life. Then he asked about me. I was a British writer, living in Tehran, speaking Turkish, doing a book about the Kurdish region. He smiled, unsure whether to believe me, and turned to look out of the window.

There is a library of books that pose the question of how we in the West view the 'other', and barely a shelf that asks how the 'other' views us. It may be that our civilisation has conferred on us, its beneficiaries, the boon of intellectual curiosity, but this seems unlikely to me. Rare is the travel book, policy recommendation or news report that does not read like a mirror on its author. Few are the commentaries that do not contain, within the honeyed empathetic phrases, the homilies to the wisdom of the East, an urgent appeal: be more like me! Or a keen regret: must do better!

The Republic of Turkey is interesting in that it contains, in a big rectangle, both a 'we' and an 'other'. Just as old Europe regarded with alarm the advance of the unspeakable Turk, so the republican elite regards with alarm the advance of the unspeakable Turk – the Islamists; the Kurdish separatists; the traitors Pamuk and Dink.

This 'we' sits next to me now, in the form of a demobbed squaddie, staring down at yellow, thirsty, camel-backed Anatolia, dreaming of Ma's meatballs, some barrack room chorus clattering around his head. And the 'other' is here too, for the lad's grandmother was from Diyarbakir and a dozen months in the world's armpit have convinced him that the Kurds deserve some slack – more slack, certainly, than his superiors would entertain. This private is a supporter of the Justice and Development Party. Flushed with re-election, anticipating the elevation, at the second attempt, of an Islamist to the presidency, the Justice and Development Party have promised to allow girls into university wearing the Islamic headscarf. The generals are furious but where's the harm – here, in a Muslim country?

In the newspaper I am reading it says that Professor Yusuf Halacoglu of the Turkish Historical Society has presented his findings after a period of 'private research' into the various ethnic groups of Anatolia. Thirty per cent of those who call themselves Kurds are of Turkic origin, states Professor Halacoglu with miraculous precision; many of those who claim to be Alevi Kurds are in fact Armenian converts. These Alevi Kurds are not, apparently, set in their new beliefs; 'it is known that they are trying to set up churches'. Some PKK militants, Halacoglu goes on, turn out not to have undergone the Muslim circumcision.

'Everybody should learn their own identity,' Professor Halacoglu recommends obscurely.

Things have come to a pretty pass when you find the top historian of a big modern country commenting on the penises of dead men.

I shut my eyes to avoid Professor Halacoglu – and the steward, prowling with sandwiches for sale. My thoughts return to the rain, the skidding clouds and the smell of mutton on my clothes. I settle on an old woman in a red smock, hugging her own brittle ribs, silhouetted in the door to her hut in the village of Emeran – the place where I had first met her. She had begun to shrivel on the day they informed her that the Apoists had shot dead her beloved husband, her Haydar, in the snow, and she had taken up the youngest of her new orphans, sat him on her lap and sobbed, 'My son! I'm here!'

A whirlwind had beaten about her, for Haydar had not only been a Firat, a relation of Mehmet Serif, but also a prominent and outspoken Kemalist; his death, immediately after the 1980 coup, had provoked a sharp military response. But the operations and arrests and bastinadoes had, for her, been a tumultuous irrelevance. She had kept herself apart, barricading her smashed-in windows, mourning furiously. Haydar had come to her in a dream, appearing from under a rolled carpet, hale and upstanding. On the fortieth day after his murder, she had draped her mourning breakfast with the Turkish flag and gone around the village. It was a way of showing that she wouldn't be beaten.

But she had been beaten, eventually, like so many other women in the rebel land, by fear and bereavement and emptiness. She had gone to live with a son in Izmir, but that hadn't worked out, and she had come back to Varto – to this life of bereavement and destitution. The winters she particularly hated. A metre of snow. Another metre of snow. Nowhere to go. Nothing to do. Just sit.

This woman had asked me to do her a small favour, to win for her the attention and sympathy of the new district commissioner. I had gone to Government House, but the diary-holder had smiled contemptuously at my request for an interview. I could have applied myself to find a different route, circumventing the diary-holder, but I hadn't done so. She had asked me to do her a small favour, this drift of leaves who had run the Apoist gauntlet and been forgotten, and I hadn't found the time.

It was the image of this woman that I carried through that last day in Istanbul. Hers and that of Lutfu Balikkaya – and, of course, that of the Armenian newspaperman Hrant Dink.

They had killed Hrant Dink, murdered him. I had heard the news in Tehran. A seventeen-year-old from the Black Sea had done the job, outside the offices of *Agos*. Three shots to the back of the head. 'I shot the infidel!' Turn tail and flee.

The boy had been identified and arrested. The police had treated him as a visiting dignitary: souvenir snaps down at the station. He had been sentenced and the awkward allegations – that the Deep State had put him up to the job; that he'd been acting not on his own, but for an organisation – had been swept away. The prime minister had affected outrage but done little. The liberals of Istanbul had marched – 'We are all Hrant!' – and gone back to work.

From Dink, mixing with the soil in the Armenian cemetery out at Zeytinburnu, to the exile Pamuk, finishing his latest novel in New York. I passed his apartment block, and the graffiti: 'Whatever you do, don't come back!' And I went down the hill, past the little mosque, and looked up at the flat that I had once lived in – back then, when I was a Turk.

The next morning, a little bleary, boarding my flight at Ataturk Airport, he came to me: the captain, standing across the land at Emeran, blond and virile and laughing.

They were his victories, Dink's death, Pamuk's flight: the captain's victories.

Epilogue: The Silver Belt

In Yerevan, in the Republic of Armenia, I was invited for tea by a philologist and his family. The philologist's wife had baked a delicious apricot cake, of which I had several slices. It was a jolly tea and, feeling quite relaxed, I remarked that I had spent five years in Turkey and that I had made good friends there. This news nonplussed my hosts. It contradicted all that they knew about the Turks. One of the other guests, a middle-aged woman, held up her arms, squeezed her bare forearm rhetorically, and exclaimed: 'No! The Turks do not bleed the same blood as us.'

During the week I spent in Yerevan, I got to know a courteous architect called Armen. In the 1970s and 1980s, when he was a young man, Armen spent many months travelling surreptitiously around eastern Turkey, taking photographs and recording physical evidence for the former Armenian presence. Armen and his companion, a Turkish-speaking European, were arrested several times. Among the Kurds, they often met with hostility.

It was now several years since Armen was last in Turkey; younger men had taken over the detective work. Their findings had been gathered in a multimedia archive in Yerevan. From this, it is clear that almost all evidence for the Armenians' settlement of eastern Anatolia has disappeared. Here, the stone wall of a church is incorporated into a new house; there, a graveyard is ripped up and ploughed over. Armen told me of an eleventh-century Armenian church that he had seen, before and after it was used for target practice by Turkish gunners.

Armen was such an engaging companion that it was unsettling to be reminded, as I occasionally was, that he was driven by hatred. One late afternoon, sitting in a room at the archive, I remarked that some Armenians I had met in Yerevan believed that relations between Armenia and Turkey should be allowed to normalise, but that Turkey should first apologise for 1915. Armen's face darkened. 'They are fools,' he said. 'Do you think we will exchange one and a half million murdered ancestors for an apology? That's our land the Turks are sitting on.'

We sat in silence. Outside, in Marshal Baghramian Avenue, municipal buses were driving people home. Armen brought in some coffee. I mentioned some villages that I had visited near Hinis, and Armen nodded; he had visited the same villages. As a matter of fact, he went on, he had a particular memory of one of them.

'It must be over twenty years ago. My German friend and I were driving through, and we stopped for a glass of tea in a tea house.

'As soon as we entered the tea house, the chatter died and everyone looked at us. We must have been the only non-Kurds. You know – those faces, those moustaches. We sat down on stools and ordered tea. We drank quickly because the atmosphere was hardly congenial, but as soon as we had finished that first glass, they brought another.

'I had been looking furtively around, and my attention had been drawn to something. There was a big Kurdish fellow sitting there; he was wearing a belt, and it glinted like silver. When they brought us our second tea, the serving boy pointed at the man and said that he'd sent the tea over to us. Then, before we knew it, the man had brought up his stool and was sitting next to us.' Armen paused. The office was dark and silent; everyone had gone home.

'This fellow had seen me looking at him but he thought I was interested in the revolver he was carrying. He whacked it down on the table so I could have a look. I spoke to him about the calibre and where it was made and so forth, and my stock rose because I know a bit about firearms. Everyone in the tea house had gathered round to hear what we were saying. The place was an enormous cloud of cigarette smoke. But I was only interested in his silver belt. There was more tea and more cigarettes and my friend kept looking at his watch and saying to me, "We should get going; we don't want to be on the road after dark." I kept having to shush him and say, "No! There's something I have to do here."

'Eventually, I summoned up the courage to ask to see the man's belt. He took it off and handed it over. It was composed of embossed detachable sections and had leather on the back. It was inscribed in Armenian, and there was a date, 1902. I was sweating and trembling, but, in the end, I managed to buy the belt from that Kurd.'

Armen fell silent. He had become a silhouette in front of the window. After a few moments, I said, 'Presumably only rich men could have afforded a silver belt.' He became animated. 'Not men! Men didn't wear such belts! These belts were given to Armenian girls when they got married. They were meant to last their whole married life; that's why they were made up of removable sections. During pregnancy, they added sections. After giving birth, when they were getting slim again, they took the sections away.'

Now, months later, I still imagine this belt being wrenched from its owner, who has been destroyed along with her family – a woman of substance turned casually to a lump. I imagine it held aloft as a trophy, and then corrupted, a woman's belt around the waist of a man. I imagine it passing, along with the dogs and a horse, from father to son, re-entering the moral economy. And I wonder how many generations must elapse before we judge this belt no longer to be stolen property, evidence in a case of murder, but to belong rightfully to the man who holds it.

I think these things in a neat, well-ordered terraced house in London, where I have belts of my own – my family; the nice reassuring things that I inherited from my mother. Supposing these people, these things, were wrenched away from me by an ancestral enemy, supposing that I were robbed of everything in a matter of minutes – I suppose that I too would disregard those principles, of love and forgiveness, that were instilled in me painlessly as a child, and abandon myself to insatiable rage.

Acknowledgements

Scores of people in several countries helped me as I researched and wrote *Rebel Land*. To many of them, being the subject of sections of the book, my debt is obvious. To the following, who also gave time and help, I am extremely grateful.

Eyup Akbal; Rusen Aslan; Murat Aydin; Nazim Aykal; Negar Azimi; Ina Baghdiantz-McCabe; Faruk Balikci; Baris Balikkaya; Hasan Balikkaya; Ismail Balikkaya; Riza Balikkaya; Turkan Balikkaya; Eric de Bellaigue; Ismail Besikci; Huseyin Bingol; Fuat Degertas; Ismet Demirdogen; Samvel Felekyan; Behcet Firat; Haydar Firat; Umit Firat; Salpi Ghazarian; Deniz Gunduz; Armen Haghnazarian; Hasan Ali Karasar; Burhan Kaya; Harun Kaya; Enver Konukcu; Fergin Melik; Violet Mooradian; Cemile Ozkaya; Hakki Ozkaya; Hamdi Ozyurt; Dennis Papazian; Sait Sever; Ismail Sever; Mehmet Emin Sever; Serif Sever; Norman Stone; Brian Sarookanian; Faysal Tas; Cemal Teker; Christine Ter-Hovanessian; Orhan Tural; Davud Vartaniyan; Ali-Riza Vural; Halis Vural; Baris Vural; Remzi Yalcin; Husnu Yurtsever; Mumtaz Yurtsever; Amberin Zaman; Armineh Zeitounchian.

To Ben and Yesim Holland, Amberin Zaman and Joseph Pennington, and Steve Bryant and Hande Culpan, I am indebted for many nights' hospitality in Turkey. I am grateful to the officials of Turkey's foreign press directorate in Ankara, who treated me with unvarying kindness and consideration, and to their opposite numbers in Iran, where I wrote much of *Rebel Land*; my thanks go to Mohsen Moghadaszadeh and his team. I am grateful also to the staff of the British Institute of Persian Studies in Tehran, where I spent many hours writing, and not a few dozing, and similarly to the committee of the Alistair Horne Fellowship at St Antony's College, Oxford, under whose auspices I was able to finish writing in 2008.

My agent when I started *Rebel Land*, David Godwin, and when I finished it, Peter Straus, and my editors, Michael Fishwick at

Bloomsbury, Vanessa Mobley and Inigo Thomas at Penguin, Detlef Felken and Jonathan Beck at Beck, deserve thanks for the faith they have put in me and in this book. Anna Simpson and Margaret Stead provided invaluable expertise in preparing the book for publication. Throughout I have benefited from the friendship of Robert Silvers, my longstanding editor at the *New York Review of Books*, whose publication sponsored several of my trips to Turkey. I am also grateful to Ian Jack, formerly of *Granta*, who published excerpts from the book under the title, *We Have No Minorities*, in *Granta* 94, under the pseudonym George Bowater, and to Roger Hodge of Harper's, who published my profile of Orhan Pamuk, *There is no East: Reading Orhan Pamuk*, in the issue of September 2007.

Norman Stone, Ben Holland and Amberin Zaman were good enough to read and offer suggestions on the finished manuscript. All responsibility for the contents of the book is mine alone.

Above all, I offer my thanks and love to my family: to Bita, Jahan and Kiana.

Bibliography

Ahmad, Kamal Madhar (trans. Ali Maher Ibrahim), *Kurdistan during the First World War*, Saqi, London, 1994.

Akcam, Taner, *A Shameful Act: The Armenian Genocide and the Question of Turkish Responsibility*, Constable, London, 2007.

—*From Empire to Republic: Turkish Nationalism and the Armenian Genocide*, Zed, London, 2004.

Akpinar, Alisan, Rogan, Eugene L., *Asiret Mektep Devlet: Osmanli Devleti'nde Asiret Mektebi*, Aram, Istanbul, 2001.

Aksoy, Gurdal, *Dersim Alevi Kurt Mitolojisi: Raa Haq'da Dinsel Figurler*, Komal, Istanbul, 2006.

Altan, Cetin, *Onlar Uyarnirken, Turk Sosyalistlerin El Kitabi*, Bilgi, Ankara, 1996.

Anter, Musa, *Hatirlarim*, Yon, Istanbul, 1992.

Arcayurek, Cuneyt, *Demokrasi Dur: 12 Eylul 1980 (Nisan 1980–Eylul 1980)*, Bilgi, Ankara, 1986.

Arslan, Rusen, *Cim Karninda Nokta: Anilar*, Doz, Istanbul, 2006.

—*Seyh Said Ayaklanmasinda Varto Asiretleri ve Mehmet Serif Firat Olayi*, Doz, Istanbul, 2006.

Aydemir, Sevket Sureyya, *Tek Adam: Mustafa Kemal, 1922–1938*, Remzi, Istanbul, 2005.

Aytar, Osman, *Hamidiye Alaylarindan Koy Koruculuguna*, Medya, Istanbul, 1992.

Barkey, Henri J., Fuller, Graham E., *Turkey's Kurdish Question*, Rowman and Littlefield, Lanham, Maryland, 1998.

Bayrak, Mehmet (ed.), *Kurt Muzigi, Danslari ve Sarkilari*, Ozge, Ankara, 2002.

Besikci, Ismail, *Dogu Anadolu'nun Duzeni: Sosyo-Ekonomik ve Etnik Temeller*, e Yayinlari, Ankara, 1970.

Brant, James, *Notes of a Journey through a Part of Kurdistan, in the Summer of 1838, by James Brant Esq., H.B.M. Consul at Erzurum*, Royal Geographical Journal (10), London, 1841.

Bruinessen, Martin van, *Agha, Shaikh and State: the Social and Political Structures of Kurdistan*, Zed, London, 1992.

Bryce, Viscount, *The Treatment of Armenians in the Ottoman Empire, 1915–16: Documents presented to Viscount Grey of Fallodan, Secretary of State for Foreign Affairs, by Viscount Bryce*, T. Fisher Unwin, London, 1916.

Buldan, Nejdet, *PKK'de Kadin Olmak*, Doz, Istanbul, 2004.

Cavdar, Tevfik, *Turkiye'nin Demokrasi Tarihi*, Imge, Ankara, 2004.

Celebyan, Antranik (trans. Mariam Arpi, Nairi Arek), *Antranik Pasa*, Peri, Istanbul, 2003.

Cuinet, Vital, *La Turquie d'Asie, Géographie administrative, statistique, descriptive et raisonnée de L'Asie Mineure*, Ernest Leroux, Paris, 1890.

Curukkaya, Selim, *Apo'nun Ayetleri: Beyrut Gunlugu*, Doz, Istanbul, 2005.

Dadrian, Vahakn N., *History of the Armenian Genocide: Ethnic Conflict from the Balkans to Anatolia to the Caucasus*, Berghahn, Providence, RI, 1997.

Deringil, Selim, *The Well-Protected Domains: Ideology and the Legitimisation of Power in the Ottoman Empire*, 1876–1909, IB Tauris, London, 1999.

Ersever, Ahmet Cem, *Kurtler, PKK, A. Ocalan*, Ocak Yayinlari, Ankara, 1994.

Feyizoglu, Turan, *Deniz: Bir Isyancinin Izleri*, Belge, Istanbul, 1991.

Firat, Kutsal, *Milletvekilligine Degismem*, Kutsal Firat, private, Istanbul, 2000.

Firat M. Halit, *75 Senelik Derbeder bir Hayat Hikayesi*, private, Ankara, 1968.

Firat, Mehmet Serif, *Dogu Illeri ve Varto Tarihi*, IQ Kultur Sanat Yayincilik, Istanbul, 2007.

Gursel, Kadri, *Dagdakiler: Bagok'tan Gabar'a 26 Gun*, Matis, Istanbul, 1996.

Guvenc, Bozkurt, *Turk Kimligi: Kultur Tarihinin Kaynaklari*, Remzi Kitabevi, Istanbul, 1996.

Halacoglu, Yusuf, *Ermeni Tehciri*, Babiali Kultur, Istanbul, 2004.

Haykakan Hanradikarani Klkhavor Khmpakrutyun, *Haykakan Hartz Hanrakidaran*, Yerevan, 1996.

Hoogasian Villa, Susie, and Kilbourne Matossian, Mary, *Armenian Village Life before 1914*, Wayne State University Press, Detroit, 1982.

Hovanissian, Richard G. (ed.), *The Armenian People from Ancient to Modern Times*, Macmillan, London, 1997.

—*Armenian Baghesh/Bitlis and Taron/Mush*, Mazda, 2001.

—*Armenian Karin/Erzurum*, Ucla Armenian History and Culture Series, 2004.

Imset, Ismet, *The PKK: a Report on Separatist Violence in Turkey (1973–1992)*, Turkish Daily News Publications, Ankara, 1992.

Inalcik, Halil, *The Ottoman Empire: the Classical Age (1300–1600)*, Phoenix, London, 1997.

Jabar, Faleh A., and Dawod, Hosham, *The Kurds: Nationalism and Politics*, Saqi, London, 2006.

Kahraman, Ahmet, *Kurt Isyanlari (Tedip ve Tenkil)*, Evrensel, Istanbul, 2004.

Karasu, Dogan; Hulaku, Ahmet; Korkmazcan, Orhan; Guleryuz, Devrim; Gungur, Ozlem, *Bingol Dengbejleri*, Peri, Istanbul, 2007.

Kaya, Ferzende, *Mezopotamya Surgunu: Abdulmelik Firat'in Yasamoykusu*, Alfa, Istanbul, 2004.

Kevonian, Armenouhie, *Les Noces Noires de Gulizar* (trans. Jacques Mouradian), Editions Parentheses, Marseille, 2005.

Kocadagi, Burhan, *Dogu'da Asiretler, Kurtler, Aleviler*, Can, Istanbul, 2004.

Koekorta, Meme, *Berxa Mi Xeribiye De*, Wesanxaneye Vateye, Istanbul, 2004.

Konukcu, Enver, *Selcuklardan Cumhuriyete Erzurum*, Erzurum Ticaret ve Sanayi Odasi Yardim Arastirma ve Gelistirme Vakfi, Erzurum, 1992.

Larcher, Commandant M., *La Guerre turque dans la Guerre Mondiale*, Chiron & Berger-Levrault, Paris, 1926.

Lewis, Bernard, *The Emergence of Modern Turkey*, Oxford University Press, Oxford, 1967.

Lewis, Geoffrey, *The Turkish Language Reform: a Catastrophic Success*, Oxford University Press, Oxford, 2002.

Lowry, Heath W., *The Story behind Ambassador Morgenthau's Story*, Isis, Istanbul, 1990.

Lynch, H.F.B., *Armenia: Travels and Studies,* Armenian Prelacy, New York, 1990.

Mango, Andrew, *The Turks Today*, Overlook, New York, 2004.

Mater, Nadire, *Mehmedin Kitabi: Guneydogu'da Savasmis Askerler Anlatiyor*, Metis, Istanbul, 1999.

McCarthy, Justin, *Death and Exile: the Ethnic Cleansing of Ottoman Muslims, 1821–1922*, Darwin Press, Princeton, 1995.

McDowall, David, *A Modern History of the Kurds*, IB Tauris, London, 1996.

Melikian, Yeghishe, *Hark Khenous*, Catholicosate of Cilicia, Antelias, 1964.

Mumcu, Ugur, *Kurt-Islam Ayaklanmasi, 1919–1925*, Ugur Mumcu Arastimaci Gazetecilik Vakfi, Ankara, 1999.

Olson, Robert, *The Emergence of Kurdish Nationalism and the Sheikh Said Rebellion, 1880–1925*, University of Texas Press, Austin, 1989.

Orgeevren, Ahmet Sureyya, *Seyh Sait Isyani ve Sark Istiklal Mahkemesi*, Temel, Istanbul, 2007.

Ortayli, Ilber, *Imparatorlugun En Uzun Yuzyili*, Hil, Istanbul, 1983.

Ozkirmli, Atilla, *Alevilik Bektasilik: Toplumsal bir Baskaldirinin Ideolojisi*, Cem, Istanbul, 1996.

Parilti, Abidin, *Dengbejler: Sozun Yazgisi*, Ithaki, Istanbul, 2006.

Pir, Mahsum Hayri (a.k.a. M.C. Yuce), *Bir Yanilsamin Sonucu*, Komal, Istanbul, 2000.

Pope, Nicole and Hugh, *Turkey Unveiled: a History of Modern Turkey*, Overlook, Woodstock, NY, 1998.

Rogan, Eugene L., *Asiret Mektebi: Abdulhamit II's School for Tribes (1892–1907)*, from the International Journal of Middle East Studies 28, Cambridge, 1996.

Sakik, Semdin, *Apo*, Sark, Ankara, 2005.

Sarikas, Ali Kemal, *Goz Yaslariyla Cileli Varto*, unpublished, 1988.

Sassuni, Garo, *Badmoutyoun Daroni Ashkharhi*, Sevan, Beirut, 1956.

Sever, M. Emin, *Kurt Tarihinden bir Kesit: Azadi Orgutu ve Cibranli Halit Bey*, from Bir Journal, Istanbul, 2005.

Shankland, David, *The Alevis in Turkey: the Emergence of a Secular Islamic Tradition*, RoutledgeCurzon, London, 2003.

Shaw, Stanford J., *History of the Ottoman Empire and Modern Turkey, Volume One: Empire of the Gazis – The Rise and Decline of the Ottoman Empire* (1280–1808), Cambridge University Press, Cambridge ,1995.

Shaw, Stanford J., Ezel Kural, *History of the Ottoman Empire and Modern Turkey, Volume Two: Reform, Revolution and Republic – The Rise of Modern Turkey (1808–1975)*, Cambridge University Press, Cambridge, 2002.

Sinclair, Tom, *Eastern Turkey: An Architectural and Archaelogical Survey*, Pindar Press, London, 1987–90.

Sykes, Mark, *The Kurdish Tribes of the Ottoman Empire*, from the Journal of the Royal Anthropological Institute (38), London, 1908.

Teker, Mehmet, *Kurt Tarihinde Hormek (Alhas) Asireti*, Kalan, Ankara, 2006.

Tekin, Arslan, *Imrali'daki Konuk*, Tutibay, Ankara, 1999.

Ter-Minassian, Anahide, *Un Exemple, Mouch 1915*, from *L'actualité du Génocide des Arméniens*, Edipol, Paris, 1999.

Ter-Minassian, Minas (Rouben Pasha), *Mémoires d'un cadre révolutionnaire arménien* (tr. from the Armenian by Souren L. Chnath), Publications de la FRA Dachnaktsoutioun, 1994.

Teymuroglu, Ferruh, *Iste Kurt*, Furkan, Diyarbakir, 2005.

Xenophon, *Anabasis* (trans. Carleton L. Brownson), Loeb, Cambridge, Mass., 1998.

Yavuz, Edip, *Tarih Boyunca Turk Kavimleri*, Kurtulus, Ankara, 1968.

Yegen, Mesut, *Devlet Soyleminde Kurt Sorunu*, Iletisim, Istanbul, 1999.

Yuce, M. Can, *Dogu'da Yukselen Gunes*, Zelal, Istanbul, 1999.

Zimansky, Paul, *Xenophon and the Urartian Legacy*, from *Dans les pas des Dix-Mille: Peuples et pays du Proche-Orient vus par un Grec*, ed. Pierre Briant, Presses Universitaires du Mirail, 1995.

Journals: *Serbesti*, Istanbul, September–October 2003.

A Note on the Author

Christopher de Bellaigue was born in London in 1971 and has spent
the past decade and a half in the Middle East and south Asia. He has
worked as a correspondent for a number of publications including
the *Economist*, the *New York Review of Books*, *Harpers*, *Prospect*
magazine and the *Financial Times*. He is the author of two books,
In the Rose Garden of the Martyrs, which was shortlisted for the
2004 Royal Society of Literature Ondaatje Prize, and *The Struggle
For Iran*, which led *Prospect* magazine to describe him as 'one of the
best new generation of Middle East experts'.

A Note on the Type

The text of this book is set in Linotype Sabon, named after the type founder, Jacques Sabon. It was designed by Jan Tschichold and jointly developed by Linotype, Monotype and Stempel, in response to a need for a typeface to be available in identical form for mechanical hot metal composition and hand composition using foundry type.

Tschichold based his design for Sabon roman on a fount engraved by Garamond, and Sabon italic on a fount by Granjon. It was first used in 1966 and has proved an enduring modern classic.